Events Feasibility
and Development

Other books in the series

Marketing and Selling Destinations and Venues: A Convention and Events Perspective by Tony Rogers and Rob Davidson

The Management of Events Operations by Julia Tum, Philippa Norton and J. Nevan Wright

Innovative Marketing Communications: Strategies for the Events Industry by Guy Masterman and Emma H. Wood

Events Design and Experience by Graham Berridge

Human Resource Management for Events: Managing the Event Workforce by Lynn Van der Wagen

Event Studies: Theory, Research and Policy for Planned Events by Donald Getz

Conferences and Conventions: A Global Industry, 2nd edition by Tony Rogers

Risk Management for Meetings and Events by Julia Rutherford Silvers

Events Management, 3rd edition by Glenn Bowdin, Johnny Allen, William O'Toole, Rob Harris and Ian McDonnell

Events Feasibility and Development
From Strategy to Operations

William O'Toole

AMSTERDAM • BOSTON • HEIDELBERG • LONDON • NEW YORK • OXFORD
PARIS • SAN DIEGO • SAN FRANCISCO • SYDNEY • TOKYO

Butterworth-Heinemann is an imprint of Elsevier

Butterworth-Heinemann is an imprint of Elsevier
30 Corporate Drive, Suite 400, Burlington, MA 01803, USA
The Boulevard, Langford Lane, Kidlington, Oxford OX5 1GB, UK

British Library Cataloguing in Publication Data
A catalogue record for this book is available from the British Library.

Library of Congress Cataloging-in-Publication Data
A catalog record for this book is available from the Library of Congress

ISBN: 978-0-7506-6640-4

For information on all Butterworth–Heinemann publications
visit our Web site at www.books.elsevier.com

Printed and bound in Great Britain

11 12   10 9 8 7 6 5 4 3 2 1

Dedication

I would like to thank all the people I have worked with in this exciting industry. Tracey Hull, Ted Tooher, Marwan Bin Beyat, Hamad Al Sheikh, Habeeb Habash, Steve Schmader, Tariq Al Asser, the wonderful event teams at Liverpool City Council, Coffs Harbour Council, Dubai Tourism Commerce and Marketing, IIRME and the Aqaba Development Authority, the EMBOK executive and the International Standard in Event Management team.

The contributors to this book are numerous and I can't name you all — it would be as long as the book.

The event industry is full of people with integrity, creativity and warmth. In the years of working with people in the events in numerous countries and cultures, I have been constantly delighted by their common humanity. To all of you, this book is dedicated. Events are organised celebrations. While people are happy they do not go to war. *God smiles when his children play.* In a world that seems to be in constant conflict, it is the celebrations of harvest, knowledge, occasions, sports and business that provide the humanity.

Contents

Foreword

Steven Wood Schmader, CFEE
President & CEO
International Festivals & Events Association (IFEA World)

Over the course of my 30+ year career in festivals and events I have had the pleasure of meeting, working with, and learning from many remarkable individuals; consummate professionals with a passion for their work, their communities, their countries and our common industry. And while my respect for them all is unquestionable, there is among them a small and special handful that I have found operate on a different plain from the norm; forces of nature, with a vision and understanding of the possibilities, and not only a desire, but a need and drive to explore and go where others have not yet imagined. Bill O'Toole may be the leader of that pack.

Bill is a unique combination of practitioner, educator and — on most days — philosopher. He sees the world as a whole, but understands, first-hand, the role that all of the many parts and pieces must play to ensure the success of the whole. He is not only about theory, nor does he stand behind his considerable experience as being beyond the need for theoretical value. It is that combination of traits that has taken Bill down many different pathways that most in our field may have walked past unnoticed, together with his willingness as a professional and individual to share his wealth of insights with all of us, that stand him out from the crowd.

While events and celebration have been a part of human history for as long as we can trace back, it is only within the past several decades that those in our own industry, and now others outside of the field, have come to recognize it more clearly as a profession and a force that can be harnessed to positively affect people, communities, and countries around the world. As economic and tourism drivers, marketing and branding tools, bonding and involvement mechanisms, infrastructure and business incentives, and much more, festivals and events are following a natural development path, much like any human endeavor; a path that can be directed, through a combination of creativity, knowledge and experience to maximize the returns for everyone.

In my role as the President & CEO of the International Festivals & Events Association (IFEA World), *The Premiere Association Enabling and Supporting Festival and Event Professionals Worldwide*, I have watched with fascination and pleasure at the continually expanding number of calls and requests from governments, corporate leadership and event organizations around the world for guidance and information about how to best use, develop and maximize this 'new' tool. As a result, the IFEA has taken on many new consulting projects, developed new programs to recognize and share best practices, and upgraded our professional education tools to help meet those needs.

In this new book, *Event Feasibility and Development*, Bill O'Toole has taken us all another giant leap forward, drawing upon his extensive global experience and knowledge to provide a textbook development guide that can be used by cities, countries, tourism organizations and other professionals as you develop your own feasibility strategies, management plans and operation systems in an effort to maximize the success of those efforts and the resources expended in the process.

As an added value, Bill shares with us a variety of successful case studies and interviews with event professionals from around the world, giving readers a rare opportunity to recognize the many similarities (and differences) that those in our industry share and a renewed understanding of the amazing impact and return-on-investment that events have had and will continue to have upon the world around us.

I always look forward to those opportunities when my own travels cross with those of Bill O'Toole's, because wherever we may be in the world I know that I will learn something new. For the readers of this book, no matter what starting point you may be coming from, I can promise that you, too, will learn something new and valuable. Enjoy the journey.

PREAMBLE

This is a textbook from the frontline of events development. I realised that the work I was doing was called events when we wrote the first textbook in 1998. Up until then I was a promoter or entrepreneur. I owned and managed an agency with a major record company in Australia, Larrikin Records. Our 'product', or line up of talent, was unusual and therefore a large part of my work consisted of coming up with ideas to employ them.

We approached major companies and government organisations with ideas for events. Although they had their marketing departments, we found that the larger the company the greater the need for outsourcing creative ideas. It was a chink in the corporate organisation's wall. The large organisations had the 'muscle' — power and money — and we had the ideas and we were in touch with the market and the trends. We could move quickly, looking for opportunities and gathering a project team to organise an innovative event.

Event management as a business, at this stage, was unheard of. Most event organisers were seen as the 'party people', the people who put on a party. It was regarded as low down the corporate hierarchy and, basically, anyone who has organised a children's birthday party could do it. This was not helped by the attitude of the event planners, who kept the secrets to themselves. At that stage, their secrecy was their competitive edge. The secret of a successful corporate function was the knowledge that gave them an edge on the competition. It has the not-so-insignificant effect that the event could not go ahead without the event planner. The concepts of accountability, status reports, management competency and cost—benefit analysis are a recent addition to the science and art of event management.

There were two trends that changed the secrecy and mystery of event management. First was the growth in importance of events. Numerous experts in the field, such as Don Getz and Julia Rutherford Silvers, have commented on the exponential growth of events. They have grown in number and importance. At the same time the term 'event' has expanded to include sports, exhibitions, meetings and community celebrations. As a result a large company found it was involved in numerous events. They organised internal events, such as staff parties, training seminars and incentives. They used events to market their products and services such as product launches and exhibitions. They supported community events as part of their Corporate Social Responsibility (CSR). They sponsored major events such as the sports and festivals. When viewed from the event perspective, the company was heavily involved in events. Exactly the same was happening to local authorities such as councils, governments and government departments. The organisation of events was distributed across numerous company divisions. The marketing department was concerned with product launches, openings and the odd travelling exhibition. The executive assistant or communications team organised the seminars and conferences. Sponsorship of events was controlled by a combination of marketing and finance. Human resources organised the training and a recruitment event. Everyone had a hand in the staff party.

The next trend was the arrival of formal risk management. I won't go into the reasons for the growth of risk management, suffice it to point out that it is here to stay. In the event context, risk management provides a pathway of accountability for any risks. If something goes wrong, the responsibility for the fault will find its way via the risk management plans until it rests with those responsible. If there is an incident at an event, the responsibility may be apportioned to the board of directors of the company. No longer can the senior management of an organisation say they are not responsible for the operations of the staff party. Although this varies with different countries, laws concerning corporate responsibility and board liability are certainly spreading rapidly around the world.

Risk management and the growth in importance of events imply that management of the event must be competent. This reflects the maturing of the event industry.

The large companies were fascinated. They knew there was a return on investment for events. The new telcos and the software companies were heavily involved in events. By sponsoring the right event the highly competitive mobile telephone companies could beat their opposition and get into a new market dominated by the government telecommunication company. This produced the new term for many promotional events-experiential marketing.

The events and festivals we organised ranged from a 12-day magic festival to a concert in the middle of Borneo (Indonesia) with the local Dayaks. In one case I organised a 2-day public awareness event in a swamp. It was a 9-hour drive from a major city and had no infrastructure. By carefully developing the event, the result was a live broadcast to Asia and the Pacific, a CD and a video that grossed millions of dollars, as well as the event itself. I had no idea when I began the project that this would be the result.

I heard the term 'it'll never work' so often that I took it as a challenge. The problem with events feasibility and development is that events are special and if someone thought they would work, it would already be happening. Inevitably, there will be many people who cannot imagine a new event.

Events development is not a linear path. The growth of an event — I refer to increase in quality and size — does not follow a simple ratio. Putting more money into an event does not necessarily mean that the event will grow proportionally. Doubling the amount of advertising or promotion does not mean doubling the audience.

Events feasibility and development are the most rapid growing areas of the industry. The fast developing economies of Asia, South and East Africa and the Gulf are hungry for events. Unfortunately, in my opinion, their first response is to 'buy in' major events with little thought to the legacy of the event.

In part this text is written to assist those countries to develop their events and gain a maximum return to their populations from the events they have bought from overseas. These major events can leave a real legacy of knowledge and skills. One must realise that the current major events — particularly sporting events — that are sold around the world were originally developed by enthusiasts. From the Grand Prix to the Olympics, it was local enthusiasts who created them. The lesson is that a country can develop its own major events (and sell them to other countries) by assisting local enthusiasts.

My recent work has been in Jordan, United Arab Emirates (Dubai) and the Kingdom of Saudi Arabia. In each of these countries there is a vibrant culture and innumerable local events. In Entebbe and Khartoum I have been training the UN event staff in event management. In the Sudan, a country ravaged by strife, events will help heal the social and economic wounds. After years in the doldrums, the economies of Uganda and Kenya are powering ahead and will be in need of more commercial and public events to assist their development. I am privileged to 'sit in the front row' and take part in this unfolding history.

About the Author

William O'Toole, BSc, MEng
Manager of EPMS Pty Ltd
Founding Director of Event Management Body of Knowledge (EMBOK)
Events Development Consultant to the Kingdom of Saudi Arabia

William is recognised as a key person in the creation and development of the event sector around the world. His experience has spanned the globe and events from operations to management to strategy development.

Recently, he worked as an events development specialist for the governments of the Kingdom of Saudi Arabia, the European Union, Dubai Tourism Commerce and Marketing, the Aqaba Development Authority and numerous councils and local authorities. He trained events staff in the UN in Khartoum and Entebbe. He originated and advised on the inaugural events conferences for both Kenya and Uganda.

William has been creating and organising events for more than 30 years. His experience in developing, managing or consulting events spans over 40 countries. He is a sought-after presenter and teacher in event management in Australia, New Zealand, South Africa, Taiwan, UK, USA, Malaysia and the Middle East. He is an Event Management Consultant to public and private organisations for events throughout Australia and Asia, including numerous tourism and regional authorities on their event support mechanisms.

He authored two international texts on event management, 'Festival and Special Event Management' and 'Corporate Event Project Management'. These textbooks are used for courses around the world and have been translated into Chinese, Korean and Portuguese. His adaptation of project management to event and festival management as published on his CD-ROM, found at www.epms.net, is used for events in USA, Europe and China.

William originated the concept of the event management body of knowledge (EMBOK) which has grown into an international body and is the basis of the International Competency Standard for Event Management. He is not only versed in theory William currently organises concerts, festivals and other events around Australia and throughout Asia.

Author with event managers in bedouin tent, Qassim, Saudi Arabia. Photo courtesy of Unaizah Governor's Office

Series Preface

The events industry, including festivals, meetings, conferences, exhibitions, incentives, sports and a range of other events, is rapidly developing and makes a significant contribution to business and leisure related tourism. With increased regulation and the growth of government and corporate involvement in events, the environment has become much more complex. Event managers are now required to identify and service a wide range of stakeholders and to balance their needs and objectives. Though mainly operating at national levels, there has been significant growth of academic provision to meet the needs of events and related industries and the organizations that comprise them. The English speaking nations, together with key Northern European countries, have developed programmes of study leading to the award of diploma, undergraduate and post-graduate awards. These courses focus on providing education and training for future event professionals, and cover areas such as event planning and management, marketing, finance, human resource management and operations. Modules in events management are also included in many tourism, leisure, recreation and hospitality qualifications in universities and colleges.

The rapid growth of such courses has meant that there is a vast gap in the available literature on this topic for lecturers, students and professionals alike. To this end, the *Events Management Series* has been created to meet these needs to create a planned and targeted set of publications in this area.

Aimed at academic and management development in events management and related studies, the *Events Management Series*:

- provides a portfolio of titles which match management development needs through various stages;
- prioritizes publication of texts where there are current gaps in the market, or where current provision is unsatisfactory;
- develops a portfolio of both practical and stimulating texts;
- provides a basis for theoretical and research underpinning for programmes of study;
- is recognized as being of consistent high quality;
- will quickly become the series of first choice for both authors and users.

Introduction

We have witnessed the growth of a new industry that crosses all borders: events. Of course, there were numerous of events happening in the past, the weddings, exhibitions, religious celebrations and sports, however, it was highly distributed in different departments, companies, divisions and regions. The event organisers concentrated on their next event and did not have time to look at a wider industry. In the last years a number of factors have driven the recognition of this new industry.

The development of the Internet and the World Wide Web allowed information and communication to anyone with a connection, a computer and training. The ability to communicate around the world quickly enabled the event managers, festival organisers, event planners and exhibition coordinators to realise that they had much in common. Google, Wikipedia and Skype were all free and some countries were quick in the uptake of these tools.

The ease of travel has created the modern tourist. With the tourism came the movement of cash. This has created a burgeoning source of income for countries. To control this new industry, the Tourism Authorities and Tourism Strategies were created by governments. At the same time the standardisation of culture and cities drove the need to differentiate the destinations. Events, such as festivals, international conferences and sport events, move people and create tourism. If a country is left out of this scheme, they loose funds as their population travel overseas for events. The competition for the tourist dollar is intense. Most major Tourism Authorities have the creation of events and the bidding for international events as one of their priorities. This applies to cities, regions and countries. It is a complex weave of competing destinations. In itself this lead to establishing international services for events, such as education, staging, production and knowledge management.

The importance of logistics and movement of goods and services around the world has created the need for the internationalisation of knowledge. Very few companies can exist without updating the knowledge and skills of their staff and professional development. Attending the international conference or exhibition is mandatory in a competitive world and now part of the ongoing business expense. The reduction of tariffs, the International Monetary Fund requirements and World Trade agreements have diminished the importance of borders and correspondingly increased the need for businesses to network internationally. The number of conferences and meetings has exploded in the last 15 years. As one small example, the requirements for their Continuing Medical Education (CME), physicians must update their skills. The CME points can be gained by attending seminars and conferences. Now multiply this with the medical developments in the Gulf, China and India and the number of new hospitals. One aspect of the industry gives us a small view of the overall growth.

Finally, the event industry has reached a stage where it creates it own reason for growth. Competition between cities, regions and countries for the event that will

FIGURE 1

Layout of the book

attract the tourists is a strong driver for more and better events. In the corporate field, competition for brand recognition drives the event sponsorship. The rise of the IT, telecommunication and services industries with intangible services to sell combined with the privatisation of government services has driven this need for brand recognition.

The industry has reached a level of maturity. At this stage the event industry must take stock, look for patterns and decide on their pathway. International companies, sponsors, organisations and governments know they have reached this point.

This book is written as a way forward and a map of the new maturity of the event industry. It is both a manual and a textbook. The examples and case studies used are fresh. They are from the frontline

The layout of this book is divided into three sections Strategy, Management and Operations. Figure 1 represents this as three concentric circles with the event operations as the core. Events feasibility and development cannot be so simply categorised in reality. Even the smallest operational issue can result in an event being unfeasible. At all times it is well to remember that the day of the event is the time when all the work creating the strategy and the management comes to fruition.

Strategic feasibility and development

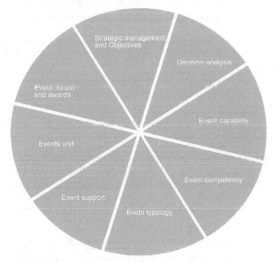

FIGURE 1

Theme of Section 1

This section refers to the bigger picture of event management. It is the feasibility and management of the programme of events or a portfolio of events and festivals. A region, city, organisation or company will rarely host only one event. Numerous events and festivals take place under their name. From the event organiser's point of view they are the primary stakeholder. They finance, host and/or sponsor the event. This primary stakeholder must decide the type and level of support given to events. They must decide whether they will organise the event internally or contract it out. A local council, for example, will organise their civic events, such as national days and they will host sports events, conferences and exhibitions. They sponsor or provide some support for community events. Another example is a major hospital. They will be involved in numerous events. They may host conferences and seminars. The modern hospital must constantly improve their doctor's skills through the continuous professional development that includes attendance at international conferences. They have launches of new wings and new campaigns. They may host VIP events and fundraising dinners. Also they may be involved in public awareness campaigns and community relations events.

It is a complex mix and the question of feasibility is central to the decision to support events and create a full programme of events and festivals. This section will consider the event and events programme feasibility from their point of view. It includes the host's or client's objectives, the process of support, the levels of support and the application process. As events and festivals grow in their economic visibility, these decisions are central to the economic robustness of a region or company. Exhibit 1 illustrates the concerns of a large annual event and is an example of an event's growing pains. Most of the operational issues have been solved over the many years of the event. The issues that come to the fore are the long-term management problems such as stakeholder management and knowledge management. These are strategic issues as they affect the sustainability of the event.

EXHIBIT 1 A SAMPLE OF THE STRATEGIC ISSUES AND GOALS OF A MAJOR EVENT

- The event has had enormous growth and the event organisation must be able to manage this growth.
- It needs the best 'structure' for the organisation to ensure long-term viability.
- The event organisation must move away from the ad hoc arrangement of the past.
- Contingency staff and committee strategies, i.e. if a committee person leaves then there should be backup as the event team loses their knowledge and experience. Every committee person has a role and looks after an area such as concert, trade sites and catering and merchandise, when they leave their skills and knowledge goes with them.
- There must be the ability to get major funding in the near future.
- The local authority's role should be more defined in relation to the event. Their level of assistance and future support should be described and agreed upon.
- At the same time the event should stay true to its origins and should always be memorable.
- The legal entity of the event must be decided by comparing the various models; such as company, association or part of the local authority.
- One goal of the event is to become international.

Inaugural Saudi Events Forum. Photo William O'Toole

Event strategy

INTRODUCTION

Events and festivals are an economic and social driver of many companies, cities, regions and countries. They need to be assessed for their benefits and placed in the development plans of the organisation. The only way to achieve this sensibly is to devise a framework for the development. This chapter describes how these frameworks or event strategies are created. It begins with the recognition of events as being part of a development portfolio and not isolated instances. A company or city has a range of events spread over the year. Each event is an asset and should be treated in the same way as other projects are developed and assessed. The returns on this asset assist the organisation to reach their objectives. The chapter has numerous real cases and concludes with a detailed example of a local authority.

1.1 STRATEGY CHECKLIST

A strategy is a long-term plan of action, encompassing all divisions of the organisation and designed to achieve organisation-wide goals. Once an organisation, such as a company or government department, reaches a certain level of complexity, it is necessary to have a common method and direction understood by all the divisions or departments. The strategy provides the common direction for all the subdivisions. It enables the various departments to work in their area of specialty and know they are helping the organisation as a whole. Generally large organisations have strategic plans with 3, 5 and 10-year cycles. Near the end of each cycle the past strategic plan is evaluated and the new strategic plan is developed. Despite insightful criticism of strategic planning by analysts such as Henry Mintzberg, organisations invariably use it.

Understanding the strategy of an organisation is essential to understand the reason for their events and the feasibility of future events. The limitation of strategic planning is that the plan, once adopted, tends to have a life of its own, regardless of the changing conditions. The plan and the objectives filter down to all the divisions of the company. Each of the divisions formulates their own subobjectives referring to the company-wide objectives. All of this takes time and the delay in implementation should be taken into account with strategic policy. Once the objectives are formulated by the organisation's departments, the strategic plan will push the organisation in a certain direction. Just like a large cruise liner, it is difficult to turn the company once its course is set. Over a period of 5 years, the basic assumptions and projections that formed the foundation of the strategic plan may no longer align with the real

Events Feasibility and Development. DOI: 10.1016/B978-0-7506-6640-4.10001-9

world. Events can assist the company in these new conditions but they will not be supported as they do not fit in with the strategic plan. Given that one of the outcomes of events is to assist change and development in a company, the lack of support for the vehicle that can realign the company is a problem.

Notwithstanding these issues, the strategic plan of the key stakeholders is a vital document in the feasibility and development of events. It provides the framework and the objectives of the future of the organisation and the events that fit into the strategic plan will be supported by the organisation.

The strategic concerns of a key stakeholder are outlined in the example of the tourism event strategy checklist (Exhibit 1.1). It is a list of the requirements of an events strategy for a region. They are set out in heading format so that they can be dealt with in a systematic way and used as a template outline to develop the strategy.

EXHIBIT 1.1 A TOURISM EVENT STRATEGY CHECKLIST

1. Definitions
   a. Reflect the region's tourism market strategy into an event strategy
   b. Extent of involvement of the event coordinator in hosting, organising and marketing an event
2. Strategy
   a. Create a vision and direction for region's events industry
   b. Identify goals and objectives
   c. Identify potential partnership between stakeholders and us
   d. Identify gaps (review)
   e. Identify challenges (review)
   f. Identify critical success factors (review)
   g. Suggestions to overcome challenges (review)
3. Policy
   a. Insurance policy
   b. Event registration policy
   c. Event proposal policy
   d. Budget policy
   e. Promotion policy
   f. Event evaluation policy
4. Funding
   a. Establish transparent and consistent process for funding events
   b. Establish clear and consistent protocols for tendering and contracting events
   c. Establish transparent and consistent process to bid for events
5. Evaluation
   a. Develop evaluation methods based on the objectives of the events strategy
   b. Develop an appropriate tool to measure the social, community and economic benefits of specific MICE (Meetings, Incentives, Conventions and Exhibitions) to enable comparisons between different festivals and events

6. Human resources

    a. Establish an advisory Board to identify opportunities, develop strategies and make decisions about MICE

    b. Develop an event industry employment and training strategy with events, professional bodies and training providers

7. Organisation and management

    a. Suggest methods for increasing the ease of producing events in the region

    b. Maintain an events organisers database

    c. Develop a handbook of relevant requirements and procedures for the production of events

    d. How to sustain an efficient management and international good practice

    e. Establish an event volunteers group

8. Reviews

    a. Review ways in which volunteers are recruited and recompensed

    b. Review long-term planning objectives for hosting major events and consider how these objectives fit into the development and business plans of tourism division

    c. Identity the institutional involvement in event production

    d. Review the MICE market covering the following points:

        – Credibility of events

        – Return of investment

        – Required infrastructure and facilities

        – Success potential

        – Timing

        – Funding and sponsorship

        – Event rotation

        – Expertise

        – Geographical location and climate

        – International participation

    e. Review of existing events

9. Expected results

    a. Execute summary of events strategy

    b. Annual action plan

    c. Refine and develop a calendar of events which caters for the diverse needs of the region's tourists

    d. Suggest an event steering group

    e. Create a database of contact people

    f. Create templates

    g. Application to hold an event (organiser profile)

    h. Sponsorship request form

    i. Event evaluation form

    j. Special requirements form

    k. Venues inventory (suggested activities for each site)

    l. Meetings and conferences facilities kit and CD/DVD

    m. Create events identity for the region

(Continued)

EXHIBIT 1.1 A TOURISM EVENT STRATEGY CHECKLIST—*Cont'd*

      n. Contact management

      o. Event manual

      p. Action checklist

10. Development

      a. How to develop an infrastructure that supports a vibrant events sector in the region

      b. Refine and develop a calendar of events which caters for concepts 'fun and entertainment' and diverse needs of residents and tourists

      c. Suggest innovative events that can be used for promotion by identifying its elements that are considered 'special'

11. Marketing and promotion

      a. Develop a comprehensive events communication tool

      b. Develop a comprehensive source of information on events in the region

      c. Develop a partnership with the communication system in the region

      d. Create an event publications listing

      e. Develop a comprehensive events promotion tools

      f. Devise how to develop local and international media networks and encourage the regional exposure involvement

      g. Suggest events marketing and related services skills development strategy

Exhibit 1 (Section 1 of this book) and Exhibit 1.1 illustrate the push for strategic development from two different directions. It is the internal need of an event organisation as the event grows to have a pathway for development. The other shows the push from the stakeholders to plot the direction of their events in the region. Both of these are a result of the growth of the events industry around the world. It is not unique to the events industry. A similar path was followed by many economic sectors as they gradually matured.

The events industry needs to adapt the tools of these other industries to make sure that the development of strategies is using the best models. The next section suggests it is time for the introduction of the tools of asset management as a way to assess the feasibility and to guide the development of events.

1.2 THE EVENT PORTFOLIO AS AN ASSET

The core of this book is that the events industry around the world has matured. The key event stakeholders are no longer solely concerned with the management of the next event. It now includes the development of an events programme, a portfolio of events that deliver on the strategic objectives of the key stakeholder be it a country, region, city, association or a company. The return or benefit realised on the investment in an events portfolio is various and distributed over time. Therefore its management cannot be solely project based. The management must take into account where an event fits into the large picture. It must consider the relationship to other events over a long period of time. The returns on the investment in an event are complex and not immediately obvious.

One of the major impediments to the development of this long term management of a portfolio of events is the lack of data on what events are worth. There are a number of disparate studies to indicate the events sector is a billion dollar industry. The Meeting Professionals International Foundation Canada claim the meetings industry

> Although the direct industry output of meetings activity in Canada was $32.2 billion, every dollar spent on meetings activity in 2006 resulted in another $1.21 in spin-off activity in some other part of the economy. Indirect and induced effects accounted for $20.2 billion and $18.7 billion respectively, for total industry output of $71.1 billion (Maritz Research Canada 2008:2).

The Business Events Strategy Group quote a figure of $122.31 billion spend in 2003 in the USA on business events (BEISG 2008:18).

Events are invisible to official economic statistics gathering. It is not hard to see why when considering the United Nations classification of industries. The International Standard Industrial Classification of All Economic Activities, Revision Number Four has the following categories:

A. Agriculture, forestry and fishing
B. Mining and quarrying
C. Manufacturing
D. Electricity, gas, steam and air conditioning supply
E. Water supply sewerage, waste management and remediation activities
F. Construction
G. Wholesale and retail trade repair of motor vehicles and motorcycles
H. Transportation and storage
I. Accommodation and food service activities
J. Information and communication
L. Real estate activities
M. Professional, scientific and technical activities
N. Administrative and support service activities
O. Public administration and defence compulsory social security
P. Education
Q. Human health and social work activities
R. Arts, entertainment and recreation
S. Other service activities
T. Activities of households as employers, undifferentiated goods-producing and services-producing activities of households for own use
U. Activities of extraterritorial organisations and bodies

This has no category for events or festivals and yet all these industries are significantly impacted by events. They all employ events to further their business.

It is safe to assume that events, although not defined, are big business and can be regarded as an asset.

Asset management is a long-standing management science. It originated with the management of the physical assets of a company or a country. These include machinery, roads, airports, buildings, parks and gardens. In an economy with a large service sector the assets are not as easily defined as just physical assets. The skills or competencies of the people are assets and can be more valuable than the buildings or machinery. Carrying this to the next step, a government or a company may regard their events as assets. Although the returns from these assets may be intangible, they still come under the definition of an asset. As will be discussed in this chapter, the programme of events is indeed a valuable asset for a country and has significant returns on the investment. Unlike many physical assets an event is one of the few assets that appreciates or increases in value over the years. The importance of the introduction of asset management theory into events management is because it recognises time and value as integral to management. An asset changes over time. It requires constant management. An annual association meeting will develop over time. A sports competition will grow as it becomes more established. It is foolish to think all events will become successful in its first year. Asset management recognises that the repeat event is an investment. Unlike many other assets, an event can appreciate as well as have a good Return On Investment (ROI). An event can create intellectual property and a brand. This is well known to the event companies who eventually franchise their events. The brand is no more obvious than the effort the Olympics Organising Committee will take to protect the name Olympics and the symbol of the rings. Asset management is concerned with the asset over its lifetime. Although the lifetime of many events can only be guessed, it takes a long view of the event. At the same time asset management understands the asset may have to be sold off, devolved or scrapped. A major difficulty with managing an event portfolio is getting rid of the 'non-performers'. A repeat public festival, for example, can be very difficult to permanently cancel. By using asset management the client or host can make these decisions using a transparent and agreed-upon system. Core concepts of time, value and development are joined with the idea that an asset produces an outcome. An asset is there to produce social benefit and financial value. This is implied in the term 'asset'. Hence it is not a matter of explaining that it produces value but the amount and extent of the value. It puts the events portfolio on the same level as the other assets of a company or a country. It then becomes a matter of deciding what assets to invest in.

The tools of physical asset management can be taken across to the event industry. They provide a readymade language to describe the event portfolio and enable the comparison of the event assets with other tangible and intangible assets.

The acquisition of the asset is the first decision in asset management. Once the need for the asset has been determined, it involves the make, hire or buy choice. This book goes into this decision in great detail for events as it is vital to the long-term life of the event and its results. With physical assets the choice can be straightforward as it is possible to compare the variations. Events, however, are not as simple. The World Cup is an example. It is a huge asset for a country and there is nothing to compare to it. It can only be hired. It is a complex decision full of uncertainties for a country to bid for the World Cup. Despite all the research and reports over the years it is still debated whether the World Cup or the Olympics gives a good return on the investment for a country.

The operation and maintenance of the assets is an important part of asset management. For the annual event to benefit the client, it will need constant management and development. Events require more than maintenance, they need renewal and innovation. This means the event can increase in value. Unlike many other types of assets that depreciate, the event can appreciate. This gives them a unique place in the assets of a county or a company. Also an event can rapidly appreciate in matter of a few years. The *Sculpture by the Sea* event, over a period of 10 years, grew in numbers and exposure. The numbers of attendees went from a few thousand to half a million.

One of the most important elements of asset management for the events portfolio is the idea of the asset life cycle. An asset will reach a stage when the costs of the asset will be beyond the benefits plus the cost of its replacement. At this point the asset must be sold or scrapped. This is factored into the decision to acquire the asset in the first place. It is known that the asset will eventually pass its use-by-date. This is rarely done in the events industry. The result of this oversight is festivals, sports events and meetings going way beyond their life cycle. They become a burden on the community or the company and are almost impossible to shed. The non-performing assets take funds and other resources from the development of new events. In part it is a result of the complexity of the event environment as outlined below, as well as the immaturity of the event industry. From an asset management perspective, the decision to shed the asset is all part of its accountable and transparent management. This problem of events is worldwide and one of the reasons for writing this book.

From the science of asset management arises the term ROI. It is the current buzzword in the industry. Most of the misunderstandings arise from a confused use of the ROI. A number of events professionals have tried different versions of the ROI such as Return on Event, Return on Objectives and Return on Entertainment. This is described in detail in the section on Return on Investment (Chapter 11). If the basis of the concept is asset management, then the ROI is quite clear. The problem is, as ever, how it is to be measured. To have the measurement based on the solid foundation of asset management is the essential first step.

From an asset management perspective there are three types of ROI. These are commercial, social capital and goodwill.

The commercial returns are numerous, highly targeted and efficient. Direct commercial returns comprise the financial income from the event itself. Much of this will flow through the region or the company. This flow provides a stimulus to the local business and enables new businesses to overcome the initial constraint to their development. Indirectly, events such as product launches, conferences and exhibitions provide the means for companies and industrial sectors to develop. There has been constant disagreement by economist over how to measure the indirect commercial returns for an event. This has not been helped by exaggerated claims by event sellers and governments who conveniently estimate the gross returns without all the costs.

Events contribute to the social capital of a company, city, region and a country. They drive many capital projects such as infrastructure. At the same time they contribute to the vital social network that enables the unification of a country and the development of morale and corporate culture. The contribution public festivals, special interest group events and conferences make to the social cohesiveness of a country is enormous. Cultural and social affirmation and development is an important outcome of events.

Finally events contribute to the goodwill of a city, region and country. This is how it is valued above its direct economic assets. In tourism, this is referred to as the 'brand'. For some companies the brand is their real wealth. If the company were to be sold, the goodwill or brand value is determined by the price of the sale minus the value of their physical assets.

As will be demonstrated by the chapters in this book, all the returns on investment fit under these three categories. This does not necessarily give the reason for the event. Not all events have a good ROI. Political considerations often cloud the clarity and the straightforward application of asset management to events. There are plenty of events around the world that cost far more than they benefit a population. Their true benefit is in terms of political power for a person, party or group of people.

The production of events strategies by countries around the world and the formation of the semi-government event corporations attest to the value of events.

Figure 1.1 is a schema to visualise the development of a national event strategy. Prior to the creation of a national strategy the events, shown as lines, develop in a haphazard way. This has numerous advantages as the events closely reflect the needs of the population and businesses. However, the events which return a national benefit and a long-term positive ROI for the country have no advantage or support. Events with immediate benefits are favoured and the events have a short lifespan. The development and implementation of a national strategy will assist the events that meet the national development objectives. At the same time the strategy, through implementing quality rewards and informing legislation, raises the excellence of all events. The next stage in the development is to devolve the national strategy into a regional support system. This pathway will create an industry that includes associations, bidding for events and event training. Once the industry is created it will support by itself. The only need for government action is to guide the industry through awarding of government contracts, training and regulation.

A similar figure can be constructed for a private organisation or a corporation. There are many companies with disparate events. A strategy enables a company to

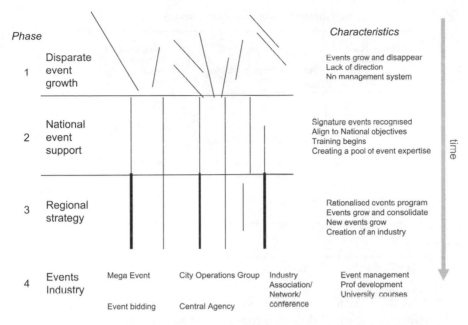

Phase					Characteristics
1	Disparate event growth				Events grow and disappear Lack of direction No management system
2	National event support				Signature events recognised Align to National objectives Training begins Creating a pool of event expertise
3	Regional strategy				Rationalised events program Events grow and consolidate New events grow Creation of an industry
4	Events Industry	Mega Event Event bidding	City Operations Group Central Agency	Industry Association/ Network/ conference	Event management Prof development University courses

Examples :England,, Scotland, Ireland, New Zealand, China, Australia, UAE, Qatar, Singapore, Malaysia, South Africa, Canada

FIGURE 1.1

The development of an events industry.

control the direction of their event programme and invest in the ones with a positive return on the investment. This book will address each of the topics in Fig. 1.1 and show how a number of organisations have created this pathway to the development of an events portfolio.

1.3 CASCADE OF OBJECTIVES

Organisations use objectives in their strategic plans as a guide for the units of the organisation such as the departments, the divisions or individual staff. Each division is expected to use their expertise and resources to assist the organisation to reach the objectives. The larger objectives may be termed global objectives, organisation-wide objectives, objective functions or goals. To derive the division's objectives is straightforward in most departments such as marketing, logistics or operations. However, as events tend to span all the divisions, the way they help an organisation reach its goals is not always obvious or stated. To establish an events feasibility and development system in a company or government, it must be aligned to the organisation-wide objectives.

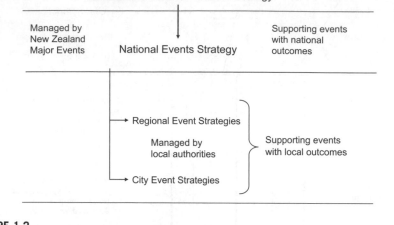

FIGURE 1.2

New Zealand hierarchy of strategies

This is the same for government authorities. They develop strategic plans for economic development of their city, region or country. The plans have a fairly set formula or template. The core of the economic plan is made up of the objectives. These are often set out in tablature and numbered form so other government departments and divisions can decipher which of the objectives applies to them. They in turn develop objectives that will allow them to direct their work and outcomes.

Figure 1.2 illustrates how this works for the country of New Zealand. There is a National Tourism Strategy that is developed by the stakeholders in the industry and the government. The National Tourism Strategy contains objectives that relate to the policy of the current government. One of the strategies under the Tourism Strategy is the National Events Strategy with its objectives. These objectives all relate to the objectives of the National Tourism Strategy. Under the National Events Strategy are the Regional and City Events Strategies. The National Events Strategy is interpreted around the country in the form of the local strategies. This represents the ideal situations. New Zealand adopted the concept of events strategies early in their event development. Most countries do not have such a rational system for the development of their events.

The next four exhibits illustrate strategic management by using objectives. Exhibit 1.2 is an example of the tourism objectives from the North East England Tourism Strategy. Although events and festivals are not mentioned in this list, it is easily seen how events can assist the authority to reach its objectives. Events and festivals in this case become part of the tools used to develop their tourism.

An example of the tourism objectives is provided in Exhibit 1.2. These objectives are similar around the world for regional authorities.

This core part of an organisation strategy is the list of objectives such as those show in Exhibits 1.3 and 1.4.

EXHIBIT 1.2 TOURISM OBJECTIVES OF A LOCAL AUTHORITY

1. Attract more domestic and overseas tourists to the region
2. Increase visitors' average spend and increase day visitor spend
3. Increase visits throughout the year, not solely in the main holiday season
4. Increase employment in tourism and tourism-related businesses
5. Improve the productivity of the regional tourism economy
6. Accelerate the rate of investment in the tourism product
7. Improve the quality of the tourism product
8. Improve the skills of the tourism workforce
9. Improve levels of visitor satisfaction in the North East
10. Enhance and conserve the region's natural, heritage and cultural assets

Tourism Objectives of North East England Tourism Strategy (2005–2010); available at: www.onenortheast.co.uk.

The tourism objectives of Exhibit 1.2 are precise as they concern measurable outcomes. The councils' objectives are more intangible but nontheless as real as the tourism objectives. The right sort of festivals and events could easily help this council reach their objectives. The way this is done is described in the case study at the end of the chapter.

EXHIBIT 1.3 SAMPLE OF COUNCIL OR LOCAL AUTHORITY OBJECTIVES

An example of a council or local authority objectives

Strategic objectives
A. People
    1. A community that enjoys and celebrates its diversity
    2. A stronger and more self-sufficient community
    3. Council facilities and services that best meet community needs
    4. An accessible and active City Centre
    5. Council and the community working together to achieve shared goals
    6. Encourage life-long learning

B. Land
    1. Well-planned and sustainable development
    2. Reduced impact of flooding
    3. Cleaner water
    4. A protected and restored natural environment
    5. Sustainable use of natural resources
    6. A healthier public environment
    7. An environmentally aware community

(Continued)

EXHIBIT 1.3 SAMPLE OF COUNCIL OR LOCAL AUTHORITY OBJECTIVES—*Cont'd*

C. Community assets/infrastructure

1. Community and economic development is supported through the provision of transport, drainage, recreation and building assets
2. The deterioration of council's community assets is minimised
3. Council's community assets are maintained, within available resources, so they are safe and functional to users

D. Services

1. User-friendly and convenient customer service
2. Services that reflect the needs of the families living, working, studying and visiting Liverpool
3. A community informed on key council initiatives and activities

E. Governance

1. Sound financial management
2. Effective, efficient and sustainable operation of council
3. High levels of governance within council and the community
4. A workplace which values learning and equity
5. A safe and healthy workplace

EXHIBIT 1.4 OBJECTIVES OF A REGIONAL EVENTS PROGRAMME

The Regional Events Programme is designed to complement Event Scotland's Major International Events Programme by showcasing specific towns and regions across the country. Whilst the majority of International Events are likely to take place in our larger metropolitan areas of Glasgow and Edinburgh, the Regional Events Programme has been created to support cultural and sporting events held outside these areas.

The objectives of the Regional Events Programme are to develop a portfolio of events that will

- Generate economic benefits for specific regions of Scotland
- Attract visitors to a region from other parts of the country
- Inspire and involve local communities
- Enhance the profile and appeal of the host region

Event Scotland's regional event priorities focus on events that meet the objectives of the programme and have

- The confirmed financial support of appropriate local agencies
- Local passion and leadership
- A viable budget and realistic planning
- The opportunity to build legacy and sustainability
- The capacity to grow in terms of spectator and participant numbers, media profile, etc.

For reference visit http://www.eventscotland.org/supportprogrammes.htm.

EXHIBIT 1.5 STRATEGIC OBJECTIVES FOR COUNCIL SUPPORT OF EVENTS

The objectives of supporting events can, for the purpose of discussion, be divided into four categories. Note that each of these categories overlap with the others.

1. Community strengthening
2. Event sustainability
3. Economic development
4. Increase tourism

The characteristics of these objectives are as follows:

1. Community strengthening
   a. Ownership of the event
   b. Passion in being involved in the event
   c. A diversity of events and yet a focus on quality events
   d. Partnerships with local businesses
   e. Increasing social interaction
2. Event sustainability
   a. Evaluating the events
   b. Tracking and evaluating the support from the council including in-kind support
   c. Up-skilling current event committees in areas such as finance and risk
   d. Training new event coordinators for succession plan
   e. Enable a workflow approach to permission and council processes for event support
3. Economic development
   a. Partnering with local businesses and assisting in other ways
   b. Actual economic impact through cash input assessment
   c. Branding the region – in conjunction with Tourism Plan
   d. Maximising the employment of local resources including parks and facilities
4. Increase tourism
   a. Grouping events as a way of increasing stay
   b. Branding the shire in conjunction with the Tourism Plan
   c. Assessing the catchment area for each event, i.e. local, regional and interstate

In both Exhibits 1.3 and 1.4 an events development strategy must show how events address these objectives. If they are tourism events the strategy must show how the future tourism events will satisfy these objectives. The next two examples, Exhibits 1.4 and 1.5, illustrate this. The list of objectives must relate back to the organisation or division-wide objectives. Note how they can be divided into the benefits of good asset management: social capital, commercial returns and goodwill.

The event support objectives illustrated by Exhibits 1.4 and 1.5 provide the parameters of the event support process for the host organisation. They are basic guidelines to decide which events to support and which ones are feasible and which event has no benefit to the organisation. These are the reasons for having the event. These two exhibits can be cross-referenced to the two previous exhibits and the event support objectives traced to higher development objectives.

The objectives are needed to obtain a consistency of support across the organisation. It may seem obvious why Saudi Aramco, for example, has a clean up the desert campaign. However, in practice, each person in the organisation will give different reasons for the event. For the event to work for the host there must be agreed-upon objectives. The event may be a success from the point of view of the attendee. They enjoyed the day and felt they contributed to the environment. At the same time this furthers the objectives of Saudi Aramco of social responsibility and goodwill.

The event support objectives are fundamental to the event's success. They provide the reason to support the event for the host. They provide the foundation to framework of the event management. The case study Local Council events describes in detail how events in one council or local authority region can contribute to the council's objectives.

Although these examples concern regions and cities, the process is the same for companies. The company's objectives must be met by their events they support. This will be further described in the section on sponsorship.

CASE STUDY 1.1 LOCAL COUNCIL EVENTS

Introduction

Events cross all disciplines and departments. Their contributions to the strategic objectives of the organisations are many and varied. For this reason, the contribution is often hidden. In particular, the regional authority, such as a council, will benefit from events in numerous ways. An events strategy clearly points out the benefits. To establish a sustainable event policy, these benefits are listed and closely aligned with the organisation's objectives. This can be illustrated by using the five goals as set out in a City Council's strategic plan. The outcomes of an event programme can be listed. Below is an example of this process. The outcomes of the events are described according to the way they contribute to these strategic objectives. Although this focuses on the government sphere, it is easily adapted to a company's strategic plans or any other organisation.

Strategic objective: Demonstrating the use of the assets and services

The facilities and services of the council are highly visible to the public and businesses during a festival or event. Parks, roads, sporting facilities and transport are used as an integral part of any event. Events provide an opportunity for the council to showcase these facilities. The services provided by the council can often remain unnoticed on a day-to-day basis by the community. However, a festival or event provides an opportunity for the council to make these essential services noticed. The council's event team provides the service of assisting the community with their events. The expertise of the council's event team is a great asset for the region. Most events and festivals are organised by volunteers or on a part-time basis. The event team and the information stored by the council represent accumulated knowledge of thousands of events and have links to similar events around the country.

Community assets are both celebrated and visibly employed for events and festivals. There is no better time for the parks, gardens and other assets to be showcased to the community than during an event. Events and festival can also be used to employ these assets during time when they are underutilised. Some events, such as the celebration of World Environment Day are a way to improve the assets and result in a clean and well-maintained neighbourhood. Other events can be a reason to improve or upgrade the assets and services. All of this is done in the spirit of community celebration.

In summary events can be used to:

1. Demonstrate the provision and utilisation of the services to the community
2. Maintain and improve the community assets and services
3. Test the services at times of high capacity and improve them

The character and heritage of existing neighbourhoods, villages and semi-rural areas are visible in their celebrations. Most community events are a means for the community to support and enhance their character and heritage. Cultural celebrations such Diwali, Chinese New Year, Easter and Eid are regarded as essential by their respective communities. Events such as school fetes and sports competitions are part of the character and express the heritage of the community.

Strategic objective: An attractive and liveable city

Festivals enliven any public space. Conference and meetings create and enhance social networks. Social life is the basis of any community event. Events and festivals revitalise the old spaces and validate the new spaces. With judicious management, events and festivals assist with the even spread of economic activity in an area and across time. The Summer Festival is an example of spreading economic activity across time. The festival was explicitly arranged so it occurs in a tourism low time. The popular event, *Sculpture by the Sea*, is used to revitalise the coastal area and corniches.

Events, by their nature, ensure an active community. Public festivals are accessible to all, attract the media and showcase the community as vibrant and active. Sports events and events with a large element of physical activity promote activities. Most sports will culminate in a yearly event. This event provides the focus for innumerable community activities throughout the year. A City Centre can provide a central site for many of these events that are widely distributed over the region.

Strategic objective: A city that respects the environment and sustainability

The concepts and aim of sustainability are found in most events through a waste wise policy and the value of events as a means of communication. Events are highly valued by corporations as a channel for their messages, as they provide uninterrupted promotion. This means that the message is an integral part of the event. In a similar way, festival and events that promote the natural environment are highly effective in delivering their message and having it accepted by the attendees. Events and festivals demonstrate these objectives by the method the festival is managed and during the event. They also provide a clear uninterrupted channel to deliver these messages to a highly targeted audience at a time when they are most receptive.

Strategic objective: A continually improving workforce

Events provide training and education in a variety of areas. Seminars, conferences and exhibitions are a part of the event industry. These represent direct learning. Most events include elements of these. As well, events provide the attendees with new experiences and new ways to look at the familiar. Some events are used indirectly to educate the public about important issues, such as being waste wise, saving water, tax issues. In particular, certain events provide the educator with a highly targeted audience and therefore an efficient way to deliver a message.

Events and festivals use a large number of volunteers. This creates a training ground for youth of the region. The knowledge and skills gained from working on events are transferable across all industries. The team environment engenders a group work culture. The event or festival is the direct and visible result of the work. For this reason colleges include working on events and festivals as part of their curriculum in marketing, business and hospitality.

Strategic objective: A tolerant work and living environment

Events and festivals strengthen the community through working together for a common goal, such as the celebration of an important date in a cultural calendar or a civic function. They promote tolerance and understanding and show the various cultures under the light of celebrations. To the

(Continued)

CASE STUDY 1.1 Local Council Events—*Cont'd*

various religious and cultural backgrounds of the region, events, such as Diwali, are seen as a way of celebrating their uniqueness. This diversity produces a robust community with a wide variety of experience and understanding.

Events and festivals provide the medium for the community to enjoy and celebrate in a safe environment. Events enable the celebration to be directed and evaluated and therefore sustainable. The positive aspects of diversity in the community are no more evident than in their celebrations. They solve the seeming contradiction of social unity and diversity.

Events are particularly good at emphasising local history and heritage. They celebrate anniversaries of historical events. Events and festivals can also create heritage and showcase a hidden heritage.

Many community events arise from the needs of the community and therefore are an excellent communication channel to that community.

***Strategic objective*: A community involved in decision-making**

Events and festivals, being project based, work towards achievable goals. The goals are explicit and in common agreement. The local authority working with community groups to create a celebration enables the parties to reach a common understanding. Most events and festivals include numerous stakeholders such as local businesses, schools, contractors and suppliers, community groups, roads and traffic authorities, and transport companies. All of these groups are working together to achieve a shared goal.

Events and festivals provide a friendly channel to inform the community of council initiative and activities. The attendees represent a highly targeted audience, and therefore the event is an efficient way to both inform the public and obtain feedback.

As well as directly fulfilling these objectives, events and festivals can be used to demonstrate the council's commitment to good governance through public awareness programmes at events. The event attracts a highly targeted audience and the awareness programme can be tailored to the specific audience.

The strategic objectives in Case Study 1.1 are typical examples of the ones a regional authority or a city government contain in their 5-year management or development plan. National government may have wider objectives. Some of these are described in the following paragraphs.

1.3.1 *Strategic objective*: Nation building through networks of common interests

Events and festivals are a part of creating a sense of nationhood. For some developing countries this is an essential objective. The post-colonial world has created countries with borders that cross ancient tribal, language and cultural regions. The Duran line between Pakistan and Afghanistan has cut the Pashtun tribal region in half. The break up of the Middle East after the fall of the Ottoman empire and the subsequent scramble for resources has left nations with highly disparate populations. Many countries in Africa suffer this complexity of nationhood. The Sudan, for example, has over 200 language groups. In this volatile situation the national and regional events can assist in giving the people a common aim and a cause to celebrate. The conferences, exhibitions and sports events all have a vital role to play in the social construction of a country. Cultural events allow the citizens to be proud of their culture at the same time as being part of the country's social fabric. As pointed out by the historian David Glassberg, the USA used events to re-enactment their history in the pageantry movement of the early 1900s. Their aim was, through events, to give the citizens a sense of common nationhood and common history. Even in highly tribal areas there are networks of common interest independent of religion differences or history. Sport is an excellent example of this. The broadcast of the World Cup in South Africa showed the citizens sharing a common space that would have been unthought of a few years ago. Associations, clubs and social networks, such as vintage car groups, doctors' associations, or bicycle clubs, provide a network on which to create a national identity. In the documentary on the USA Spelling Bee competition, Spellbound, the mother of one young brilliant contestant comments that this is the one place her child can feel normal.

1.3.2 Keeping the tourist at home

The leakage of tourism money is serious for some regions and cities. Events can minimise this by providing a reason to 'stay at home'. In one country over a million people, a tenth of their population, travel overseas in the one short season. The aim of events in this situation is to make the place more enjoyable than going overseas. The same can be said of sports, conferences and exhibitions. By not having these events in a city it encourages people to travel outside to attend them. If all the doctor's conferences are overseas then a large amount of money is following them.

Making the place attractive for families can be a strong objective in the development of cities and the new integrated developments. If a town is to attract people to work, they need to provide an environment that is conducive for families. There are many places around the world they have been designed for logistics with perfect roads and shopping centres, but lack the soul or life that events and festivals can give.

The above discussion shows how strongly events can contribute to a company or regional development. The next logical step is to find a way that the organisations can promote and support events. Traditionally in the corporate field this is done through sponsorship. However, as the new generation of companies have found, passive sponsorship is not enough. Companies such as Red Bull and Zain have highly active event development section. For the government the next step is to support events that assist in the strategic plan.

Chapter 2 examines the best practice method to support these events.

DISCUSSION TOPICS

There are many event strategies published on the web by UK and New Zealand, collect these and find the similarities. Each event strategy will have slightly different priorities. Discuss the reason for these differences.

Using the development strategy of your local authority construct an objectives for an events strategy.

Using the mission, vision goals or objectives of a major company construct objectives for their events.

Sculpture by the Sea, Bondi Beach. Photo William O'Toole

Preparing the strategy

INTRODUCTION

The events development strategy must be thoroughly prepared if it is to guide the future events in a clear and accountable manner. The key tool for this is the decision table as it assists the authority or company to assess future events. The application of this tool from engineering to events is never perfect. However, in the complexity of a large organisation with many projects competing for resources, it is the most efficient way to gain support for a future programme of events. The number of stakeholders of an events programme is large. It includes varied interests and rarely do these stakeholders have an understanding of events and their impacts. For this reason stakeholder engagement and stakeholder meetings are vital to success. By using a template for the strategy the meeting can be highly productive. Finally, the ability of the area to host events is assessed.

2.1 DECISION CRITERIA

The next step in creating a system to assess event feasibility from the host's or client's point of view is to establish criteria for event support and sponsorship.

The accountability of the event support process is vital to its sustainability. Events, festivals and related projects are competing for government support. A clear-cut way of deciding on priorities in funding and other support must be developed. The most common system used in government comes from the allocation of funds in the field of civil engineering and Department of Defence. It may be regarded as an engineering approach to decisions. It has its limitations and its advantages. As with many aspects of government, it is a compromise to enable the accountable development of an industry. This section outlines the process, its origins, methods for constant improvement and its limitations.

Using a decision criteria matrix is a well-known method used in many fields. It is now more common in large organisations through the work of Norton and Kaplan from the Harvard Business School. Their system, called Balanced Scorecard (BSC), was introduced as a way to measure the intangible aspects of a company's performance. Before the BSC, the main indicator for senior executive of the health of an organisation was the financial metric, i.e. money. As a comparable figure, money is an excellent measure assuming it is the only objective of a company. However, there are many intangibles, difficult-to-measure aspect of any organisation, that are not indicated by one figure. The quality of the service provided and employee morale will not be obvious in financial report.

Events Feasibility and Development. DOI: 10.1016/B978-0-7506-6640-4.10002-0

The key was to have a more robust measurement and management system that included both operational metrics as leading indicators and financial metrics as lagging outcomes, along with several other metrics to measure a company's progress in driving future performance.

(Kaplan, 2010, p. 17)

The BSC's emphasis on operation and the intangibles is similar to measurement of the possible success of events. Many objectives of an event are intangible.

Another area of management to introduce a form of decision criteria is its use by the International Olympic Committee (IOC). They have been using a decision criteria software program to decide on the best city to host the future Olympics. The process is similar to the process outlined below when deciding the future events to be held by an organisation. The first step is to decide on the criteria necessary to host the Games. These include the support of the government and its level of commitment, public opinion and infrastructure. The country applying to have the Olympic Games is assessed by a grade of 1–10 according to their comparison with each of the criteria. Some of the criteria, such as the quality of the sporting facilities or accommodation, will not be ready at the time of decision. Therefore, a risk factor is introduced. If a sport facility is not built but likely to be built then it is scored according to the likelihood. The process is complex and involved weighting and fuzzy logic. However, it is clearly explained in their public documentation (IOC, 2008). The need to make the right choice and the need for transparency in decision-making drives the sophistication of the Olympic process. The criteria, weighting, risk, and fuzzy logic model can be adapted to the decision on the feasibility of an event.

The decision matrix or decision table may be regarded as a solution to a highly complex problem when deciding the allocation of resources and when there is a degree of uncertainty.

This process can easily be understood if an event application to an authority is followed. In the first place the event application for support has to pass a filter. This is a go/no go decision on whether the event application will pass to the next phase. The initial criteria for a tourism event could be as follows:

- Does this event clash with other events?
- Is the event culturally unacceptable?
- Has the event been duplicated?
- Are there any budget constraints?
- Does the event meet the objectives of other Government Departments?
- Does the event benefit the region?
- Does the event does fit in with authority's overall policy or image?
- Does the organiser or company have a good reputation and experience at event management?

An answer of *yes* to the first five or a *no* to the last three means an immediate rejection by the authority. If the event applicant does not understand the initial filter, a lot of time can be wasted applying for support that will never eventuate.

The next criteria are derived from the event support objectives. The professional method to use for decision criteria is to use a weighted table. The criteria are weighted according to their importance to the strategic direction of the host. With local councils and companies this is found in their policy and priorities. If it is not obvious it can be derived by a survey of the host. The survey asks the key individuals to prioritise each of the decision criteria.

The advantages of this system are numerous and include the following:

- The decision for event support is based on company or organisation's objectives
- The decisions are defendable and disagreements can be rationally resolved
- It takes the decision process out of the hands of any one person
- It is transparent
- It can be improved with each event
- It can adapt quickly to any changes in policy of the host organisation
- It is simple
- It is the same process that is used in other divisions of the organisation such as Procurement or Sponsorship

To assist the decision process, the decision criteria are assigned a value. Although these will not be the only way to decide on each criteria, they assist the process of understanding the meaning of the criteria. The process involved in producing a decision matrix for an event support system is illustrated in Fig. 2.1.

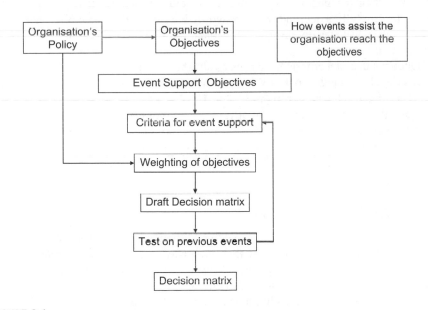

FIGURE 2.1

Producing the decision matrix

EXHIBIT 2.1 SAMPLE OF ECONOMIC DEVELOPMENT CRITERIA

Economic development

Criteria: (a) Partnering with local businesses and assisting in other ways
  Measure:
    I   Number, size and period of local business partnering
    II Direct and indirect benefits to local businesses
Criteria: (b) Actual economic impact through cash input assessment
  Measure:
    I   Measured by expected number of visitors (attendees, participants), length of stay and a description of the target market
Criteria: (c) Branding the region – in conjunction with tourism
  Measure:
    I   Promotion and marketing plan – measured in reach, target market, length of promotion
    II   Brand message quality and fit with the Tourism Strategy
    III Media impact measured by expected coverage, target market and media attractiveness

---

The criteria for support are often in the form of a general statement. To enable the criteria to be used, it needs a measurable component. Exhibit 2.1 illustrates the metrics for the decision criteria for the economic development.

Some people may resile at such an engineering approach to the art of events and festivals. It is well to remember that events and festivals involve thousands of people, huge liability and often millions of dollars. Any other decision with those parameters would be carefully made and documented. It is also well to remember that if the event industry is to become truly professional, transparent and accountable, a decision system is mandatory.

Once the decision criteria have been established, the host organisation can decide on their level of support and the exchange. They can stipulate what they want from the event in exchange for supporting the event. This is vital from both the host's point of view and the event company's point of view. It will impinge on the event's feasibility.

The event company must satisfy the decision criteria of the host organisation in order to obtain support. The process of application is illustrated in later chapters. There is a variety of types and levels of support for events and this is described in detail.

2.2 SITUATION ANALYSIS

Situation analysis for an events development strategy concerns the research and collation of the information about the current events, events programme, infrastructure and event support. It should include the event social, political and economic environment. For a tourism body the analysis would be constrained by a geographic region, such as a city, state or country. For a corporation, a Government Department or association, there may be no geographic constraint. The analysis is, basically, taking stock of the situation and presenting a report.

The situation analysis must have a clear objective. Is the ultimate aim is to increase the number of events or develop the quality of the current events? This must be clearly stated at the outset. There are many assumptions about events and the effects which are often hidden. There may be higher objectives, such as increasing the way the events allow a region to economically develop or increasing the number and appeal of events as a means to social harmony. Each of these objectives will influence how the situation analysis is performed and what data are considered relevant.

A key analytical tool to the situation analysis is the Strength, Weakness, Opportunity and Threat (SWOT) method. It is a disciplined way to divide the situation according to its predicted effect on the events programme. A tourism region on the coast could have the SWOT analysis as shown in Exhibit 2.2.

EXHIBIT 2.2 SAMPLE OF AN EVENT SWOT ANALYSIS OF A TOURISM REGION

SWOT

Strengths

1. Easy access to the region by road, air and sea
2. Possibility of air/sea/land events
3. Long recorded history and unique culture
4. New market
5. Local government support
6. Tax-free and duty-free area
7. Small tourism development community
8. Coral deepwater nearby
9. Gateway destination to other historical areas
10. Rain-free climate
11. Strategic location of importance to a number of countries
12. Waterfront
13. Infrastructure available (water, electricity)
14. Future hotel and integrated resort development plans approved and financed

Discussion. The above multiple strengths would frame the event strategy. Many of the strengths are found in the regions nearby. The culture and history are unique to this region and should assist in the product differentiation.

Weaknesses

1. Located near a volatile zone of the world
2. Lack of regular flights to the region
3. Bureaucracy
4. Lack of a culture of funding/sponsorship
5. Small market
6. Culture
7. Lack of proper facilities
8. Lack of a nightlife
9. Price levels

(Continued)

EXHIBIT 2.2 SAMPLE OF AN EVENT SWOT ANALYSIS OF A TOURISM REGION—*Cont'd*

---

10. No. of rooms (capacity)
11. Community awareness and local mentality
12. Trained manpower/education
13. Lack of services
14. Lack of venues
15. Lack of rooms
16. Lack of experience/expertise

Discussion. The weaknesses can be easily subdivided into capacity issues and marketing and promotion issues. The solution to a capacity problem goes hand in hand with the increase of events. Promotional issues are solved by a concerted marketing and branding campaign supported by a flagship event.

Opportunities
1. High-level government support
2. Real estate and major developments
3. Tourism as a key issue
4. A lot of foreign interest
5. Virgin market
6. Stable political situation
7. Cultural aspects

Discussion. The region is supported by the United Nations and the European Union. There are not many public events held in the region.

Threats
1. Political situation
2. Regional competition
3. Price comparison
4. Local community objecting to change
5. Negative media

Discussion. With the exception of the 'political situation', the threats can be minimised by a good media strategy based on risk management. Number 4 'Local community objecting to change' is similar to the capacity problem and can be minimised by judicious use of events that originate from the community rather than imposed on the community.

The situation analysis process will include the following:

1. Desktop research into the current information on the region
2. Consultation with primary stakeholders such as event organisers, event support suppliers, venues and compliance authorities
3. Consultation with secondary stakeholders such as local associations, sports bodies, clubs, education institutions and chambers of commerce
4. Research into similar regions/cities and their events
5. Collation, analysis and synthesis of the data

The situation analysis of a company includes consultation with all the divisions directly influenced by the events programme. In most cases this includes marketing, legal and finance departments.

The consultations are the key to a successful situation analysis. Meeting with the stakeholders allows the information to come out into the open. In the first place, the organisations with an interest in events have to agree on the basic definitions. In a rapidly developing industry such as events and festival, many terms are not clearly understood. An effective description of the current event situation requires a solid bedrock of clear definitions on which to build the strategy for events development. Like the 12 blind men and the elephant in the Hindu story, each will have their own version of what comprises events and 'Though each was partly in the right, And all were in the wrong!'. Each of the stakeholders will have a different view on what constitutes the event industry and what is important. The Silvers' classification (Chapter 3) is a good handout to remind the participants that the event industry includes many kinds of events. Once there is a consensus on the terminology and the scope of the industry, the consultation process can begin. The attendees at the meeting can be representatives from these areas:

1. Government officials directly involved in event permissions such as roads, parks and gardens and maintenance
2. Venues and hotels
3. Property developers, heritage and theme parks, shopping precincts and malls with a portfolio of events
4. Private event companies
5. Associations
6. Insurance companies
7. Training colleges and universities
8. Community events and festival committees

All of these stakeholders will have a direct interest in the event development of a region. A consultation meeting is not just method of gathering data, as many of these organisations would not have talked to each other before. The meeting provides an opportunity to create an informal network for future communication and support.

2.2.1 The limitations of the SWOT analysis

The SWOT analysis is a relative analysis and can be subjective. Like many formal management tools, it may have the appearance of rigour but lack substance. It is constrained by the experience of those who are undertaking the SWOT analysis. An example in Exhibit 2.2 is the term 'price'. This is a relative expression. There are events in London, one of the most expensive cities in the world. Therefore, the price is not a weakness. The term is really 'value' — it is the value that is important. Value is subjective. It is the value that the attendee obtains from the event or festival and the surrounding experience. The term price is misleading. People will pay for value.

The problem with events is that the people do not experience the value until they attend the event. Therefore, the most important aspect is to create preconceived value or expected value. This is done through creative ideas and promotion. Even the more conservative exhibitions and conferences must create a preconceived value to obtain the decision to commit by the exhibitors, speakers, buyers and other attendees.

To create this preconceived value or expected value, the event company or events unit must have a positive attitude and complete support from the host organisation. The strength of support for the events unit is directly related to the host's return on investment for any event.

To analyse the SWOT we must be aware of the two issues of capacity and financial support. Capacity is related to the incoming finance and incoming finance is related to capacity. The most common example is the 'number of rooms'. This is seen as limiting the number of events. However, the lack of events is not bringing the financial incentive to create more rooms – or to enable the hotels to predict the need for more rooms. It is a common mistake to assume that by simply increasing capacity events will come to a region. Increasing the number of hotels is a major financial commitment and to assume that philosophy 'build it and they will come' has led to very costly mistakes. The most common example of this is the numerous sports stadium built to host international sporting events and then lie idle for years afterwards.

The opportunities represent opportunities to promote the positive aspects of the region. When a Professional Conference Organiser (PCO) or an exhibition seller makes their decision for a venue site, the beauty and culture of the region can sway the decision when the other variables are the same. Conference, incentives and meetings, such as the yearly association conference, are a tax deduction in many countries for the attendees. The attractiveness of the destination and its unique features are a major part of the decision to attend the conference. In particular, the accompanying person programme will be important in the decision mix. The attractiveness of the destination will play a big part in this decision mix. As one event organiser commented, 'our conferences occur in Venice and it's not because the data projectors are better there!'

One must be aware that a SWOT analysis is a poor substitute for a competitive commercial environment. To a commercial event organisation, such as an exhibition company, PCO or a corporate event company, the SWOT is obvious and part of their operating environment. The SWOT is embedded in the commercial decisions and its successful use creates commercial viability and sustainability.

Exhibit 2.3 is an analysis of the limitation faced by South Africa (SA) in developing events. These can be compared to the outcomes of the World Cup 2010. The hosting of the World Cup allowed the various event stakeholders a focus to minimise these challenges. The challenges are faced by many developing countries. It illustrates the way a successful event can raise the quality of related industries and the competency of host population. The World Cup was also used to test the part of the National Competency Standards in training and education.

EXHIBIT 2.3 SOUTH AFRICA EVENT TOURISM CHALLENGES

Challenges

There are challenges[1] that relate to the hosting of major events like the 2010 Soccer World Cup as well as to other major events that may be held in the country in the future. For major events to occur successfully in SA these challenges must be addressed.

Lack of strategic focus

- There is no collective agreement within the tourism industry on which types of events to support to strategically maximise the tourism benefits from these events
- There is an absence of a set of criteria that will determine which events will receive SA Tourism support
- There is a lack of awareness of the types of support that SA Tourism can offer events
- SA Tourism is not part of the decision-making processes to bid for major events especially by some of the major sporting codes

Poor information management.

- There is no information available about the profile of visitors who attend sports and cultural events
- Information about the attractions in a location and the facilities available are not provided to visitors
- Information about the numerous events available in a destination is not always available to visitors
- There is a lack of information dissemination and coordination about the schedule of various sporting and cultural events held annually in the country to enable the tourism industry to plan effectively

Insufficient accommodation and transportation

- There is often an inadequate supply of graded accommodation in certain provinces
- There is no national accommodation booking platform
- High pricing of accommodation and transport during demand periods
- Inadequate transport linkages especially to rural areas and small towns
- International air routes are constrained
- Public transport services such as the mini-bus taxis are inadequate
- There is a shortage of accredited hired vehicles
- Constraints within the transport regulatory framework create barriers to entry for tourism transport operators

Poor service levels and skills shortages

- Lack of adequate skills within catering, event management, language training and service standards sectors
- Poor skill levels of administrators and managers of certain sports federations

Insufficient compelling attractions and activities

- Limited events and activities available such as cultural and entertainment events before and after a major sporting event that appeal to an international audience. Currently, most events and activities appeal to a domestic market
- Limited diversity and attractions available in certain destinations within SA
- Cultural products and events require improvement
- Insufficient packaging and awareness creation of tourism products and experiences

(Continued)

EXHIBIT 2.3 SOUTH AFRICA EVENT TOURISM CHALLENGES—*Cont'd*

Insufficient focus on tourist safety and security
- Limited specific focus on tourist safety
- Negative perceptions around crime
- Limited tourism-related crime prevention
- No implementation of the national tourism safety and security plan
- Safety concerns exist around some sports venues and facilities

Lack of coordination
- There is no coordination between the tourism industry and the sports and cultural sectors
- Domestic events are not coordinated nationally to ensure that the tourism industry benefits significantly
- Events are not used effectively to market the destination
- Bidding for major international events is not coordinated at a central point
- Events organised at a local level are not aligned to SA Tourism's branding and marketing strategy

[1]2010 Soccer World Cup Tourism Organising Plan, 2005 and meetings with tourism stakeholders

---

2.3 STAKEHOLDER CONSULTATION

The creation of an events development strategy must have the support of the numerous stakeholders. Exhibit 2.4 is an example of the guidelines for the event stakeholder meeting. The success of the event development will rest on the mutual understanding and respect between each of the stakeholders and the event team. This makes the initial meeting a key to the future of events in the area. The various agencies, suppliers and other parties have the opportunity to contribute to the strategy in its planning phase. In the example provided by Exhibit 2.4 a template for the strategy was provided to the regional authority. The filling out of the strategy template gave the meeting focus and the document was the deliverable of the meeting.

2.4 THE STRATEGY TEMPLATE

The information gathered at the stakeholder meeting will form the basis of the strategy template. The strategic questions listed in Exhibit 2.5 will be the foundation of a formal regional events strategy.

An example of the consultation to produce a major event strategy is provided by the work of Event Wales. The government called for a review of their draft strategy by interested parties. The mission statement of the strategy is as follows:

> *Developing a sustainable portfolio of major events which enhances Wales' international reputation and the well-being of its people and communities.*
>
> **(Event Wales, 2010)**

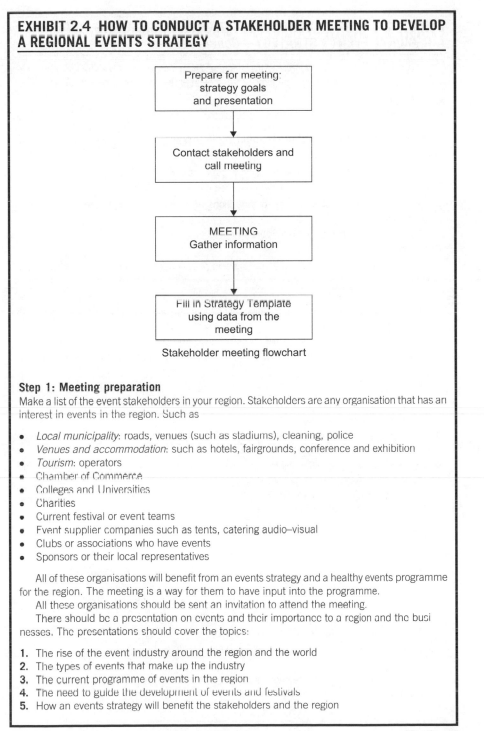

EXHIBIT 2.4 HOW TO CONDUCT A STAKEHOLDER MEETING TO DEVELOP A REGIONAL EVENTS STRATEGY

Prepare for meeting:
strategy goals
and presentation

↓

Contact stakeholders and
call meeting

↓

MEETING
Gather information

↓

Fill in Strategy Template
using data from the
meeting

Stakeholder meeting flowchart

Step 1: Meeting preparation

Make a list of the event stakeholders in your region. Stakeholders are any organisation that has an interest in events in the region. Such as

- *Local municipality*: roads, venues (such as stadiums), cleaning, police
- *Venues and accommodation*: such as hotels, fairgrounds, conference and exhibition
- *Tourism*: operators
- Chamber of Commerce
- Colleges and Universities
- Charities
- Current festival or event teams
- Event supplier companies such as tents, catering audio–visual
- Clubs or associations who have events
- Sponsors or their local representatives

All of these organisations will benefit from an events strategy and a healthy events programme for the region. The meeting is a way for them to have input into the programme.

All these organisations should be sent an invitation to attend the meeting.

There should be a presentation on events and their importance to a region and the businesses. The presentations should cover the topics:

1. The rise of the event industry around the region and the world
2. The types of events that make up the industry
3. The current programme of events in the region
4. The need to guide the development of events and festivals
5. How an events strategy will benefit the stakeholders and the region

(Continued)

EXHIBIT 2.4 HOW TO CONDUCT A STAKEHOLDER MEETING TO DEVELOP A REGIONAL EVENTS STRATEGY—*Cont'd*

Next step is to decide on the goals of the meeting. The aim is to develop a strategy. However, this is too vague for the meeting. The aims of the meeting are listed under section *Aims*.

Step 2: The meeting

Below is a guideline on how to get the most out of the stakeholder meeting.

How to run an event stakeholder meeting

Aims:

- To find out what the stakeholders currently think of events
- To allow them an equal opportunity to put their considered views
- To gain a database of interested organisations and individuals for future event agency meetings
- To allow the stakeholders an opportunity to meet each other

Outcomes

A list of objectives, benefits, future directions and risks to the development of a viable events programme for the region.

In the lead up to the meeting

- Invite all the businesses and organisation that benefit from a viable events programme in the region
- Invite the government agencies that are affected by events
- Email the questions (below) to them so they have time to formulate a considered response

Equipment needed

- A white board and pen
- Paper and pens for each of the delegates

Tips on how to run the meeting

1. Appoint a sensible chairman. This person's job is to produce the outcomes in a fair and equal way. They are not to take part in the discussion.
2. Appoint a person to write the points made on the white board. They are not to take part in the discussion or to censure what is written.
3. At the beginning, the chairman asks each person to state their name, company or organisation. Keep this to one minute.
4. The following questions are asked by the Chairman and the answer and discussion points are written down on the white board.

    Questions to the group:

    1. What are the benefits of having events and festivals in the region? What are the outcomes sought from events (or what do you want events to achieve)?
    2. What are the problems faced by event companies and event teams in putting on events?
    3. What events would you like to see happen in the region?
    4. What needs to happen to attract or develop these events?
    5. How can you help us put together a good events programme?

Further tips

- Do not let any one person dominate the meeting. When a person has an opinion write it down and then move on.

- Do not let the meeting get stuck on one issue. Always bring the meeting back to the aims.
- Do not let anyone dismiss an idea. Write it down regardless of the discussion.
- Make sure that everyone has their say. It is often the quietest people who have the best ideas. The chairman must actively make sure that each person has an opportunity to speak.
- Make sure there is an informal time for talking, such as morning coffee break.
- Let the attendees know that they can also write any points on their pads and it will be taken into consideration.

EXHIBIT 2.5 STRATEGY TEMPLATE

The answers to these questions provide the foundation to the events development strategy

1. What is the vision?
2. What is role of events in your region?
3. What are the objectives? (You can use the national objectives and apply them to your region.)
4. What is the main target market for your events?
5. Overview the venues (do not forget that an event venue can be an open field, beach or a park). What time of the year you would like to attract more tourists?
6. Overview the infrastructure: roads, airport, ...
7. Overview the event management companies.
8. Overview the suppliers: audio–visual, catering, wedding planners, conference and exhibition companies.
9. What are the developments in the region that will affect events – e.g. universities, new businesses, new roads, airport development, and housing developments.
10. What events worked well, what events did not succeed and why?
11. List of the events and programme developments, such as expansion or consolidation that will occur.
12. Identify measurable aspects of the strategy that can be used to monitor the success or otherwise of the events.
13. List of tasks that need to be completed and completion dates to enable the strategy to progress.
14. This section should describe the risks and possible future problems to the development of the events.

Event Wales asked for views on the core criteria for events development and the framework for evaluating events. They identified three problems with the current state of event support. The lack of a cohesive structure in which to plan the best event programme for Wales. There was no way to maximise the benefits or assess the real costs of events. There was an ad hoc approach which was reactive to event proposals. The government needed to 'have in place a robust strategic framework to enable us to assess and prioritise our investments in events in a fair and objective way' (Event Wales, 2010).

This is a further indication of the development of the events industry worldwide. Events feasibility is no longer assessing the feasibility of a single event based on operational criteria. It now takes place within a strategic framework. Events development strategy provides this framework.

2.5 LEGAL AND REGULATORY ENVIRONMENT

To enable a region to host international standard events and festivals, it needs a rational regulatory environment that is easy to access and similar to other countries. If the current rules and regulations are disparate, unintegrated and difficult to find, an event programme will be stifled and destined to be a major cost. Lack of consistent and comprehensible regulatory environment increases the risk for an event company to bring a professional world class event to the region.

Many international hotels have strict procedures for events held within their premises. They have adopted the rules and regulations from other places. The regulations that are fundamentally important to event operations are as follows:

1. Public safety including temporary structure, assembly and fire
2. Transport
3. Food and beverage

Other regulations include the following:

1. Use and handling of fireworks
2. Entertaining children
3. Using volunteers
4. Occupational health and safety
5. Copyright
6. Security arrangements
7. First aid requirements
8. Incident reporting
9. Insurance
10. Traffic management plans and road closures
11. Noise
12. Waste management
13. Water management
14. Provision of adequate parking
15. Entertainment rides
16. Toilet facilities
17. Legal status of an event company

All of the above rules and regulations would be part of the risk management strategy. Therefore, the most important of all of these is the need for training in risk management and the development of a risk management plan. Risk management is mandatory in most countries with a successful event programme. A tourism region only has to have one disaster caused by incompetence at an event or festival and the tourism industry will slump.

Risk management is not just a compliance issue. The modern attendee is highly conscious of safety and risk issues at an event. They are unlikely to bring their family to an event that does not have a risk management planning.

The health and safety codes around the world differ in many ways. It is out side the scope of this book to survey them. However, there seems to be the gradual standardising of these codes and regulations. The latest risk management standard, ISO 31000:2009, will assist in a rational worldwide system.

Perhaps, the most comprehensive legislation for events has been developed in SA. Their recently approved Safety at Sports and Recreation Events Act 2010 was a result of the commission into the Ellis Park soccer disaster when 43 spectators died. Risk management is central to the Act. The legislation will possibly create the impetus for other countries and states to follow.

2.6 VENUES

Obtaining the capacity and infrastructure data for purpose-built venues is straightforward. The venues are commercial operations and generally publish these details. The only risk is the exaggeration and the problems hidden for promotional reasons. Venues that host business events, such as meeting and conferences, post this information on their websites. The capacity and infra-structure data of sporting venues, such as stadiums and fields, will be specific to the type of sport. However, these data can be extrapolated to other types of events.

The problem for the situation analysis is that many events do not use purpose-built venues. Festivals, for example, may use the streets for parades and market places. They may use the harbour for fireworks display or a ferry race. A product launch may use a community park, a beach front, a mountain side or a factory floor. The choice of the venue is discussed in a later chapter.

Therefore, the conclusions of the analysis may be skewed towards the easily obtained information and biased to business events in purpose-built venues. Exhibit 2.6 shows the SWOT analysis of the venue in a tourist region.

An assessment of venues will consider a number of physical and social char-acteristics. The physical ones include the size, shape and number of function rooms, food and beverage facilities, breakout rooms, Internet access, three-phase power, first aid facilities and soundproofing. The social characteristics will include the history and the type of past events held there, the normal clientele of the place, age and style of the building, the appearance and friendliness of the staff, the view and the surrounding area. This is discussed further in this book.

Table 2.1 is an example of a capacity table for the venues of a region. Once the table is filled in for all the venues of the region, the local authority or council can direct events to the most suitable venue.

EXHIBIT 2.6 SAMPLE OF VENUE CAPACITY ASSESSMENT FOR A REGION

The problems with the standard event venues in the region are that they are of a low standard when compared to regions nearby. The hotels, other than the Five Star, are not of a standard to host international events. The seven major hotels were not clean or of high enough quality (fitting, elevators, rooms, carpets) to attract events with a high return on investment.

The Five Star hotels are isolated from the town life. This means that any events occurring within the hotel are unlikely to benefit the wider community except indirectly. They do not teach the community the benefits of events and help them to become familiar with the advantages of local events. The flow on benefit from an event is called the 'Paddington Effect' – where an event is occurring in a neighbourhood, the community benefits from the attendees using the restaurants, buying souvenirs, etc.

The unique venues in the region and the numerous malls, wide streets and historic buildings are a major advantage for developing events. The abundance of unique venues is extraordinary when compared to other possible destinations for events. All of these have been used for corporate events. However, there is no record of their use. This is a missed opportunity. Even given the conditions of the hotels outlined, the decision to choose a venue for a business event is often swayed by the conference dinner and accompanying person programme. A PCO of a conference often does not have the time or skills to identify interesting venues for the entertainment. All the venues have privacy and therefore are suitable for ticketed events. One natural and historical park is particularly suitable with the entrance way, natural 'fence' and plenty of parking.

Streets, malls and other non-purpose-built venues

In the region, there are numerous public spaces that can be used for events such as concerts and community celebration. However, a lack of guidelines on the use of spaces for events impedes the growth of these events. The advantage of a common public place is that it will help familiarise the public with events and public entertainment.

The malls are excellent for promotional and public entertainment events. They have been successfully used in numerous countries such as the Summer Surprises in Dubai.

The areas around the port are currently not an area suitable for events. The 'seedy' nature is not conducive to events. If the local authority cleans up this area, it would be the perfect area for a festival or outdoor exhibition. It is quite common in many towns that the area near the port is underutilised. A number of municipalities have undertaken solid clean up programmes of these types of areas. Sydney, San Francisco, London, and Johannesburg have all used events and festivals as part of their urban renewal.

Given the right security, the historic buildings are perfect for corporate events and special events. Other areas that can be used for events and festivals include the beach, the harbour and the container terminal.

In summary, almost any area can be used for events and festivals. Commercial event companies only need to be told of that they are there. This is an important part of the Events Units responsibility to communicate the availability of numerous possible sites for events

Purpose-built venues are unlikely to change except through infrastructure development. The new integrated developments will dramatically change the availability of venues in the region. Any disruption to their construction, such as political changes, credit crisis or major competition could slow down the growth of business events in the region.

Business events are a good way to fill hotel rooms during low tourist periods. However, there is an extra cost to attracting these events. It is far better to attract business events by promoting the positive attractions of the low period such as ease of movement, low traffic and availability of accommodation.

Table 2.1 Venue Assessment Table

General facilities	Number of toilets	M
		F
		Disabled
	Single phase	
	Three phase	
	Water	
	Outdoor lighting	
	Internet access	
	No. of change rooms	
	ATM facilities	
	Ticket booths	
	Function rooms	
	First aid rooms	
	Meeting room	
	Access/storage	Car parking spaces
		Loading dock
Length of vehicle loading area can accommodate		
Crane and gantry available		
Storage compound		
Catering facilities	Canteen facilities	
	On-site restaurant	
	Off-site catering allowed	
	Bar facilities	
	Licensed venue	
Audio–Visual (Y/N)	PA available	
	Data projector	
	Video	
	Screen	
	Scoreboard	
	Computer	
Accommodation	Disabled access	
	Fire alarm	
	Wet/dry fire system	
	Types of accommodation	
	Maximum capacity	
Security (Y/N)	Fencing	
	Surveillance	
Insurance	Insurances held	
	Insurances required by event organisers	

EXHIBIT 2.8 A LIST OF GAPS FOUND IN AN EVENTS UNIT WHEN COMPARED TO WORLD'S BEST PRACTICE

1. Lack of an accountable outsourcing system
2. Lack of management objectives to create a framework for the successful creation, bidding, management or evaluation of events
3. Lack of risk management assessment
4. Lack of an accountable application for support process for external or internal events
5. Lack of an evaluation of events and their measurement against objectives
6. Lack of an exit strategy for events that fail to meet the objectives
7. Lack of a system to assess and prioritise support
8. Lack of a national events network to compare and support event management and the management of the event portfolio
9. Lack of an expansion and training plan if successful

---

accomplish this in a more sustainable way. Four examples of events creating capacity are as follows:

- Deni Ute Muster Australia: www.deniutemuster.com.au/
- The Wildfoods Festival, Hokitika, New Zealand: http://www.wildfoods.co.nz/wildfoods/. Both these regions have populations below 20,000
- Gilroy Garlic Festival, http://www.gilroygarlicfestival.com, in USA with a population of 41,000
- Riverfest 2006 Brisbane Australia, www.riverfestival.com.au/, with a population of 1 million

In each of these examples the events or festivals drove the increase in capacity of the region or city. The venue suppliers and other event suppliers increased their services incrementally to accommodate the event. The gradual growth allowed other events to be developed or brought into the region. Also in each of these examples the local authority supported the event through their events unit.

2.6.4 Past events

The situation analysis report must have a snap shot of the current and past events and their management. Unless there is some archiving of information, this can be time-consuming. Perhaps, the most difficult information to obtain is the past problems at events. The immaturity of the industry is illustrated by its inability to capture problems in a knowledge management system and to learn from them. Too often they are swept under the carpet. The lack of evaluations of past events means the host and the events team cannot leverage an event. In other words, they cannot suggest other events or improve on the repeat event. This is perhaps the most obvious indication of the early stage of the events industry. In some ways it is a problem because events cross so many boundaries, department divisions and the intangibility of many of the outcomes. So there is no one current department that has responsibility for the whole industry.

For the strategic feasibility and development of an events programme the situation analysis must be performed. It is far more than a snap shot of the current condition as the history, cultural and social situations must be assessed. Events do not suddenly appear. Many take years to develop. It is the same with capacity of a region or company to develop an events programme. Capacity can be developed as the events are developed. The right infrastructure and logistics are only part of the solution.

DISCUSSION TOPICS

There are two views on developing the event industry. One is to bring in the mega event and by focusing the country's resources on one major event, the industry can quickly grow. The other view is to support numerous local events so they grow. Discuss the pros and cons of each approach. Research the mega events in cities around the world and find out if the event industry did benefit.

Undertake an events development situation analysis for your organisation — such as a University or your local region.

Create a stakeholder meeting with each person representing a different organisation with an interest in event development. Who would oppose development? What would the time frame be for the event development?

Korean Drums. Courtesy of IFEA

Commonwealth Games Queens Baton Relay. Courtesy of Maxxam Events International

Event support: directing the development

3

INTRODUCTION

A company or government must direct the development of their events to maximise benefits and minimise problems. It needs to establish guidelines for their future events. In many parts of the world this is achieved by an events unit within the organisation. Initially, the events unit may be one person who works in the marketing, communication or tourism department. With the growth of importance of events the events unit has grown around the world. A specialist events unit enables the organisation to support events through a number of strategies. They initiate an event support application system. By adopting an accountable system the events loosing value can be retired. The first step in directing an events portfolio is to understand the variety of events. The classification of events is essential to this process. This chapter discusses the techniques used to achieve a viable events portfolio. The examples and case studies represent the leading edge in this field.

3.1 EVENT SUPPORT

For a large organisation such as a regional government most support for events will vary from simple advice to partnering with the event organisation. Advice and facilitation are services such as providing advice on event best practice, assisting with a development application and advice on compliance issues such as liquor licencing requirements. This can come through the provision of the event guide, website information or personal contact. It can also include providing training for event organisers, such as seminars and workshops on local rules, traffic, risk, compliance, marketing, promotion, safety, 'dealing with the Host organisation' and general good management. The event guide is discussed further in chapter 6.

The next level of support is through providing facilities or indirect services. For a regional authority these are services that are not purposely created for events such as road closures, use of parks and gardens and cleaning up after the event. The trend in many countries is to cost this type of service. It is called *user pays*. It can be a direct cost to the event or a form of sponsorship of the event. A private company may provide support through assisting the event with their marketing or legal services.

Directly supporting the event with money is the next level of support. In the corporate world this is most common in the form of sponsorship. More and more cities, regions and tourism bodies regard their support as a form of sponsorship and

Events Feasibility and Development. DOI: 10.1016/B978-0-7506-6640-4.10003-2

expect a service in exchange. The exchange could include promotion, naming and other actions that further the organisation's objectives. Grants and gifts without any requirement for an exchange are becoming rare in the event industry.

The event unit or the company can partner with the event organisation. This level of support implies being an internal stakeholder and taking part in the event management decisions. They become part owner of the event with the liabilities that partnership implies. Finally, there is full ownership of the event. A Local Authority or a company may decide to buy the event and have complete control over it.

The five levels of support are not static. They develop with time. A company may decide to sponsor an event and eventually move into being a sole sponsor and partner with the event company. In the other direction, a Local Authority may own an event, such as National Day celebrations, and put it out to tender for a private company to manage it. The event industry is dynamic and constantly evolving.

Within these levels of support are guidelines for the amount of financial support. For example a city council may have three levels:

1. Under $1000 – contributions to events that partially fulfil the council's objectives.
2. $1000–$5000 – contributions to event that may contribute fully to the council's objectives.
3. $5000 plus to main events in the regions that significantly fulfil the council's objectives.

Based on the decision criteria the next step is to have a development strategy for the event. In most cases the event, such as a festival, conference or exhibition, is not a once only affair. To maximise the effort put into organising the event, they tend to be repeated each year. The science of asset management is referred to at this stage, as the alternatives are similar to those of physical assets. They are develop, devolve, or close.

3.1.1 Develop the event

A successful event will require ongoing support and development. The support may change and move between the different forms of event support listed above.

Event development can include the following:

- Event growth – events may grow under their own dynamics.
- Event consolidation – event may have to 'downsize', shed some parts and focus on the successful parts of the event.
- Event partnership – partnering with an outside body to organise the event.

3.1.2 Devolve the event

This can be subdivided into distribute or handover.

a. *Distribute*: An event may be more successfully organised if it is distributed to the interested parties and overseen by the events unit. An example of this is where one shire council no longer organises the National Day. It assists the various communities within the shire to have their own National Day celebrations.

b. *Handover*: The event or festival organised by the events unit of the Local Authority may be handed over to a private company to manage. If the event is currently financially viable or appears to be in the near future, the event may be put out to tender. Some council-supported events may come under competitive neutrality principle whereby the government must not manage an event if it can be managed by a private company. Council support and/or management of an event or festival may result in an unfair marketplace for services. Outsourcing events is common in the corporate world. As mentioned elsewhere in this text, private companies often swing between managing the events in-house and outsourcing for their events.

3.1.3 Close the event

Events and festivals can reach their 'use-by date'. Many events follow the standard product cycle. The principal sponsor needs to have an exit strategy. Without some idea of an exit strategy the full feasibility of the management of events cannot be ascertained. This is one of the most powerful reasons to set up an asset management approach to the events programme. Many government organisations have come to grief in their event strategy on this issue. Local festivals can gain an 'event inertia'. The festival has been going for years and the local council has lost the reasons for supporting it. The festival soaks up resources and the opportunity costs are enormous. The only way out in that situation is to re-establish the objectives and measure the festival against the objectives. Corporations, as they have clear corporate objectives, generally have a better record in 'event exiting'. At the same time as developing the event the host organisation may actively seek or bid for events and festivals to further their objectives. The events unit within the host organisation can provide the expertise necessary to assist this process. The events unit can be proactive in this area. The advantage to seeking existing events, the event or festival has already been tried and tested in other areas. Many aspects of the event have already proven they are viable. There is further discussion on this topic in later chapters.

To create an events portfolio, the local or regional authority or the company needs a clear event application and approval process. Figure 3.1 illustrates an example used for a number of regional authorities.

Figure 3.1 shows the process of event support by following an application from an event team. The flowchart is similar to the one calling for proposals for event tendering and applying for sponsorship of an event. In this case the event team applies to the organisation or client for support. The organisation in this case could be local, state or federal government body such as a tourism agency. The event applicant selects the level of support they require. The next step is to ensure the event team understands the support objectives. It is pointless for an event team to apply for assistance if their event is unrelated to the objectives of the organisation to which

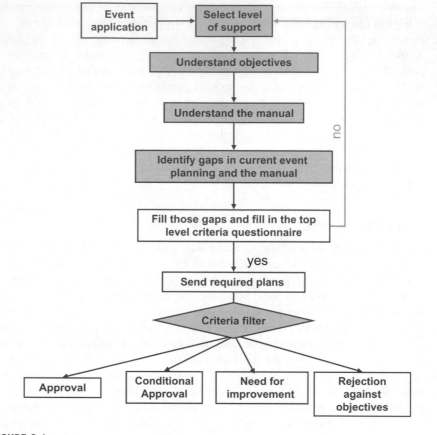

FIGURE 3.1

Online event support process

they apply. For example, if the event does not have tourism outcomes then there is little reason to apply to a tourism agency for support. The event manual is the next step. The manual describes the policy of the organisations. The event manual is described in later chapters. The event support applicant identifies any difference between their event planning and the expectations set out in the manual. The next step is to submit the application for support. The events unit of the client or organisation compares the event and its plans to the criteria for support and decides on the appropriate response. The organisation should not just reject the application if it does not correspond to the criteria. There may be aspects of the event that can be developed. The organisation can give conditional approval or suggest improvements to the event and its planning.

Using this flowchart the events unit can direct the event support and, at the same time, improve the quality of the events.

3.2 EVENT TYPOLOGY

A classification system for events is essential in the development of an events strategy and in understanding the feasibility of future events and events portfolios. As pointed out by numerous authors, the event industry is disparate. There is no common event terminology and communication between different event companies, across borders or between industry sectors is difficult. Events are found in almost all industry sectors as well as in civic life. The backgrounds of the event managers, festival organisers, sports coordinators and all the rest of the people who make up the industry are hugely varied. They can be appointed to be the event organiser for a company on the flimsiest of reasons — 'no one else will do it' or 'you've organised a wedding so you can do this'. It is not surprising that we lack a coherent classification of types of events.

Most of the current classification systems are pragmatic and single purpose. The widest attempt at classification was adopted by the Event Management Body of Knowledge from Julia Silvers' work shown in Exhibit 3.1.

EXHIBIT 3.1 SILVERS' CLASSIFICATION OF TYPES OF EVENTS

Business and corporate events
Any event that supports business objectives, including management functions, corporate communications, training, marketing, incentives, employee relations, and customer relations, scheduled alone or in conjunction with other events.

Cause-related and fundraising events
An event created by or for a charitable or cause-related group for the purpose of attracting revenue, support and/or awareness, scheduled alone or in conjunction with other events.

Exhibitions, expositions and fairs
An event bringing buyers and sellers and interested persons together to view and/or sell products, services and other resources to a specific industry or the general public, scheduled alone or in conjunction with other events.

Entertainment and leisure events
A one-time or periodic, free or ticketed performance or exhibition event created for entertainment purposes, scheduled alone or in conjunction with other events.

Festivals
A cultural celebration, either secular or religious, created by and/or for the public, scheduled alone or in conjunction with other events. (Many festivals include bringing buyer and seller together in a festive atmosphere.)

Government and civic events
An event composed of or created by or for political parties, communities or municipal or national government entities, scheduled alone or in conjunction with other events.

Marketing events
A commerce-oriented event to facilitate bringing buyer and seller together or to create awareness of a commercial product or service, scheduled alone or in conjunction with other events.

(Continued)

EXHIBIT 3.1 SILVERS' CLASSIFICATION OF TYPES OF EVENTS—*Cont'd*

Meeting and convention events
The assembly of people for the purpose of exchanging information, debate or discussion, consensus or decisions, education and relationship building, scheduled alone or in conjunction with other events.

Social/life-cycle events
A private event, by invitation only, celebrating or commemorating a cultural, religious, communal, societal or life-cycle occasion, scheduled alone or in conjunction with other events.

Sports events
A spectator or participatory event involving recreational or competitive sport activities, scheduled alone or in conjunction with other events.

Without going too deep into the theory of classification systems, suffice to say many aspects of events can be used to classify them. An efficient and robust classification system should have three characteristics. It should be *exhaustive*, that is, there should be a place for all types of events within the system. The categories themselves should be *exclusive*. An event should be unambiguously placed into one of the categories. Finally, it should have *utility*. It should be able to be employed in the management and operation of events and events portfolio. This implies that the terminology is easily understood across the events sector. The utility of the classification system is the most important and as can be readily seen by the examples in this chapter, the categories are not exclusive. A festival can be a major event and a sports event at the same time. Although the event classification system would be regarded as too vague by an expert, it does allow a lot of slack or leeway. This may be seen as room to move that allows development, in preference to a rigid system. When an industry is developing rapidly, the 'room to move' may be an advantage as it does not set the constraints. The impressions can be the source of development.

Events may be categories according to any of their attributes such as:

- *Number of attendees*
- *Primary aim*: such as selling goods (fairs), celebration (festivals) and recognition (awards)
- *Industry or sector origin*: religious events such as the Hajj, Ashura Festival, World Youth Day and marriages
- *Resources needed*: has implication with sports, exhibitions and conferences
- *Time*: established events, annual, new events, off season or shoulder events
- *Ownership*: community, associations
- *Budget*
- *Risks*: extreme sports
- *Ability for development*
- *Size*: mega, major, local

- *Industry*: such as sports, medical, marketing, tourism, business, government and community
- *Target market*: such as youth events or third age expos
- *Major objective*: religious, promotion campaigns and celebrations
- *Economic impact*: such as used by the UK Sport

Exhibit 3.2 is a classification used to assess economic impact of events by UK Sport. The economic activity is measured by size and level of certainty.

EXHIBIT 3.2 UK SPORT EVENT CLASSIFICATION

* Type A – i.e. irregular major international spectator events generating significant economic activity and media interest such as the Olympic Games;

* Type B – i.e. major spectator events generating significant economic activity, media interest and part of an annual domestic cycle such as the FA Cup Final;

* Type C – i.e. irregular one-off major spectator/competitor events generating an uncertain level of economic activity such as Grand Prix Athletics;

* Type D – i.e. major competitor events generating little economic activity and part of an annual cycle such as the national championships in most sports.

http://www.uksport.gov.uk/pages/economic_impact/ (accessed Jan 2008).

Each of these attributes has a different priority to different stakeholders. The economic impact, for example, will be important to countries using events to develop their businesses.

An example of this is found in the detailed document from the US Department of Transportation. As they state in the section on classification and categories:

> *A planned special event impacts the transportation system by generating an increase in travel demand in addition to possibly causing a reduction in roadway capacity because of event staging. The first step toward achieving an accurate prediction of event generated travel demand and potential transportation system capacity constraints involves gaining an understanding of the event characteristics and how these characteristics affect transportation operations. In turn, practitioners can classify the planned special event in order to draw comparisons between the subject event and similar historical events to shape travel forecasts and gauge transportation impacts.*

US Department of Transportation, 2003, p. 2-1

The characteristics of an event of interest to the Federal Highway Administration are those impinging on the flow of traffic around the event site. Hence, the peak arrival and departure times, surrounding transport facilities, numbers of attendees and audience catchment area are examples of these event attributes.

The categories for the US Department are as follows:

- Discrete/recurring event at a permanent venue
- Continuous event
- Street use event
- Regional/multivenue event
- Rural event

All of the classifications have advantages and disadvantages. An events feasibility and development strategy must be comprehensive. If events are not supported, there has to be a reason for the lack of support. The disparate nature of the industry may allow events to be ignored or not even come into the radar. For example, the size of the wedding industry is often forgotten in any classification system for events. On any estimate the wedding industry in a region is worth millions of dollars. If this is multiplied around the world, the wedding industry is as big an economy as sports events. The social network impact of weddings is rarely if ever analysed. The importance of youth events such as rave parties is often hidden from official data. The microevents of 10–20 people such as street soccer or the community cricket match fall under the radar and yet these microevents can be the support structure for the major events. A further limitation of any current classification system is the lack of the relative priority of the types of events. A classification system tends to be a snapshot of the event situation at that time. It does not take into account how some events can grow rapidly and others may quickly disappear. This is a conservative force on a dynamic and evolving industry. It will reinforce the situation it describes. Given that the data for a classification may take a year to compile, the information should be seen as helpful but slightly out of date.

A robust classification system for events will simplify communication and be employed in many areas of a development strategy. It is used as a framework for the awards for excellence, for the funding criteria, education and training, communication throughout the regions and internationally as well as for gathering and collating data, research and to identify gaps in the strategy.

Below is a classification for events used in the development strategy from a tourism perspective.

3.2.1 Community events

A community event is directed at the local community and has a local audience. It is staged for reasons of community participation and enjoyment. Many of these events bring the local community together to celebrate or specific sectors of the local community. Small sports events are good examples such as a local football match. It is from these small community events that the local community is trained in events. These smaller and often special interest events can grow into larger events. The local backgammon group may invite the national competition to the region, for example. They are sometimes called microevents and can be below the radar of tourism strategies. They do not have any direct and immediate tourism outcomes. However, they represent the real community culture and they bring support for larger events. The smaller community events allow the community to become 'event literate'. They understand the major events and are more likely to appreciate their value. Examples include chess competition, fishing competition, swimming competitions and community fetes.

3.2.2 Official events (also called civic events)

These events are regarded as the direct responsibility of the council or local authority. They are often organised by cities around a country at the same time and celebrate a significant date or issue. They include the one-off events such as civic reception and welcome home parade for sports teams or the military. They generally do not lie directly with the Tourism Authority. If the event is large enough, such as a National Day Parade, the tourism sector will be involved. Examples include senior's week, National Day and refugee week.

3.2.3 Major events

Major event can be a repeat event or a special event that attracts large numbers of people. A significant percentage of the event audience will be visitors to the region. It has media coverage outside the region and creates economic benefit. They often develop from the growth of a local community event or a special interest group event. The event can result in significant branding of the region, city or town in which case it can be termed a hallmark event. These events are very difficult to create artificially and they generally are driven by personalities or special interest groups. Examples are Ramadan Nights in Aqaba, the New Orleans Jazz Festival, The Wild Food Festival in Hokitika and the Dubai Shopping Festival.

3.2.4 Business events

The aim of business events is to enhance commercial activities. They include the conferences, conventions, exhibitions, product launches and meetings. Some of these events have a large impact on the community such as car shows and international exhibitions. The attendees — often called delegates — are motivated by the desire to increase their commercial opportunities through networking and information. They can have a large economic impact on the host region as a result of attracting 'high spend' international attendees.

Examples include the Riyadh Economic Forum, Nairobi Bridal Fair and Dubai Event 360.

3.2.5 Special or touring events

These are events that may only occur once in the city or region. They can generate intense publicity and awareness. They are often sold to the city on their branding impact. As they have not been tried before in the region they can be high-risk asset. At the same time they may have a high return on the investment. As pointed out in many audits of these events, the risks arise when the host city bought the event without expert advice. Examples of special events include the major concerts such as Desert Heat, Picnic on the Sydney Harbour Bridge Festival, opening of Atlantis in Dubai and the Commonwealth Baton Relay.

One last classification system is worth exploring as these events have a large amount of government support, intercountry competition and publicity. This is the subclassification of events within a larger category of Major events. Events Wales divide the events they will support into Mega, Major, Signature and Growth.

Mega events are those that reach the world and are preceded by major new infrastructure development. Smaller versions of the mega event are the major events. These are international events, such as the international sports finals that are hosted by Wales. The third are the large events owned by the country, the signature events. As in the tourism classifications, the signature events are important as they are unique to an area and culture. The Welsh classification identifies the indigenous events with a long cultural history and the new events such as the music festivals. The category that makes the Welsh classification of interest to this book is the fourth category of 'growth events'. This introduces a dynamic and development into the classification as they understand that events have the potential to evolve and become signature or major events.

A useful classification system allows the collection and collation of data on the development of the events industry. It can assist in recognising result of any changes. The affects of changes over time, such as improving infrastructure, can be tracked to changes in the events. As an industry grows these statistics are vital to understanding its development and informing the planning strategies. They are of particular interest to large organisations such as national governments and the United Nations. For this reason a classification system and the categories that comprise it can have a long-term influence on the sustainability of the industry.

A classification system is essential in the development of events and an events strategy. It helps in communication and allows the apportioning of event support by providing a framework. There are limitations. It can be rigid and therefore events that may be future successes are unrecognised. The classification is too often based on a snapshot of past events. In a dynamic industry this will slow down development. The classification system and the categories are generally decided by the characteristics of the event that are of most concern to the stakeholder. The event classification systems outlined in this section are not ideal. However, their very imprecision does allow for new events to find a place.

When the strategy does not work

The event support system outlined in this section has its limitations. It depends on the political environment and the culture in which it is immersed. An accountable and transparent system is an ideal state and most countries and companies are not in the ideal state. This points out the major limitation to the triple bottom line approach to event impact analysis. The triple bottom line concerns the evaluation of an event through its economic, social and environmental impacts. It has great value for the study of events and its proponents sought to emphasis that event impact was not solely economic. However, to imply that it fully describes the reasons for event support is naive.

Regardless of the reasons for an event, a company CEO or the mayor of the city can overrule the decision. This is too often the case in the event industry for it to be ignored. Political decisions have an enormous impact on the reasons to go ahead or cancel an event. The reality is that the jazz festival goes ahead because the mayor is a fan of jazz, for example. A city may bid for a major trade event, because the current political party has low ratings in the opinion polls. They hope that the trade deals occurring during the meetings will generate good publicity for the city government. A company may sponsor a tennis match, because the company executive knows a lot about tennis and it gives her a chance to show off to their clients. A minister in a state government ignores their event advisory body and commits taxpayer funds to an event that has demonstrated time and again it looses money. All of these are true and occur more often than is supposed by those who study events. The people who actually develop and manage events know politics plays a large role in the decision to support events. In particular if the negative effects of the event are not felt until years later, after the average term in office of a politician, and the positive effects are immediate, there is an incentive for politicians to support it. Needless to say this type of political decision is rarely investigated or recorded. Therefore, the results of any research into events will be skewed away from the political decision. In countries that do not follow the western democratic model or in companies that are privately owned, the political reasons for events can be more obvious.

In summary, the event support process that is described in this section on strategy is found to a degree in many countries. It is the ideal state. It implies that accountability and transparency are the normal or desired characteristics of business and government. Politics, the play of power, can always invalidate the system. But at least the event industry will know the background of the decision to stop the event, if not the actual reason.

DISCUSSION TOPICS

1. Using the event strategies and event support programmes published on the Internet, list and compare the event classification systems. Look for the characteristics used to create the event classification.
2. Develop a classification of events used by Multinational Corporation such as Red Bull or IBM. Discuss which events they would support.

Event setting up on Lord Howe Island. Photo William O'Toole

Wedding in the Gulf. Photo William O'Toole

Implementation of the strategy

A relationship manager will be the key point of contact for any council business with the event organiser, including regulatory processes, funding and other forms of support.

(Auckland City Council, 2005)

INTRODUCTION

The strategy is merely a written plan unless there is a way to set all the tasks in motion. Organisations around the world have come to the realisation that a specialist position is needed to assess the feasibility and develop the events portfolio. Befitting a dynamic and rapidly growing industry this position goes by many names. The events unit or events office is the most descriptive. This chapter investigates and describes the role of the events unit and the recently created semi-government events agencies. It includes an interview with a Group Manager Events at Tourism Victoria from one of the more successful events units.

4.1 EVENTS UNIT

To implement an events development strategy and to make recommendations on the feasibility of future events, a specialist unit is often established within an organisation. This may be called the events unit for governments or the event office for private companies. It is becoming more common for regional authorities such as councils and city governments to hire or train dedicated staff to take care of their burgeoning event programme and to handle enquires for support. Table 4.1 shows that many councils and shires around Australia and New Zealand have a dedicated events unit with trained event staff. For the public sector, the size and scope of work of an events unit depend on a number of factors such as the number of people in the administrative region and the tourism value of the events. For a private company the size of the events unit will depend on the number of events and their importance to the creation of value.

The assessment, management and bidding for events are often spread thinly through the various departments of an organisation or company. The events unit should be regarded as the expert in this area and they enable the organisations to manage a portfolio of events. The unit acts as a one-stop shop so that any external event can minimise the unnecessary communication by dealing with one team. The

Events Feasibility and Development. DOI: 10.1016/B978-0-7506-6640-4.10004-4

Table 4.1 Sample of Events Units in New Zealand and Australia

	Nelson, New Zealand	City of Wodonga	Colac Otway Shire	Albury	Latrobe City Council
Events staff/ unit	Events office 2 people – festival office	Four staff (2 × 4.5 days a week, 1 × full time and 1 × 3 days a week)	Events unit consists of 2 staff. One full time member and one part-time who works 2 days per week	Events team – 3 people	Yes – 2 full time; 1 part-time; 1 × Coordinator; 1 × Senior Events Officer; 1 × trainee/ intern
Role	We organise Nelson Arts Fest 12 days; Summer in Nelson Programme such as Lanterns Opera in the Park	Delivery of community events and projects	Primarily to oversee coordination of Council Event Approval process, administer funds under the Council Festival and Support Scheme and to deliver the FReeZa programme and Australia Day events	Civic and community events and conferencing. Facilitating and supporting external event	Manages Council events, supports and sponsors community/major events and has regulatory/ compliance role with all events
Pop	70–75,000	35,000	21,000	110,000	70,000

efficiency of this process is essential for a successful event programme. At the same time it allows the organisation to collect information about all events in the region or in their industry. This information can be used to direct the future support for events, planning new events and assessing their feasibility.

To organise and host events is highly complex. Each task is dependent on all other tasks and there is a web of responsibility. To streamline one of the processes such as the interface between the event and the host organisation is to make it easier for all parties. If this one difficulty is resolved, it will invite events to the region, city, town or state. Bureaucratic hurdles are often identified by professional event organisers as the major constraint to the introduction of their event into a city or region.

The current situation around the world is moving towards the one-stop-shop approach. Quite a few local authorities have an event coordinator who is providing many of the services listed below. Quite a lot of corporations have an event office. The event coordinator assists with the applications for permissions and sponsorship. At the same time, they can ask for information from the events. The information should be formalised and this is outlined below. With the collection of these data the local authority will have a whole picture of events in the region. In other words, every enquiry to event coordinator is an exchange of information. For example, if an event company asks about a suitable venue for their event, event coordinator will provide the information and at the same time ask a few simple questions. Of course, this is the simplest level of event support. However, it should not be underestimated in its affect on an events programme. The event organiser benefits from the information.

The function of the city or regional events unit can be summarised as below:

- *One-stop shop*: the events unit is the first place for an event company, community group or festival organisers to find out their responsibilities to local authority, the resources in the region and the possible support for their event. All initial event enquiries to authority are routed through the events unit.
- Data collection and research.
- Assess the event application to determine the level of support from the organisation with the assistance of the staff of the events unit.
- Hosting and convening the cross-departmental events within the organisation and with external clients.

The core functions are expended in the following description of the scope of work.

4.1.1 Events unit: scope of work

The overall initial scope of work of the events unit is to implement the recommendations of a strategic report. There are seven primary tasks of the events unit in implementing the strategic plan. These are explained in the following paragraphs.

Task 1: event support

There are many events in a region that do not need funding or any physical support from the local authority. Business events are often independent of any local authority. However, there may be many enquiries asking for information on the formal

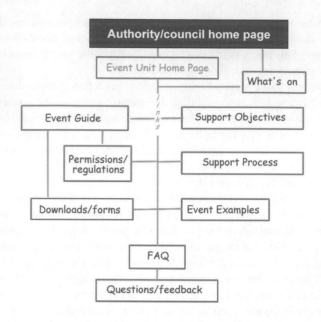

FIGURE 4.1

Schema of the events unit website for a regional authority

processes and permissions necessary to allow the event to go ahead. The first stop for these event organisers is to go to the events unit's website, as illustrated by Figure 4.1, to download the guide which will have a list of local rules and regulations. Once this is understood, the events unit may provide other advice to help the event organisers. If the event rates highly in the decision criteria the organisation may decide that a higher level of support is necessary. Below is a list of the levels of support. They are from the perspective of the events unit and correspond to the list in Chapter 2.

Advice

This is the entry level for any event. The event team is given free advice on aspects of events in the region such as rules and regulations. The forms of advice can be as follows:

1. How to contact the relevant stakeholders — such as roads authority, emergency and police
2. How to fulfil the requirements and other regulations such as Place of Public Entertainment
3. List of suppliers
4. Provision of the organisation event guide
5. Contacts for other events in the region or nationally
6. Venues in the region
7. History of similar events

Most of this information can be placed on the website and would be found in the event guide or manual. There is always a 'lag' of information on websites and guides. The events unit staff can provide the current updates. The advice can lead to the event company not going ahead with the event. In this case the events unit may be saving the event from failure.

The events unit should become the 'one-stop shop' for any events in the region. It needs to consider the legal and regulatory requirements and how these can be streamlined so as to attract new events and allow current event teams to apply for permission with a minimum of 'form filling' and so it is all completed in a timely manner.

Facilitation and in-kind support

This includes indirect assistance in the form of training seminars and conferences. The seminars/workshops may include the topics: how to make the most of council and the region, marketing, promotion and safety. The website is an essential part of the facilitation process. In-kind support includes the free provision of services such as assisting with the development applications and the use of council facilities for free. In order to assess the cost and benefits of the event, the events unit must cost these services for future planning. It is easy for a community group to assume that the council should provide the services for free. After a few years, this attitude is difficult to change. To minimise the risk all the services provided by the events unit should have a costing. Marketing and promotion via the council website, banners, at other events and on council property is another area of in-kind support. The most cost-efficient in-kind support is the support the council can give the event that uses minimum council resources and, at the same time, saves the event team the use of their resources.

Sponsorship/funding

Sponsorship is the exchange of money for the provision of a service, generally public recognition and promotion of the sponsor. Funding implies certain obligation in exchange for the funds. The line between funding and sponsorship is not exact. The events unit can regard all sponsorship or funding as an investment in the event and its management. The return on the investment is the way the event assists the council to meet its objectives to the people of the region and its legal obligations.

Partnership and management

The most involved form of event support is being directly involved with the management of the event. The council can own the event and it is completely managed by the events unit. This implies a large increase in workload for the events unit. In a number of regions the events unit manages major events and this keeps their expertise up to date.

Task 2: data collection and research

The events unit should have a systematic method to collect and analyse data on events. In particular, the comparison of the outcomes of the event with the event support objectives is essential. The level of detail and amount of information received from the event should be tied to the level of support. This must be part of any communication with the event management team and the event's stakeholders. The application for financial support will be a starting point for all data collection. However, whenever an event organiser emails or telephones for advice or help with permits, the events unit can use the opportunity to gather information about the event. The information from the event is seen as an exchange for the service/advice the council is providing. An important task of the events unit is researching events around the world. A percentage of time resource must be devoted to researching and upskilling. The proactive research should include the latest developments, such as:

- Risk management including legislation and compliance
- Quality of event service suppliers and opportunity
- Trends that affect the industry
- Audits of past events
- Events in other regions
- Possible events to bid or attract to the region

Task 3: opportunities

Events unit must be constantly aware and informed of opportunities for the organisation to bid for and host events. As the event industry is dynamic and opportunities are easily lost, the staff of the events unit should attend industry training and conferences. This is essential for the events unit to keep current with the standards in the event industry. The industry standard is often used in risk management and in liability cases.

Task 4: capacity planning

The events unit should have an advisory role in the planning of facilities in the region. They can provide event information needed to attract events to the facilities. The trend towards creating an 'events precinct' as part of city and town developments allows the events unit a unique opportunity to influence future venues. There have been numerous problems in the past with these event venues and the decision to build them has to be carefully considered. To quote from the Port Macquarie/Hastings Council Public Inquiry Report:

> *Despite Council's evidence that the Glasshouse project has been included in financial modelling since 2003 and the building appeared in the Council's 10 year rolling works program from 2003/04, there is no evidence before the Inquiry that the council took into account all the costs of the centre, both current and future or how they addressed the escalating costs of the project*
> **(Port Macquarie/Hastings Council, 2008, p. 144)**

The existence of the purpose-built venues does not guarantee a full event programme. In many cases these venues turn into 'white elephants' and council resources are tied up in fixed physical asset maintenance with little or no return. The constant controversy over the return on investment for the various Olympic stadiums around the world is a case in point.

Task 5: dissemination of information

The website is a major communication tool to disseminate information to the event stakeholders of the region and event organisers proposing to come to the council with their event. It can also be used to collect information on events. Once again there should be an exchange of information. If the event organiser wants information on the region, the events unit can use the opportunity to obtain information on their event. The website can also be used to filter the applicants for support. It can allow the applicant to self-assess before applying to the events unit. This will limit the number of applicants to those with a chance of success and allow the applicant to become familiar with the process of application.

Task 6: events development

The organisation's events unit must at all times be aware of developing, consolidating or expanding the events programme for the region or company. There are a number of business and marketing tools to assist the unit. One of the more difficult tasks in the ongoing quality improvement of an events programme is the shedding of events that take up more resources than is needed to produce the benefits. The events development quadrant, shown in Fig. 4.2, is a tool to assist the events unit to analyse their events portfolio. The portfolio can be subdivided into outstanding, unknown, standard and non-performing. The outstanding events attract publicity and are used as an example of the effectiveness of the events programme. There are the standard events that occur with little fanfare and satisfy the objectives. There are the events which may graduate into outstanding or become a failure. These are the unknowns. Finally, there are the non-performing events.

The events programme must be seen as a group of projects, each competing for fixed council or company resources. Supporting non-performing events takes away resources from events that are of benefit to the people and businesses of the region. Any event that is no longer supported must be given the reasons referring to the over all events strategy of the council, as part of their responsibility to the region.

A similar quadrant can be used in analysing the corporate events portfolio. It is not uncommon for events to be sponsored by a company long after they have passed their positive return on investment date. Corporations can be highly conservative and the quadrant assists in the constant development of the events programme, identifying failures, supporting innovation and dynamic events.

Task 7: convening meetings

Within organisations there are a number of departments and people responsible for events. It is important that the events unit knows about these events. From a risk management point of view and to minimise the organisation's exposure, the events unit should be aware of all events. Foreseeable risk is judged according to the

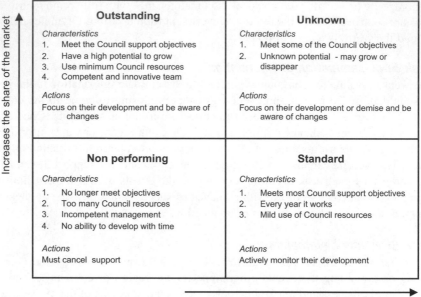

FIGURE 4.2

Events development quadrant

standard in the industry and the various departments are not necessarily abreast of the standard.

There are two methods to make sure that the events unit is 'in the loop':

1. All events sponsored by the company or supported by the authority should be directed to the events unit website for information on how to conduct events according to council or company policy.
2. For an organisation with an active portfolio of events, there should be meetings of the parties at least once a month. At these meeting the coming events are discussed and any exception issues are tabled. The events unit should chair the meetings.

The task list of responsibilities of the events unit recognises the work already performed by the organisation's staff. It reflects best practice in this area of management as evidenced by government authorities around the world with a vibrant and rewarding event programme. At the same time, a professional events staff supported by a cross-departmental staff minimised the risk and exposure of the organisation to faulty and mismanaged events.

The two areas in particular in need of a repository of expertise and local knowledge in events are risk and event portfolio development.

As set out further in this text, risk management is more than compliance with the law. It concerns the duty of care the council or company must have to the staff and event attendees. At the same time there are financial and reputation risks. Events and festivals represent a unique collection of risks. The relationship between organisation and the local event must be managed with event management expertise. It is not just insurable risk. There is reputation and 'duty of care' which are beyond insurance. Hence, this issue is vital to all events in the events portfolio. Risk management takes place within a culture and environment. Hence, there are risks in local area that may be overlooked by events coming in from outside. An essential role of the events unit is to understand these and continually collect information on the risks and the 'near misses'.

Events and festivals are not static. For the organisation to gain the most from the new and existing events, they must develop. In the case of councils the development should be to the advantage of people of the region. Event portfolio development must be based on historical information. This can only be done with expertise residing in a professional events unit using the world's best practice.

4.1.2 Events development position

An important part of the event support process is the job positions to enable the development of events. A position that seems to have been advertised only recently is the event development manager. They are responsible for the application of the event policy as well as for feedback to improve it. They ensure the successful implementation of an event development policy.

City or regional event development officer's duties and responsibilities include the following:

1. Attract events to the region
2. Assess the event's ability to contribute to the region's social capital
3. Implement an event evaluation system
4. Liaise between events, communities and sponsors
5. Ensure the effectiveness of the interagency committee
6. Develop capacity building workshops for the current event organisers
7. Develop the events programme for the region
8. Assist community, business, sports and special events with their compliance to local rules and regulations

Within a company, the events development manager's core responsibilities would include the following:

1. Identify and assess events that further the company objectives
2. Align all events with a specific business plan
3. Assess current company events and provide an ongoing plan to increase their quality, range and efficiency
4. Manage the current portfolio of events including the AGM
5. Provide support to other divisions of the company involved in events

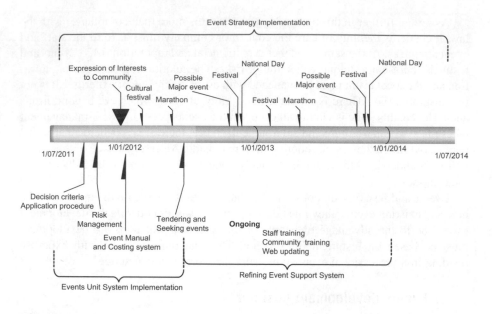

FIGURE 4.3

Timeline for event strategy implementation

6. Source and develop new events
7. Review all outsourcing and in-house decisions concerning the management of company events and the event service suppliers

To implement a strategy from which to develop an event will take time.

Figure 4.3 illustrates an example of this timeline for a government authority such as a local council or city. The strategy and its effects cannot be expected to be understood by all parties. The implementation of the strategy must be explained to all the departments. The concept that events are important for a company or a council to achieve its objectives is still very new for many people. The strategy must be implemented while the regular events are still being organised. The change over period to fully adopt an accountable system may take up to a year. Then the system must be refined as new events are developed and others are deleted. The criteria for event support will need to be refined and change as the policy of the organisation changes. If the events strategy is too far removed from the real life of events it can be a stranglehold on development.

The events unit or event office will not act on its own. Its responsibilities will cross all departments and the success of the development of events will be determined by their relations with the rest of the organisation. A major hospital, for example, will have event occurring for the doctors, nurses, staff, suppliers, local people, VIP's and many more. Exhibit 4.1 illustrates an example of this relationship for a regional authority.

EXHIBIT 4.1 SAMPLE OF THE RELATIONSHIP BETWEEN THE EVENTS UNIT (EU) AND THE OTHER DIVISIONS OF A LARGE ORGANISATION

Department of Tourism and Marketing
Role of EU: the Marketing and Tourism will be part of the advisory group for the staff. In particular to give advice on maximising tourism value of future events. Also it can provide assistance with major events such as advice on resources. It would continue to attract events to the region. However, event approval will be part of the role of the events unit.

Department of Sports
Role of EU: the events unit will assist sports events with event management and risk expertise. Plus assisting on an event-by-event basis with spare resources.

Risk Office
Role of EU: liaising with the risk unit to have input into event training of event organisers in risk management. EU to collect a database of the risk management tools, forms and incidents at events. Relevant documents and the risk management process put up on the website.

Department of Parks and Gardens
Role of EU: there is need to streamline this process. When relevant, the Parks and Gardens section of the council will be represented on the Events team.

Traffic Control Committee
Role of EU: liaise with the traffic control to provide information and training on road closure approval and other traffic-related issues.

Development Application Approvals Office
Role of EU: communicate about future events and simplify the necessary process to allow for the event deadlines.

Community Services
Role of EU: allow the community service events to come under the guidance of the events unit.

The primary role of the events unit is not event operations. Any time taken in assisting an event 'on the ground' is less time spent working on the events programme (portfolio). Valuable experience can be gained by the staff by being involved in the event operations and this is gained by managing a flagship event. Any other operational work must be weighed against the waste of resources and the use of experts.

The events unit should be the primary liaison between the organisation and the other government bodies. The roads authority or the police, for example, is highly involved in some events. These authorities often have guidelines or manuals to outline the necessary processes of their role in public event. The events unit should be familiar with all the processes and relationship between the council and these bodies.

The state of the development of the events units in government authorities and the events office or desk in companies is varied. Table 4.1 shows a number of small cities and their event staff. Case study 4.1 is an interview with one of the most successful of the events units. Their success derives from a proactive policy of researching, seeking events and looking for opportunities to improve the event outcomes.

CASE STUDY 4.1 EVENTS UNIT IN VICTORIA – INTERVIEW

What is the background to the work you are currently doing?

Victoria's events provide significant opportunities to boost the profile of the State and provide major economic benefits. Its impressive list of annual hallmark and one-off special events is already a major tourism drawcard. These include sporting, food and wine, cultural and aerospace events and they have become the recognised 'brand' for Melbourne.

Tourism Victoria is a State Government statutory authority which markets Victoria in Australia and overseas as a premier tourism destination. It is committed to ensuring that Victoria retains its reputation as the events leader. It contributes significantly to not only attracting and delivering major events, but also ensuring that they are viable and provide increased benefits.

As Group Manager Events at Tourism Victoria, I oversee the identification and determination on how best to develop appropriate events to maximise their tourism potential. The events programme helps to increase not only the number of visitors to Melbourne and regional Victoria, but also their length of stay and yield. These events attract visitors to Melbourne and regional Victoria where they spend money on accommodation, shopping, sightseeing, eating out, theatre and attractions. The programme also addresses the quality of the visitor experience and destination-branding opportunities.

Please describe Tourism Victoria's policy of 'proactivity' when it comes to developing events?

Events assist with the tourism branding of the destination. Some destinations are recognised for their ability to attract tourists – whether it be cultural tourism opportunities, adventure-related activities, food and wine produce or perhaps its scenic attractions.

Tourism Victoria's events programme aims to link the destination branding to an appropriate event. To further explore this, the cooperative relationship between Tourism Victoria and the City of Greater Bendigo is a good example.

Bendigo is a major regional Victoria cultural tourism destination and it has the appropriate infrastructure to host cultural exhibitions. It is also considered to be an ideal short break tourism destination as it has a good variety of accommodation and dining out options, has magnificent architecture and is within 2 hours drive of Melbourne.

Tourism Victoria and the City of Greater Bendigo recently identified an opportunity to develop a major event that would attract significant visitation to the region on an ongoing basis. The event, a Regional Blockbuster Exhibition held annually over 4 months, will further promote Bendigo as a cultural tourism destination as well as generate increased visitation.

Following a commitment by both organisations to fund the study to determine the most appropriate event, a comprehensive process was undertaken by a qualified consultant. This included an audit of existing events, event infrastructure and stakeholder support; a review of the event-related assets and disadvantages in the immediate region; a review and assessment of event opportunities across a range of event segments including cultural and sporting; value analysis of best event options; feasibility comparisons and assessment of stakeholder responses; recommendation of the preferred event option; a viability study including event budget of the preferred event option and finally recommendations for action.

Once the event was identified, Tourism Victoria financially committed to supporting the initial 3 years of exhibitions and discussions regarding the further development of the exhibitions following that period have commenced.

Another example of Tourism Victoria's proactivity is the work undertaken to maximise the broadcast opportunities associated with those events that attract an international and/or national broadcast. The value of event broadcasts has also been recognised by the Victorian Major Events Company (VMEC) and Tourism Victoria and the VMEC now looks to attract events that not only provide substantial economic impact, but also have significant global broadcasts.

The value of profiling a destination via event broadcasts is significant. Specific studies have been undertaken to provide Tourism Victoria with a benchmark for exposure levels and return on investment. With the internationally recognised events that are hosted in Melbourne and regional Victoria, Tourism Victoria has identified opportunities available to generate national and international exposure for the destination via event-related broadcasts. It has also determined what is required to maximise these and in most instances, a proactive approach made to the broadcasters is required.

Opportunities that have been identified and negotiated with event operators and/or broadcasters include signage on playing surfaces and around venues that are included in the broadcast, the provision of vignettes to the broadcasters for screening, on-screen graphics and interview and studio backdrops.

It should be noted that Melbourne's major events have a major impact on the accommodation sector at specific times of the year. The March and October–November periods are traditionally busy times. Tourism Victoria aims to ensure that appropriate accommodation is available for visitors attracted to Melbourne because of its events and that issues associated with multiple events in crowded timeslots continue to be addressed. Tourism Victoria also assists in developing events that are held during the not-so-busy periods.

What are the constraints, risks and opportunities for the proactive policy?

The constraints associated with a proactive policy tend to relate to the fact that the nominated event has not necessarily been held previously and as such, there is an element of doubt associated with the financial viability and capacity of the organisers to deliver. There is also the mindset of some regarding going against what has occurred previously. The risks tend to relate to these constraints, in particular those relating to the financial risk.

The opportunities relate to the fact that the event organisers can initially host a 'manageable' event that can grow over time. It is normally better to 'start small', do it well and then grow an event over time. The event's potential can then be realised and cooperative relationships can be developed as the event demonstrates its ability to meet the needs of a tourism market.

How does this fit into the overall Tourism Strategy?

Tourism Victoria plays a key role in generating tourism to the State by implementing innovative and effective marketing strategies to position Victoria as a distinct and competitive tourist destination. Its events programme supports this by increasing the tourism impact and leverage opportunities associated with these events and by developing and marketing new and innovative events for key regional Victorian locations. By attracting, developing and cooperatively marketing appropriate events in Melbourne and regional Victoria, economic benefits along with increasing the profile of the host destination are achieved.

How does Tourism Victoria's Events Unit know if it works?

Any funding contract associated with the events programme requires some form of event evaluation. The more money allocated to an event, the greater the reporting requirements. All event organisers must provide a written post event report within 3 months of the event being held. Issues addressed include financial viability, tourism implications and the effectiveness of marketing strategies. In most instances, Tourism Victoria maintains a close association with the event organisers in the lead up to the event so that any issues that may impact on the event's success can be monitored and/or addressed.

What is broadcast impact and how is it important to the development of events in Victoria?

Tourism Victoria's *Events Broadcast Strategy* highlights the opportunities for generating additional national and international exposures for Melbourne and Victoria via event-related broadcasts. The

(Continued)

CASE STUDY 4.1 EVENTS UNIT IN VICTORIA – INTERVIEW—*Cont'd*

strategy also addresses what Tourism Victoria could do to maximise these opportunities. It has identified specific events that provide the opportunity to include destination footage in television broadcasts. In most cases, these events have an ongoing or year-by-year funding arrangement with the State Government.

In particular, the global broadcast evaluation associated with the 2006 Australian Open Tennis Championships indicated that the tournament broadcast reached an audience of 241 million and that it generated $283 million worth of coverage for Melbourne. Other research has been undertaken of various other major events held in Melbourne. Some of the studies include recommendations on how to increase and improve exposure for the host destination.

What are the trends in the formulation and implementation of events strategies around the world?

Major events should deliver more than economic impacts – they need to generate positive promotion of the destination. This allows an event to have a longer lasting impact as ongoing tourism opportunities can be realised through increased visitation in the future.

Attracting major events to a destination is costing more as the interest now demonstrated by many destinations throughout the world increases. The cost of bidding for events, associated rights fees, and the desire to ensure that the event is 'the best ever', all of these factors contribute to the ever-increasing costs of hosting major events. Another major factor is whether the event attracts an international broadcast and if so, what can be achieved through working in cooperation with the broadcaster.

The events also attract a transient population that work on the events. The number of event professionals continues to increase and this assists with ensuring that the event will be delivered appropriately.

4.2 EVENTS AGENCIES

The next step up from an events unit within a council or an event office within a corporation is the events agency. These are established by city, state or national governments to develop and direct the events portfolio. With the rise of the mega events and the increase in international sporting events and their media attention, the events agency has taken a large role in tourism marketing through events. As noted in Case study 4.1 one of the unintended results of this sudden growth of the agencies is the driving up of price of major events. With the growth of the new economies of Asia and the Arab Gulf countries, the bidding for events has been fierce. This has led to a further funding of the event agencies and an increase in their number. Below is a sample of these semi-government agencies.

4.2.1 EventBritain

EventBritain was set up as part of VisitBritain, the agency to market Britain in the tourism field in late 2007. It is part of the reinvigoration of the event industry leading up to the Olympics.

'Our mission is to provide focussed support to partners so as to identify, win and market the maximum new events for Britain.' It is a service to be used by the existing event industry and the event industry stakeholders.

The primary role of EventBritain is to attract events to Britain by streamlining the bidding processes. It includes halting the competition between the companies in Britain to bid for events and presenting united front. Hence 'building partnerships' with the event stakeholders is vital to its work. Its role is also to 'Maximise benefits of the games' — the 2012 Olympics — by ensuring there is a positive legacy. The organisation, Events for London, has a larger brief as they are also a 'one-stop shop' for events seeking to be held in London. Its focus is currently on the lead up to the Olympics.

4.2.2 EventScotland

EventScotland was formed in 2003 as one of the key recommendations of the 2003–2015 Major Events Strategy 'Competing on an international stage'.

In December 2008, EventScotland launched their new strategy for the event industry in Scotland 2009–2020 called 'the Perfect Stage'. This was a move away from supporting major event programme to a wider role of supporting the event industry. It represents the next phase in a country's event strategy, whereby the Government agencies recognise that their role is to *facilitate* and not to *determine*. They understand that the key drivers of events are not government agencies, they are individuals, communities, private companies and associations and the role of the government agency is to guide the development of the event portfolio. Their role is to construct a legal/business/social climate conducive for the key drivers to create and develop the variety of events.

Their major contribution to the event strategies is the division of the impact of events so that the approval, support and assessment process can be measured. These areas are as follows:

- Tourism
- Business
- Image and identity as a nation
- Media and profile
- Participation and development
- Environment
- Social and cultural benefits

An important part of the EventScotland strategy is the nationwide event called 'Homecoming Scotland 2009'.

'Homecoming Scotland 2009 is an events programme celebrating Scotland's great contributions to the world. In 2009 join us to celebrate the 250th anniversary of Robert Burns' birth, Scottish contributions to golf & whisky, plus our great minds and innovations and rich culture and heritage'. It is a year-long series of events to celebrate Scotland. It was aimed at overseas tourists.

4.2.3 Dubai Event Management Corporation

There is very little information about the Dubai Event Management Corporation except their budget of 150 million Dirham over 2 years. *Dubai Event Management Corporation (DEMC), which was established, in March 2008, by a decree issued by His Highness Sheikh Mohammed bin Rashid Al Maktoum, UAE Vice President and Prime Minister and Ruler of Dubai with the mandate to create, manage and organise live events in the fields of sports, arts and culture, exhibitions, conferences and entertainment in the emirate.*

After a very short-life the Dubai Event Management Corporation seems to be inactive.

4.2.4 EventsNSW

Australia, like New Zealand, has been at the forefront of events development. For a country with a small population and a long distance from Europe and the USA, Australia had to 'think smart' to attract major sporting events such as the Olympics or Grand Prix. They were the first to create the management systems for major events such as the Olympics and the first environmental programme called the Green Games. These mega events enabled the cities to develop a multiagency approach to major events.

In 2007 the State Government produced a report named *Review into a Possible Events Corporation for New South Wales*. It recommended establishing an events corporation with a budget of $30 million AUD per year for 3 years. EventsNSW was set up in 2007 with the mission:

> *Events New South Wales works to position Sydney and New South Wales as a preferred destination by working with government and industry partners to develop existing events, attract new events and maximise the economic, strategic and community benefits of events.*

EventsNSW has funded a number of sporting and cultural events to enable them to take place in NSW. Australia has a comparatively long history of the State Government event agencies primarily concerned with major international sports events. The West Australia EventsCorp was one of the first in the world set up in 1985 to maximise the benefit of the America's Cup yacht race. There is no national event agency and the state agencies compete fiercely for events.

4.2.5 Other countries

Most other countries have a dedicated unit within a larger Government Department. An example is the New Zealand Major Events.

New Zealand Major Events is a unit within the Ministry of Tourism and its existence shows how seriously events are being taken by the government. The unit administers the Major Events Development Fund, which has an annual budget of $3.4million. Funding decisions are made by an Interagency Events Group, *which has members from various government agencies, who are all involved with events.*

Their budget does not include the cost of bidding, hosting and building infrastructure for the Rugby World Cup 2011.

The aim of many of the event corporations or agencies, in particular the Tourism units, is to identify, evaluate and nominate the country's or region's interest as a candidate city for a mega and major event. It is to position the country/region/city in the bidding process for foreign events.

CASE STUDY 4.2 DEVELOPING THE EVENTS STRATEGY FOR MAJOR SPECIALIST HOSPITAL

To maximise the benefits of the professional approach to event management and the minimisation of event risk at the hospital, it is suggested that the hospital aligns the event portfolio with the business strategy.

Currently, events are spread across all the administration departments of the hospital. Events are the public face of the hospital, an important incentive for the medical staff, a link to international days and an opportunity for staff to learn and participate in best practice medicine. All of these outcomes depend on the quality of the event, which depends on the quality of the planning and management of the events. The first step in the quality management is training. The next step is establishing a strategic framework for future events.

The hospital's conference and training events are growing in importance – estimated to be a 5% growth for the first few years after 2006 and a rapid growth of 25% in 2009. The public and media events are growing faster. There are no data to compare this growth to hospitals and other services. This rapid growth of events in number, type and size is common to all modern institutions and companies as they realise the importance of events.

The table below is a list of the departments, offices and committees which are involved in events. In summary, the events cross all the management and operational divisions of the hospital. They require resources and deliver direct and indirect positive outcomes to all the departments.

Public Relations Department
Security and Safety Office
Logistics Department
Human Resources Department
AC Services, CME
Information Technology Office
Transport Department
Catering Department
Maintenance Department
Housing Department
Finance Department
CEO Office
Quality Control Committee
Environment Office
Religious Affairs Committee

To optimise the benefit of events to the hospital it is essential that the event portfolio, the calendar of all the events, has direction and purpose.

(Continued)

CASE STUDY 4.2 DEVELOPING THE EVENTS STRATEGY FOR MAJOR SPECIALIST HOSPITAL—*Cont'd*

The first step in the development of the strategy is to analyse and acknowledge the contribution events make to the objectives of the hospital. For example, conferences and other educational events are essential to the Continuing Medical Education (CME) credits and professional development of the staff. They profile or brand the hospital to the medical profession and other hospitals. The public awareness events are needed to tell the media, VIPs and general public of the hospital services. This is a constant need as the services are developing. A few simple tasks are required to maximise the benefit of events and reduce their risks.

Events website

The hospital should have a part of their intranet, an event website or portal, accessible to any member of the hospital staff who is planning an event. This is a repository of knowledge and contains templates and checklists from the workshops employed in the management of the events and improved with time. Note that it is not the calendar of events. The website is devoted to best practice management of events. To improve the events at the hospital it is essential that the event managers benefit from the lessons of past events from an easily accessible website. The contents of the website should include the following:

1. The objectives of the hospital having events
2. Event templates – the management system
3. Checklists
4. Past events
   Seminars

   Conferences

   Public awareness

   VIP events
5. Links for further education – events websites
6. Event terminology, contacts and suppliers
7. Online consultation

Event office

Events are currently spread over the divisions of the hospital. As a result each event is a new undertaking with many risks. Instead each event should adapt the management framework from previous events and learn from the past mistakes. An event office or event desk should have a staff of one or two people who are highly trained and experienced in events. They coordinate all the events of the hospital. If the departments want to undertake a new event, the event office will help them. In many cases the event office or the event desk will manage the events, such as the public awareness programmes and they will liaise with outside events, such as international conferences.

One task the event office could undertake immediately is to consolidate and expand the sponsorship of the events. Currently each event, individually, tries to find sponsors or does this through the Public Relations Department. This is a large waste of resources. The event office can offer to a sponsor a number of events over a number of years. It is far more attractive to sponsors and requires far less resources of the hospital.

Multidepartment meeting

A monthly meeting of department representatives concerning the upcoming events and their interdepartmental responsibilities would assist the events. The purpose of the meeting is to ensure that the departments know of future events and can coordinate their support and maximise their benefits.

Clarity of departmental support for events

There seems to be miscommunication between the events and the various departments. Responsibilities and timelines are not clear. This can be easily solved by an event office. The most common miscommunication seems to be with the IT Department. This can be solved by taking an event-wide approach and defining the mutual responsibilities.

Event mentor

Some members of the hospital staff have wide experience in events and others had no experience. The hospital can acknowledge the staff with experience and ask them to assist the newer event managers with advice. They could be called Mentors. It would greatly assist with the problems faced by the events.

An event strategy should be a detailed document showing the direction for the hospital and their staff to enable and rationalise events in the future. Currently this is difficult because:

1. Events are cross-departmental and there is no central expert group to assist in their management.
2. Events are not valued. Their contribution to the objectives of the hospital is not analysed and therefore cannot be improved. The true cost and benefit of events need to be done so that the hospital can maximise their benefit and understand exactly why they support some events and not others.
3. The departments do not understand the importance of events and the deadlines that are crucial part of events.

The hospital has taken an important step by providing training to their event staff. The training cost is an investment. To optimise and leverage this investment the hospital must implement some or all of the tasks described. The costs of an intranet website, an event office and the others are tiny. The benefits are a risk-free environment where successful events brand the hospital to the world and keep the staff up to date with the health care profession.

DISCUSSION TOPICS

Discover the equivalent of the events unit in the local regional authority. Compare their tasks with the tasks listed in this chapter.

Describe the proactive role of Tourism Victoria in the case study. Discuss why they needed to be proactive. Compare this to the other event agencies.

Research the other government and semi-government event agencies around the world — such as Singapore, Beijing, Cape Town, Abu Dhabi and Wales. Discuss if there is a maturity model for these agencies.

Interview the local organisations and companies such as the hospitals, road and transport office and taxation office and compile a list of their events. Compare the different organisations with their types of events and their management style.

Curry Festival in Woolgoolga. Photo courtesy of Coffs Coast Marketing

New Zealand Festival of Body Art. Photo courtesy of Warwick Hall

Techniques and tools for events development

On comparing the events development around the world there are numerous common tools and techniques used to implement a strategy. In some countries the development is piecemeal and not integrated under a national strategy. However, there is a definite convergence towards these methods as the industry matures. Bidding for events is increasingly employed as the regions and cities realise that they are missing out on a significant revenue from major events. The immaturity of the bidding process for events results in major mistakes. An alternative is to develop events in-house and one method to do this, the flagship event is explored. The events precinct, whereby an event friendly area is part of the construction plans of new cities or housing developments, is a new concept to assist the development of events. As the event profession grows the issue of government licensing event companies is raised. The chapter concludes with a brief exploration of the meeting of event professionals and other event stakeholders at the yearly event forum. Each topic is illustrated with current case studies and examples.

5.1 BIDDING AND REQUESTS FOR TENDER

In numerous countries the management of a major event is 'put out to tender' or a 'request for bid' is announced. Procurement of event services is a central process to the development of an events programme and is part of event feasibility. Tendering is a key process in procurement. Event companies compete for the right to manage the event. It is part of the outsourcing decisions of the event support process outlined in Chapter 3.

The application of the formal procurement process to events services is relatively new for government and major organisations around the world. They tend to adapt their standard tender documents to the event industry. Most of these come from the civil projects and the construction industry. These Requests for Tender (RFT) stress the compliance and measurable aspects of the project and tend away from the more intangible nature of the events. As time goes on, the tendering process will become more accepted, refined to the event industry and reflect the needs of event development. In this section the tendering process is outlined. The terminology is explained and a number of examples of successful tenders and RFT are examined. There are two parties to the tender process; the client and the tenderer or event company.

Events Feasibility and Development. DOI: 10.1016/B978-0-7506-6640-4.10005-6

The advantages to the client of employing event tendering as a method of procuring event management services are as follows:

1. There is a choice of event companies to manage the event.
2. The choice can be narrowed down using criteria to ensure the client benefits from the event.
3. Tendering is an objective, accountable and transparent process.
4. The process is common to other areas of business such as engineering and information technology.
5. The tenderers often have better ideas for the event than the client.

There are disadvantages to this process. It is difficult to describe the intangible aspects of the event in a tender document. Goodwill, brand image, attendee enjoyment, surprise and VIP hospitality level are difficult to unambiguously describe in a formal document. It is often the intangible outcomes that make the event a success. The decision criteria to award the successful tender will be biased towards measurable aspects of the event and the tender. As a result the job may be awarded to the company who underbids on price. The penalty for an incorrect proposal may be far higher for the client than the event company. If the event is a fiasco, there may be no suitable compensation for the client to minimise the damage. This is common in a number of recent government/private construction partnerships not just in the event industry. The assessment of tenders can be time consuming. Once again this favours the measurable aspects such as cost of the tender as they can be compared between the applicants.

The formal tendering process is illustrated in Fig. 5.1. It illustrates the ideal model. It implies a clear step-by-step flowchart. In the corporate arena there may be more interaction between the tendering companies and the client on the feasibility of the event.

The legal requirements driving the move towards RFT in the event industry are the concepts of Fair Markets (USA) and Competitive Neutrality (UK, EU).

Competitive Neutrality is a policy in place to prevent government departments and semi-government organisations using their advantages gained by public ownership, government influence and protective legislation to compete with private companies. The aim is to encourage efficiencies in the economy and within the government organisations. It is to ensure fairness in the marketplace and in the awarding of work. The monopoly status of government organisations gives them an unfair advantage in a competitive market. It ultimately results in an inefficient and protected economy. Often government-run projects, such as events, are placed out to tender so that their management can be compared to privately run projects.

The tendering process may begin with an expression of interest (EOI). It is advertised prior to the request for tender. The EOI contains a summary of the event and key points in the scope of work. It may also contain compliance guidelines. It enables the client to filter out the unsuitable candidate before the proposal assessment process. A response to an EOI is straightforward compared to a full tender

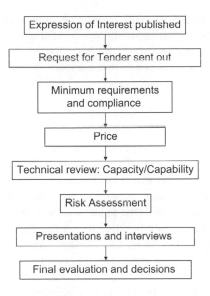

FIGURE 5.1

Process map of the tendering process

document. The preparation of a tender by an event company can take weeks and tie up resources. The EOI benefits both the client and the event companies.

5.1.1 Assessment of the tender

The tender can be assessed either by an individual or by a committee. They may ask for additional information and call on experts to assist in the assessment. This will depend on the importance and complexity of the event. Their first task is to filter out all the proposals that do not meet the minimum requirements. These include the following:

- Not meeting the tender requirements
- A low standard of submission
- Overpriced
- Not meeting the overall decision criteria
- Presenting a risk to the client

The tender document then passes through a number of stages before it is directly assessed against the criteria. If the client is a government organisation there may be political and legal compliance issues that must be met. The compliance will include legislation such as workplace/industrial relations, worker's compensation, affirmative action, diversity in the workplace and economic empowerment. A corporation will add 'not working for their competitors' and 'not having a bad public image'. For this reason a government or local authority can use their RFT to change the work culture of the event industry. By only awarding events to compliant organisations, the government acts as a gatekeeper. In South Africa, the government will only award work to event companies with a minimum rating on a scorecard to measure compliance with the Black Economic Empowerment. Some local councils will only award work to event companies that can demonstrate their environmental policy.

5.1.1.1 *Probity and collusive tendering*

If the client is a government organisation, the assessment of the tender must be completed within strict guidelines. Each of the tenders must have the same information, they must be assessed using the same criteria and there can be no conflict of interests. The legal system under which this process is placed will be described in the RFT. For events taking place in a number of countries, the jurisdiction is a vital issue. Collusive tendering refers to the tenderers, the event companies, agreeing to anticompetitive conduct prior to submitting the tender. One event company may, for example, submit an inflated price so that another company's bid will be seen as reasonable. In such a case the competing event companies are said to be a cartel. Cartel behaviour comes under the Competition or Antitrust laws in some countries and can result in large fines for the companies and their executives.

5.1.1.2 *Tender assessment software and electronic lodgement*

Numerous templates to create RFTs can be purchased over the web. They contain the standard headings found in this chapter. The next step is creation of software that can automatically assess the tenders. For this reason, recent RFTs contain questions created so that the answers can be assessed by computer software. The answers must be anticipated and the choice restricted to a menu list of options. This is a form of multiple choice. An example is found under the compliance heading of an RFT, with a menu of three choices, namely, 'comply' 'partially comply' and 'not comply'. Other questions are answered in text fields or with supporting attachments.

A robust software tender assessment process is yet to be developed. The limitation for some events is that the tender software favours standard answers. For some events such as meetings and conferences, the tendering can be straightforward. However, for events that are unique, complex or uncertain, the tendering software does not capture the subtle information needed to make the choice. The intangible nature of the main outcomes can be a problem for automatic assessment of the tender.

5.1.1.3 *Capacity and capability*

The client in the event industry is concerned with the competency of the event company. So much of the management of an event and the success of the event are dependent on the competency of the event team. The two dimensions of a competent event company are capacity and capability. In other words being able to manage the event and having enough resources to accomplish it.

The decision on the capacity of the event company to deliver the event concerns the resources available to the company. The company should have skilled and experienced staff. They need to have a network in businesses, access to the necessary subcontractors, the right equipment and an office.

The assessment of the capability of the event company must take into account the experience of the event company with similar events. It may include experience and knowledge in the type of industry such as tourism, banking or pharmaceutical. Risk management knowledge and experience these days is fundamental to the ability to organise events. The tender document should include the risk management process that will be used and how the client will be informed of the risks. Also it must include the management tools and techniques, such as performance measures, stakeholder management, using objectives and status reporting used by the event company. Innovation and the ability to respond to developments and redesign the event to take advantage of changes may be a core necessary skill depending on the type of event. Finally, the event company may include the credentials in event management and related fields.

Under the capability heading may be the question asking for a description of the methodology used in delivering the event. Exhibit 5.1 shows a successful reply to the request to describe the methodology in a recent tender.

EXHIBIT 5.1 SAMPLE OF A TENDER

The submission below is a sample of a successful tender for a series of public events addressing the requirement to describe the methodology. The event company 'ExpressStop' is a fictitious company.

Methodology

ExpressStop incorporates the employment of a comprehensive event project management system (EPMS) underpinned by the Federal Government Standard in Risk. The EPMS is an adaptation to the event industry of the PMBOK (Project Management Body of Knowledge) and Prince2. This supports the creative and design techniques developed by *ExpressStop* over many years of successful event practice. Planning and implementation capacity is met by our expert system and staff experience. A full risk register is produced for this event and includes the Occupation Health and Safety (OHS) codes, contingency planning and the Event Risk Planning in consultation with the event stakeholders. Progress reports are created within the project environment and can be produced at anytime on request.

ExpressStop recognises the two work flows essential to successful event delivery within the objectives of the client:

- Event design
- Event production

These management areas are integrated by the overall project management.

The design component is led by our highly experienced creative team and closely coordinated by the project team. At all times this includes close consultation with the client's event committee and relevant stakeholders.

The deliverables of the event project are as follows:

1. Event programme
2. Event risk plan
3. Event project plan – including site design, communication and logistics plan

(Continued)

EXHIBIT 5.1 SAMPLE OF A TENDER—*Cont'd*

The *communication plan* includes consultation via meetings and work in progress reports to the key stakeholders including the following:

1. Client
2. Venue management
3. All subcontractors – such as entertainers, audio–visual and security
4. Relevant legal entities necessary for compliance

The *logistics plan* includes sourcing and scheduling the flow of equipment and resources to and from the site as well as around the site during the event. This will input to our risk register to ensure compliance with OHS and a safe and secure site for the attendees, media, artists, VIPs and suppliers. The other schedules include run sheets for the artists and the overall production schedule of the event.

The efficacy and efficiency of the event will be tested by rehearsals. This will further identify any risks and opportunities. On the day of the event the stage manager will be able to direct and control the proceeding.

An important part of our event planning is the ongoing evaluation of the event and the project. A Project Implementation Review will be undertaken and a full assessment report is made to the client.

ExpressStop regards the event planning and delivery as a transparent process with close consultation with the client committee to produce an event that will meet all their objectives in safe and secure environment.

The financial viability of the event company will be important to the client. Many event companies are small operations and their assets are mostly the goodwill from their reputation rather than physical assets. The RFT usually asks questions concerning any possible legal or financial actions that could affect the ability of the event company to deliver the event. These include bankruptcy, insolvency proceedings or litigation.

The use of subcontractors is essential in most events. They range from the suppliers to the event site such as sound, catering to event support services such as legal and marketing. The RFT can stipulate that the subcontractors must be approved by the client. This may be impossible to do as it is unclear which subcontractors will be used. Hiring suppliers and contracting them generally takes place after the planning of the event, not during the initiation phase. It is particularly the case with special events, where the design of the event is constantly developing.

5.1.1.4 *Alternatives*

Quite often the RFT is written by a person outside the field of events. It may be approved by a committee and the members have little knowledge of events. For this reason a smart RFT will include a section permitting the event company to suggest alternatives to the proposed event. To do this, the event company must understand the aims of the client in wanting to stage an event. A major conference in one city may be expensive compared to a small conference with a linkup and interactive website – such as a Wiki or Blog. By allowing the event company to submit an alternative, the client expands their ability to innovate.

An interesting assessment item in the RFT is the case study or event scenario. The scenario is an outline of an event or part of the event, with a budget and the event company is asked for their response. The response may include their event plan, an event programme and how the budget would be spent. It may also include a logistics plan and marketing ideas. It enables the client to assess the abilities of the tenderer in response to a specific problem.

5.1.1.5 *The event services*

The core of the RFT is the list of services required to deliver the event. It can be a general description or a detailed list of responsibilities and tasks. It is a draft of the scope of work and may be used as the basis of the event management framework. An example of a list that can form the basis of the management framework such as the work breakdown structure is shown in Exhibit 5.2.

EXHIBIT 5.2 LIST OF SERVICES FOR A CONFERENCE RFT

Conference programme
- Engage speakers suggested by the conference committee
- Develop conference programme
- Collate presentations
- Produce conference booklet

Finance
- Development and control of the conference budget
- Receiving and banking all income
- Payment of suppliers
- Financial reporting to the conference committee

Registrations
- Develop the online registrations system
- Ongoing reporting of registrations

Conference management
- Complete management of the conference including all staffing and communication
- Procurement and negotiation with all conference and exhibition suppliers
- Develop the project and risk plan for the complete event
- Develop an event evaluation system to demonstrate the level of success of the conference

Logistics
- Accommodation and transport for delegates and speakers
- Negotiate advantageous rates for all operations
- Transport and other issues for the exhibitors
- Liaise with venue management on all issues

(Continued)

EXHIBIT 5.2 LIST OF SERVICES FOR A CONFERENCE RFT—*Cont'd*

Marketing
- Preparation of a marketing ideas and system
- Preparation of promotion schedule
- Engage promotion staff/company
- Develop web-based marketing

Social programme
- Develop a social programme for delegates and accompanying personnel
- Design and programme the evening dinner in consultation with venue management

---

In the RFT it is important to understand what is not in the scope of work. Exhibit 5.2, for example, does not include the event management services such as *source the speakers or the exhibitors*. Nor does it list the responsibility to *develop the contracts*. These tasks are outside the scope of work. To be perfectly clear in such a tender, the event company should make sure that these are purposely left off the list, not accidentally overlooked. In some tenders the limits of work are described under the heading of 'Assumptions'.

The amount of money spent on an event is measurable. Hence, it tends to attract most of the attention at the stage of tendering. Other aspects of the event, such as the surprise, the goodwill or in the case of seminars, the value of information imparted, tend to take a second place to the cost. A quality RFT will have a spreadsheet attached to allow the event company to estimate the costs. As is described elsewhere in this text, the cost of the event really can only be an estimate until the event actually happens. For this reason, it is common to hear about cost 'blowouts'. Many of the major sporting events, such as the World Cup in South Africa with the extra money needed to build the stadiums, have these problems. Often they successfully solve them by finding other sources of money to cover the cost — such as extra sponsorship or more volunteers. This cannot be anticipated during the RFT phase. It is a quandary. It illustrates that the RFT is not perfect and should be used with common sense as well as a sense of the history of successful events.

The assessment of the tender is performed by using the decision tables found elsewhere in this text. Exhibit 5.3 shows an example of the decision or assessment table for the procurement of event services. The capacity and capability are given a weighting which depends on the policy of the client. It reflects the relative importance on the criteria. The criteria are based on the headings used in this chapter.

An RFT may also ask for a detailed plan for the event. A major fashion show event, for example, would use the criteria and weightings:

- Forty per cent for management experience and capability based on past events, experience in fashion events and theatrical events, past work with the government authorities and current work

- Thirty per cent for the event plan of the fashion show including schedule, responsibilities, budget, concept development, risk plan, organisation structure and plan for building the relationship with clients, retailers and fashion suppliers
- Ten per cent for cost
- Twenty per cent for occupational health and safety and quality assurance plan

The aim of decision matrix or decision attribute table is to facilitate the choice of the event service supplier. It is fallible and its limitation should be understood. There may be aspects of the decision that are difficult to quantify in the table, such as political decisions. There may also be sudden changes in policy of the client, such as the government changing legislation, that are not transferred to the weightings. The criteria in the table are separate, whereas in real life they are often linked. The criteria may not capture the subtle aspects of event management. One method of improving on the decision table is to see procurement of event management services from a risk perspective. The tenders are rated by assessing the financial risk to the client.

EXHIBIT 5.3 SAMPLE OF ASSESSMENT TABLE

Attribute	Weight (%)	A	B	C	D
Skilled staff	10	2	1	1	3
Networked	10	4	3	4	3
Access to subcontractors	5	2	2	4	3
Equipment and office resources	5	2	1	3	3
Experience with similar events	20	3	3	1	4
Risk management knowledge and experience	15	1	3	3	3
Management tools and techniques	20	1	3	3	2
Innovations	10	4	1	3	1
Credentials	5	2	2	2	2
Total		225	240	250	275

Attribute rating: 4 = well exceeds criteria, 3 = exceeds criteria, 2 = equals criteria, 1 = below criteria, 0 = fails criteria.

As the event industry matures, the process of requesting event proposals or request for tender will become widespread. It is mandatory for many governments to put all their projects out to tender if the project's budget is greater than a set amount. As events grow in importance and their budgets increase there will be more and more put out to tender. The RFT process is an accountable system that encourages competition in the production of events. At the same time, it allows a government department to compare their in-house event management with the management provided by private companies. For corporations, the request for tender or proposals ensures they employ the most efficient event company. In both cases, civic and corporate, it is part of the organisation's responsibility to their constituents, either their community or shareholders. There are limitations as this process is adapted to the ever-changing event environment. The major limitation is that the tendering process favours measurable criteria.

5.2 FLAGSHIP EVENTS

The support for the development of major events poses the problem of how to distribute the funding so that events industry is allowed to grow and thrive. The limited amount of support a government can give may result in the money being spread too thinly among hundreds of events. The event teams and companies will spend too much time competing for these small resources. In such a situation the government agency work is not efficient and too many resources are used in administrating the support scheme.

A solution to this problem is to concentrate the government support in events that are unique to a region with broad appeal and have the possibility to grow into major events. The tourism authorities are particularly interested in this type of support. These events are called flagship or signature events. They can encompass almost all types of events including exhibitions, sports, conferences, concerts, public festivals and business meetings. Generally, they become a major festival comprising a variety of smaller events loosely based around a theme.

The festivals can incorporate extra elements in keeping with the theme of the festival. This enables established signature or flagship events to expand with a minimum of risk. It is similar to the marketing strategy of product bundling. Many of the flagship events began as one idea with a core organising team and a passion for their area of interest. An agricultural festival, car rally or sea festival can be easily expanded by incorporating new elements. In particular, the conference and exhibition on the same theme can be added. Involving the local university or college is a straightforward method of doing this. Many festivals become financially self-sufficient by attaching a commercial exhibition to the event. Air shows often are accompanied by the demonstration and sale of aeroplanes. The same can be done for the sea festivals with the exhibition of boats and sea sporting equipment. The Olive festival in Al Jouf, Saudi Arabia is an excellent example of this inclusive development. The region has a rapidly growing olive industry although it dates back over 3000 years. In 2007, the local businesses decided to start an event. Over 13 million olive trees are grown. The festival's core was the exhibition of olive oil products. This created a solid economic foundation to the event. At the same time the social aspects of the event developed including the children's show of Mr and Mrs Olive, Zaytun and Zaytuna, poetry, traditional arts and crafts and photographic competition. The result is a highly successful event with visits of over half a million and olive sales in excess of $10 million USD in 2010. The Riverfestival outlined in the Exhibit 5.4 is used as a model for the development of many of these events by the author.

EXHIBIT 5.4 RIVERFESTIVAL – ANNUAL COMMUNITY ENVIRONMENTAL FESTIVAL

The community festival in Brisbane, Australia is an example of the incremental development of an event to become world famous and a flagship event for the city. It began as a small community festival in park beside the Brisbane river. The organisers decided to use the event as a way to clean up the river. At that time the Brisbane river was treated more as a waterway than a special environment. They asked the local businesses to support the festival by coming down to the river to help remove the rubbish. This was very much a hands-on operations as the rubbish had built up over many years and ranged from plastics to car parts. The companies that did help gained publicity in the local and national press. The corporate responsibility was, at that stage, a growing issue for private industry. The publicity generated with photos of the Board members of various companies helping drag out old cars from the river was so successful that the event organisers had no problems in convincing other companies to take part in the next year.

The next milestone was to start the River Symposium to highlight and discuss the issues of river management. The Symposium has grown to include international awards and speakers. In 2007, due to the drought in the state, the festival committee asked for water-saving ideas and included public discussion of the water crisis. At the same time all the other programme elements, such as the concerts, the food events, arts, such as the underwater sculpture and liquid lens, increased. The increase in the festival programme allowed an increase in the sponsorship. Each programme elements had an opportunity to attract sponsorship. In 2007, when the young scientist award started in the Symposium, it was sponsored by the international project management company, GHD. The ideas for developing the event never stopped. In 2008, an idea for gardens on the roots of the major buildings in Brisbane was discussed.

By 2009, the River Symposium became separate event. This allowed it to expand worldwide and partnered with Nature Conservancy International. The Riverfestival was then merged with the Brisbane Biennial Arts Festivals to enable the Arts festival to become an annual event.

According to their website, the Riverfestival has achieved:

- *Impressive audience reach in 2008 with 1.3 million people, including QBE Riverfire live audience of over 600,000 people and a peak television audience for the QBE Riverfire television broadcast of 650,000 across Greater Brisbane and regional Queensland.*
- *Recognition as Brisbane's signature event by 9 out of 10 Brisbane residents.*
- *High brand awareness with 96% of Brisbane residents aware of Riverfestival.*
- *Valuable economic contribution to the City of Brisbane with the economic impact of Riverfestival 2006 valued at $21.2 million.*

http://www.riverfestival.com.au (accessed 2009).

The lesson from the growth and development of the Riverfestival is the way events organically develop. It develops from a small local festival into an international one. Along the way it spawns subevents, such as educational events, concerts, arts events, conferences and exhibitions. The more successful parts of the programme eventually have a life of their own and grow. It took the festival at least 3 years to establish itself. The event grew through constant innovation, discussion and looking for opportunities. The new events were able to attract individual sponsors. Finally, the event did not see itself as just community entertainment. Education and business were all part of the package.

A flagship or signature event has the potential to attract publicity and has support of the tourism authority as it distinguishes one region or city from the others and therefore promotes the movement of people. It has the ability to grow into a major event and become the main showcase, the region from which other promotion can be used.

The strategy used by governments is to identify potential flagship events in each region and city and concentrate their support on these events. Successful flagship events promote tourism and assist the development of other events. The Taif Rose Festival in the city of Taif, Saudi Arabia, for example, has all the qualities of a flagship event. If the festival was promoted throughout the Arab world, Taif would benefit by brand acknowledgement. This would flow into conferences and other events in the city and region.

A flagship programme allows the government agency to have a direct input into the regions and their event programmes with a minimum of risk. As described in the Riverfestival, the flagship event can grow into a major event and eventually split into a number of other events. Regional or city flagship events can show off the unique aspects of their region. It differentiates the destinations and promotes the internal and external tourism. Public festivals show the local people in 'celebration mode' and are a boon for tourism. The link between the government agency and the flagship events through its support programmes means that the agency can gather data on events in the region. The staff of the government agency will develop a relationship with the festival teams and this communication channel lets the government keep abreast of the developments in the regions. The events can be used for training people in events and at the same time allow the local population to become familiar with events as a benefit to them. It is not unusual for the local community to be hostile to events. They can cause major disruption. A flagship event programme based on the local community will involve the local community and create jobs and finance for them and the local businesses. The people who work on these events often go on to create their own festivals and events. The raising of the competency of the local population can be a significant legacy of events.

By means of a flagship programme, the government agency can evenly distribute their support over the regions and the cities. If the support is for a fixed time with the aim of self-sufficiency, a flagship programme can have a large influence on the growth of the events industry.

The flagship programme has been used in a number of countries and regions. Korea is successful with its events development programme. In 1995, Korea hosted three cultural festivals when the government decided to support and foster the development of major cultural festivals for each of the eight regions. Through a system of careful support, monitoring and improvement, the programme of festivals in Korea grew. As a result of the concerted implementation of a strategy, Korea in 2009 has over 1200 festival, 36 of which are supported by the Ministry of Culture and Tourism. These festivals include the Ginseng, Science, Martial Arts, Butterfly and Icefish festivals.

5.3 INTEGRATED COUNTRY PROMOTION

Events are a powerful tool to engage the media. They have all the qualities needed for a story in a media that is seemingly full of tragedies. There are photo and video opportunities, plenty of goodwill stories, interviews and people are shown celebrating. There is no time lag as it is an immediate experience and can create an immediate story. This is one of the reasons governments support festivals and sports events. Some of the countries realise that the plethora of events can be brought under one promotion banner. Using an economy of scale produced by rationalising the marketing, the events can all be promoted with the one themed campaign. An integrated promotion can also help to kick start the event industry if it is failing. It can be an efficient use of the funding to assist a country or region reach its economic development objectives. It requires cooperation from a large number of stakeholders and competing events. To be successful on the international arena an integrated promotion needs complete political and bureaucratic support.

Due to their focus on inbound tourism, most event strategies and successful event programmes around the world are related to a mega event. The Olympics for the UK, China, Greece and Australia, the World Cup for South Africa, the Rugby World Cup for New Zealand (NZ) and the Asian Games for Qatar are some examples. All these mega events expect to accelerate the development of the host country's event industry. However, not all countries or regions need to outsource a mega event in order to produce the same results of a unified and developed event industry. Recently, a number of countries have employed an umbrella concept or theme. Denmark developed the bicentenary of Hans Christian Andresen to launch nationwide festivals and events for the year 2005. The UK was the first to start this trend with the 1977 Silver Jubilee of Queen Elizabeth 11. Events and festivals occurred throughout the UK for the year.

The use of celebration events as nation building was successfully employed in the USA at the beginning of the twentieth century in a huge number of events called the Pageant Movement. This was pivotal in the history of the USA as it created a sense of nationhood in a country made up of separate states. The Integrated Country Promotion (ICP) is not only a promotional tool but it can also have significant social benefits.

ICP is used as a promotion of a country or region in another country. For example, the Australian government developed a programme called New Horizons comprising a series of events in India. These ranged from trade seminars to cultural events. It was successfully used in Japan and Russia. The 300 events that make up the integrated promotion in Scotland is a further example. According to their website:

> Homecoming Scotland 2009 is an events programme celebrating Scotland's great contributions to the world. In 2009 join us to celebrate the 250th anniversary of Robert Burns' birth, Scottish contributions to golf & whisky, plus our great minds and innovations and rich culture and heritage.

(http://www.homecomingscotland2009.com)

This ICP comprises a variety of types of events including:

- World Pipe Band Championships with 8000 pipes and drums and 200 bands
- Wigtown Book Festival
- A number of exhibitions under the theme *Great Scottish Minds and Innovations*
- The Scottish Diaspora Forum and the International Genealogy Festival that make up the Ancestral and Heritage Events
- Gatherings of the clans from around the world.

According to the Scottish government projections:

We have a target of an eightfold return on core investment generating an anticipated additional £40 million in tourism revenue. Our target of 100,000 additional international visitors is already expected to be exceeded

According to the 2010 economic impact assessment by the consultancy EKOS Ltd (2010) the actual return on core investment was 10-fold.

The Homecoming provided far more than a series of events and direct tourist spend. It included a lively discussion on nationalism and what it means to be Scottish.

ICP represents the ultimate tool in the event development strategy toolbox. By bringing together all the event stakeholders and directing their effort to a single objective, a national government can use the expertise and experience of a highly skilled sector.

5.4 THE EVENTS PRECINCT

The island property developments in Dubai and Abu Dhabi are a publicised version of what is happening in developing economies around the world. From the large countries such as India and China to the smaller states such as Qatar and Azerbaijan, modern cities are being constructed. They are termed integrated developments, multifunction or multipurpose developments and include resorts, hotels, business parks, housing, shops and malls. The construction of the major population and business centres, cities and tourist areas in many developing economies allows an opportunity for these countries to ensure these regions are able to host and grow business events, sports events and festivals. Many countries have made the mistake of building new infrastructure and cities without understanding that people want and need a quality of life. The infrastructure alone, as efficient and elegant as it may be, does not engage the people, develop business or celebrate life. The vibrancy of a city or region is an attractor and retainer of families and high-quality employees. One of the major factors in people deciding to live and visit a region is the quality of life. Therefore, part of an events development strategy must discuss the long-term infrastructure development to assist the growth of events and create, what may be termed, an eventful city.

The physical requirements of an eventful city are as follows:

1. Public parks with access and infrastructure to allow temporary logistics necessary for festivals and celebrations.
2. Sports venues including the smaller and highly distributed sports as well as the main stadia sports.
3. Exhibition and conference areas such as buildings and temporary areas that can be used for exhibitions and return to their former state after the exhibition has left.
4. Distributed smaller venues and areas where local events can be hosted. The smaller community and association-supported events are the ones that can grow into major events.

The planners of the mega property developments need to understand the characteristic of events if they are to be successful in developing and hosting them and produce an eventful city. The need for temporary structure is important to many events. Marquees, pole tents, frame tents, temporary flooring and pathways can all be set up, taken down and removed in a matter of hours. A public event is similar to a temporary mini city. The logistics is complex and over a very short time in comparison to a permanent structure. Once it is set up there is the constant movement of people. The pathways, roads, access points, parking and much more has to work in this temporary city at maximum load for its short time. The services and utilities such as sewerage, water, electricity, telephones, gas, food and beverages and security rarely have a rest period until the event is over.

The eventful city must be able to host this frenetic activity.

At the same time it must be able to encourage new events that are unique to the region. There are social enablers to this as well as physical ones. The existence of the social network is essential. This is indicated by the number and variety of clubs and associations. Sports associations are the most obvious. However, the unseen special interested groups can bring huge events to a region. Everything from pumpkin growers to the Quarter Horse association to a bhangra dance group have events. They comprise public festivals as well as sports events, exhibitions and conferences. The special interest events can have large community support and enable other events to be hosted in the region. The association and special interest events assist the local people to become 'event literate'. They can see the benefit of events and appreciate their existence in their community.

Some of the physical characteristics of an event-enabled development are as follows:

1. Areas set aside for public use that can be converted into temporary event structures with a relative ease of access to utilities and facilities.
2. Area of public parking and transport for sudden large crowds.
3. A human scale to the area so it is attractive to celebrations.

The last point is a common problem for multipurpose developments with areas specifically set aside for events. They are often planned purely from the logistical or operational point of view. There are large areas of concrete with geometrical roads and wide pathways that are able to take the largest of trucks and deliveries. With their emphasis on efficiency in operation and fixed infrastructure, they have ignored the all important event experience and created an unfriendly site. This eventually influences the bottom line in an event economy. The event experience is not just about the field of play or the show area. It is the total experience. Ultimately, the events precinct must attract people. The operations and logistics are a support function for the event. Many of these areas have become a significant financial liability as they are vacant for a large part of the year and require large sums of public money to continue.

A further consideration is the weather at the events precinct. Large expanses of concrete and roads are windy. Wind is one of the major dangers at events. The shade is another factor overlooked in the current design of event precincts. There are number of post-Olympics sites that suffered from these problems. Once again it seems the need for efficient logistics for a mega event takes precedent over the comfort and enjoyment of the attendees of all other events.

Many multipurpose resort developments are next to the water which presents another risk. The lake or seaside is an important feature that sells the shops, houses and hotels. However, this can present enormous difficulties with the safety and management of crowds. These problems must be understood if the events precinct is on the foreshore.

The non-physical attributes of the events precinct are important to event success. Supportive agencies such as police, emergency services and ambulance will assist the development of an event programme. The surrounding area of the events precinct can assist in attracting people and event companies to the area. Restaurants and shops can create a vibrant environment. In many cases the people who attend the events will stay after the event and experience the region.

Planning the events precinct and the integrated developments must include experts with knowledge and experience in the development of events. The process is to audit the region from an event management perspective and the trends should be researched. The target market for the property development will play a large part in the type of events that would be expected to develop over time. A suggested events development programme would be a good attractor to prospective buyers. Many of the multipurpose development will attract families and public festivals play an important part in the social network. Businesses may be attracted to the conference and exhibition facilities and the businessperson will be attracted to the social life for their family.

5.5 LICENSING

The problems many countries had with their events led a number of governments to consider issuing licence to event companies and event personnel. Licensing has been considered as a method for assessing the feasibility of events through the qualification of the event company. It is considered as a way to direct the growth of the events sector. In an industry based on innovation and quick response to changing conditions, licensing could be an unnecessary hurdle to the development of a viable and sustainable events programme.

A scan of event companies in Canada, Australia, USA, UK, EU, NZ, South Africa indicates that there is no current system for licensing event companies. There are numerous systems for licensing particular events or aspects of events. South Africa has legislation for the licensing of all events over 2000 people. Most event licensing concern control exercised by the local authority over high-risk areas such as:

- crowd numbers
- beverages
- extreme sports
- transport disruption

The disadvantages of a government-controlled event company licensing system far outweigh the advantages in most countries.

In some countries there are licences for trade where there is specific danger such as for security guards and electricians. In the UK, for example, under their Licensing Act 2003, the venue that hosts the events will need licences. The type of licence will depend on the number of people and the number of events hosted by the venue.

A licensing system transfers the risk to the licensing body (Licensor). This was illustrated by the tragedy at a corporate event in Bahrain. The Al Dana, a dhow, was used as a venue for an event. It capsized killing 56 people. During the case the lawyers threatened to take the licensing body, the Bahrain government, to court. According to the acting lawyers in this case Irwin Mitchell (2008):

> *The Al Dana then received its Tourism Licensing Certificate on 18th February 2006 and was inaugurated on 9th March 2006 by the Under Secretary of the Bahraini Ministry of Information. Marine Consultants reported a number of safety deficiencies in their report of 22nd February 2006 but despite the dangers, and despite the Captain being unqualified to sail, the Al Dana set sail on the evening of 30th March 2006 leading to it's capsize.*

**http://www.irwinmitchell.com/PressOffice/PressReleases/
BahrainiBoatVictimsMarkSecondAnniversaryWithRenewedCallsForCompensation.htm**

There have been many disasters at events where it was found that all the parties were licensed. The government, as the licensor, is at fault if it can be shown that they have been negligent in the licensing process and its enforcement.

The second disadvantage of licensing is the cost in resources to set up and police the licensing. The set up costs are small compared to the ongoing costs of ensuring that the licensee keeps to the terms of the licence. In the practice of licensing, governments and their departments have been shown to be underresourced. They are unable to enforce the requirements and the necessary inspections.

The licence can be regarded as an extra tax on the event industry. The bureaucratic requirements and the cost could drive event companies to look to other countries to stage their events.

The third disadvantage is that government licensing favours established companies. The event industry, particularly in a developing country, needs innovation. Small companies, often one-person operations, are dynamic and innovative. Successful events grow from these small beginnings. Almost all flagship and mega events were created and developed by a small group of enthusiasts. The Grand Prix and the Olympics are examples of this. A licensing system, administrated by a government bureaucracy with its necessary complexity and delays, does not fit with swift moving operation that can take advantage of opportunities limited by time.

When compared with certification and permitting, the licence has a negative connotation. A certificate is recognition of professionalism and assists the event manager in their work.

As demonstrated in this book, the final argument against licensing is found in the characteristics of the event industry at this time. The events sector includes events of various size and type. Wedding, exhibitions, sports competitions and fundraisers are examples. The definition of what can be described as an *event* is unclear. Many events are organised by volunteers or a mix of volunteers and paid staff.

An event company licence needs to navigate and control this complexity. The question of who will be licensed must be resolved. Each event may involve numerous owners and stakeholders such as the event host, client and the event coordinators and managers. Event companies can be part-time individuals as well as established international companies. Unlike many industry sectors, the events industry is highly fluid, dynamic and comprises numerous individuals working on a project basis. Adding to the complexity is the early stage of development of the event sector. Although there are a plethora of associations and training courses, most of these have been created in the last 10 years. There is not a universally agreed set of knowledge and skills for the management of events.

A viable alternative to a government licensing system of event companies is to use a combination of permission for specific events and certification of event companies. Event companies can be accredited by event associations or a peak industry body such as the International Festival & Events Association or the Meeting Professionals International. To gain the certification, event companies undertake training in areas of need, such as risk management. The training can be provided by government departments, such as Regional Development and Tourism, education institutions and private training providers.

The certification is not enforced. However, the government and local authorities will favour accredited companies in their requests for tender. Certification and training provide a measure of the competency of an event company.

Certification is an incremental way to improve the event industry without loosing the dynamic thinking and new ideas necessary for its development. Provided the certification is based on a sound competency system closely linked to industry and international trends, it assists the event companies in producing better events. Ultimately, it results in a sustainable industry responsive to the country's development.

Certification and special licenses/permissions are successfully used in most professions such as engineering, accountancy and project management and in many trades such as carpentry, building and gardening. Accreditation encourages best practice, skill development and indicates the quality of the event company. As it derives from the industry bodies, it is attuned to the needs and the operational requirements of the industry. If it is linked to secondary and tertiary education, it can provide an educational research and possibly a career pathway to the student.

The final word on the issue is given by Janet Landey who pioneered this area of event management and is at the frontline of events competency development in South Africa.

My mission has been that the industry needs a Professional Body which would be the Certification Body against standards set by industry standards setting body, and certification criteria set by the Certification Body — pretty much like the CSEP (CSEP Certified Special Events Professional, awarded by the International Special Events Society) — you need a minimum of 3 years experience, x amount of attendance at CPD (Continuing Professional Development), y for the 'greater good' — altruistic/ giving back etc. and as a result of this the individual can challenge for Certification and this then against:

- *the theory for the given event — against a defined outcomes for each of the competency areas*
- *the proven industry experience*
- *the documented proof of CPD (which needs annual points — which could be the role of industry associations)*
- *applied competency — an industry experienced Assessor can assess the applied competency and*
- *Certification awarded*
- *Renewable every 5 years (against written proof of CPD points and greater good)*

(Landey, 2008 personal communication)

The licensing of event companies is impractical and would require a huge continuing commitment of resources. The industry is developing and needs encouragement of excellence provided by training and certification. Licensing would favour the established large companies and therefore stifle the industry's development. Eventually, it would lead to stagnation and the moving of events to other countries. The event industry is based on taking calculated risks and innovation. The small players of today produce the successful events of tomorrow.

5.6 EVENTS FORUM

The establishment of an events forum or conference is integral to the development of events and festivals of a region. Most profession and industry sectors convene yearly conferences. There are both practitioner and academic forums and conferences with published papers in all professions. The practitioner conferences stress current issues and operational topics. The academic conferences provide the long-term study and research in the area of knowledge. Both of these are important to the relevance and currency of the profession.

The aims of an events conference or forum are as follows:

1. To upskill the events sector through information and workshops
2. To enable the networking and cross-communication on important issues within the event sector
3. To gather information on the quality, size and potential of the event sector
4. To minimise the financial impact of the current 'sellers' market in events by sharing information and forming alliances
5. To discover commonalities and opportunities for each of the cities, councils and related organisations

In the numerous events forum the author has been responsible for developing such as Dubai, Singapore, Uganda, South Africa, Kenya and Saudi Arabia the local government has always been surprised at the large number of attendees. Once again it indicates the invisibility of events to many governments. Exhibit 5.5 is an example. The large number of exhibitors, sponsors and attendees even took the organiser by surprise.

EXHIBIT 5.5 KENYA EVENTS FORUM

The 2010 inaugural Kenya Events, Festivals and Conferences Forum was conceived by the author and the Makini College in Kampala in 2009. It came 'at the right time' according to the director of the International Kenyatta Conference Centre. The venue is a tall landmark in the centre of Kampala and was undergoing renewal. Hosting an events forum would assist the conference centre to promote the venue to event companies in the region of East Africa. According to the governments report titled *Kenya Vision 2030, A Globally Competitive and Prosperous Kenya*, Kenya was improving its economy at a rate of 7% and aiming for 10% in 2030. Their strategy is based on the three pillars, namely, economy, social and political governance. Not surprisingly, the event industry was growing rapidly at the same time. The size of the event industry in East Africa is unknown. The forum would assist in assessing the size of the industry in Kenya. The initial objectives of the forum were as follows:

- To assist in the development of the event industry in Kenya
- To involve the key stakeholders and beneficiaries of events including the government, its departments, in particular the Ministry of Tourism, the colleges and Universities and the key suppliers
- To use the opportunity to train event managers in world's best practice
- To demonstrate the importance of the events to the future of Kenya
- To pave the way for a pan East Africa events conference in 2011
- To introduce the expertise and experience of the world event industry and demonstrate the importance of training to the local industry
- To establish event and festivals as a driver of economic, social and tourism capital

The organiser of the forum, Joseph Okelo, obtained sponsorship from the main telecom company in Kenya, Safaricom. They also assisted with the session on event sponsorship.

The forum was able to take advantage of the World Cup South Africa to demonstrate the power of events in economic and political development. The 2-day programme of the forum reflected the nascent state of the events as a cohesive industry in Kenya. The topics included the following:

- Conferencing
- Sponsorship
- Marketing
- Creating the event experience
- Music and sports events

The keynote speakers delivered presentations on the World Cup, Tourism, Certification and Project/risk management of events.

The forum also hosted an exhibition of event service suppliers.

Over 200 event company representatives and other event stakeholders attended the event. The large size of the industry and its diversity was a surprise to all the attendees and the local press. The national paper carried the heading: 'First ever Kenya festival and events forum a huge success'.

Refer: www.kenyaevents.org.

DISCUSSION TOPICS

1. What events favour the tendering process and why?
2. Analyse the tendering in terms of cost–benefit analysis. What are the costs for the event company and the client? List the benefits.
3. Choose a major international conference and develop an outline of an RFT.
4. Discuss the limitations of the tendering process for the following events:
   a. International forum on the environment
   b. A ticketed rock concert
   c. A fundraising dinner
   d. The launch of a new integrated property development
5. Assume that you are the event company and send out an RFT for aspects of the event. What parts of the event will be put out to tender? What are the risks?
6. Trace the development of a flagship or signature event in your region. How did it start? Who were the event initiators and initial stakeholders? Compare its origin and growth to the well-known events such as the Baalbeck International Festival, Munich Oktoberfest and the Grahamstown National Arts Festival.
7. Discuss the themes that may be used for an ICP for your country.
8. Research the licensing issue in other professions and compare it to the event industry.
9. On the Internet search for *integrated developments* and the building of new housing estate developments. Discuss the target market for the development, the types of events that would work and where the events precinct could be placed.

Camel Race, Saudi Arabia. Photo courtesy of IFEA

Dayak and Aboriginal dancer at event in Borneo. Photo William O'Toole

Building competency: associations, awards and training

INTRODUCTION

The scattered growth of the events sector has produced a number of associations and numerous event training courses around the world. They are all at different levels of development. It is demonstrated by the growth in awards for excellence in the public and private spheres. This bewildering variety of associations and courses is a benefit to nations and regions starting anew as they can learn from the mistakes and pick and choose the best. Untimely, the events development is dependent on the abilities of the people to come up with ideas and organise the events. There is sufficient event history now to deduce a pathway for developing these abilities. This chapter explores the way to build competency of the population through forming event associations, recognising excellence, education and training.

6.1 EVENT ASSOCIATIONS

In the development of any professional sector there is a time when a critical number of companies and stakeholders are reached to support a professional association.

Part of any event development strategy is the role of the professional association. A survey of the industry shows numerous 'product'-based associations. These are associations based on the end product — or type of event. The International Special Event Society, Meetings Professional Association and International Festival and Event Association are the three examples of the 147 identified by Arcodia and Reid (2003) in their study.

The advantage of an association or a network of event professionals is it provides a common source of information on best practice and risk for all its members. Most event professionals work alone or in small groups and are widely distributed geographically. The association meeting, website and conferences provide an opportunity for them to exchange knowledge. Eventually, the professional association assists with developing industry standards and code of conduct. If a legal action is taken against an event team or company, it is common for the judge or magistrate to compare their actions or lack of action to the standard in the event industry. The event association assists in establishing this standard. The concept of duty of care can only be understood in relation to the whole industry. An association

Events Feasibility and Development. DOI: 10.1016/B978-0-7506-6640-4.10006-8

can establish a standard of practice to be employed in the assessment of fault in insurance claims and litigation. They can provide the expert witness needed in trials when event competency is involved.

The professional association can have a guiding input into the education system. This is common in medicine and engineering. The professional association endorses degrees and courses. As importantly, it provides the government with a peak industry body in the ongoing development of policy and legislation.

From the association, the government can create an event development Advisory Board. The role of the Board is to advise the government on event-related policies.

The New Zealand Association of Event Professionals is a model of the event association. It was set up in 2002 at the Eventing the Future Conference. The Board is a mixture of corporate and public event companies and managers and representatives of education bodies and government.

EXHIBIT 6.1 NEW ZEALAND ASSOCIATION OF EVENT PROFESSIONALS (NZAEP)

The NZAEP is one of the world's most successful event associations. It began in 2005 and its membership is over 200. This is significant for a country with a population of 3.8 million. Similar to other associations around the world it is based on the profession rather than the event type.

Its goals are as follows:

1. To provide advocacy for the events industry
2. To increase the knowledge and skill level of practitioners in this industry
3. To establish and maintain a robust events industry accreditation system
4. To provide professional and effective management and governance of the NZAEP

Below is an interview with Peter Burley a founding Board Member and current CEO of Sports Guidance.

The Major Event section of the Ministry of Economic Development of the New Zealand Government had an idea of setting up an event association. They set up a group but the membership was expensive. They wanted high profile members initially and were not looking for the operational people or those at the forefront of event delivery. This reflected government policy which was focused on "major" events and the big picture. So a few of us at Christchurch Polytechnic within the Business School where we were running a successful Graduate Event Course decided to run a seminar for events professionals on the applied areas of learning. The Qualification we ran had a large internship component necessitating a close relationship with industry, and this seminar was indicated to be a good way of achieving connection. The seminar quickly grew into a conference. The conference became the national event conference. It focused on vocational learning for event professionals. Although other countries have academic conferences, it was our preference to involve event organisations around the country and their staff. We targeted well known, respected and successful event managers. The people we involved were high profile in the event industry. They were highly respected by the working event organisers. This gave us a credibility in the profession. We realised that events organisations are often temporary and do not have the funds to pay large amounts for information. So we ensured the price was reasonable for the working event teams. At our third conference we surveyed the attendees about starting an event professionals association. Immediately we had 75 members.

At that time NZ had a well publicised court case as a result of a death at an event, a cycle race. The event director was being charged. This gave the conference and the formation of an association an immediacy. The event teams felt exposed and wanted information with possibly some representation at a government level. There was no common voice for event management at that time. It was the right time to start an association for the teams and was based on a core group of people who were willing to serve as Board Members, in a sense they fronted the development of this association.

The conference and the awards program provide a source for new members for the NZAEP. A member is given a significant discount on the conference fee. We are used to obtaining at least 30 new members from the conference.

Our latest efforts include the Events Update Broadsheet and establishing regional chapters of the association. A private company published an event listing called Events Update. It was well known and accurate. NZAEP purchased this and uses the broadsheet as the communication tool. In our third year NZAEP set up regional chapters and regional seminars. Although the chapters existed before NZAEP, they are now part of the association. An example of these is Auckland City that has upwards of 400 people attending a one day seminar.

We can now tour seminars around the country. Environmental sustainability and Volunteering are examples of the topics of the seminars. The links with other countries particularly key event professionals in Australia have been very important for us. We are able to bring in experts from the USA, South Africa and Singapore and many more. The festivals and events around NZ now have a voice within the government, and an ability to lobby at various levels. As a result NZAEP can provide the Government with services such as helping with bidding, resource development for events, developing the standards for events and accreditation for quality of events.

The future will involve the World Cup. We are heavily involved in this and hope that it will enable us to go the next step and develop financial and business model for the association.

6.2 EVENT AWARDS

An award system for events and festivals is an effective method for a tourism body, local authority, an association, industry sector or government to influence the development of events in their region.

Quality awards for any industry as well as government departments are recognised as having a positive effect on the development of that industry. Studies of the effect on market value of a company as a result of receiving an award claim that it results in an increase in stock price of the company. At the same time an award system reduces the perceived risk of investing in the company. Both of these results are of benefit to the corporate and public events as well as the tourism sector. In particular in the event and festival industry, the perception of 'worth' and 'risk' is vital to sustainability. Festivals and events have intangible products and an award system will guide sponsors and other organisations in their support for events. Quality awards recognise models of excellence used to compare with events and festivals.

The winners of the awards become the examples of how quality is expressed in events. They provide the universities and training colleges with case studies to enable their courses to produce quality graduates. The quality events create benchmarks for other events to strive for. Sponsors can be guided into future investments in events. Suppliers will favour quality events and therefore increase the quality of their supplies. The attendees will favour quality events and therefore increase the revenue for these events. This in turn allows these events to succeed. At the same time the events of low quality can either improve or will disappear. There is a diffusion of excellence throughout the industry. This increase in quality is produced by celebrating success rather than being imposed on events by procedures and legislation.

In summary, an award system for excellence in event and event management has a substantial influence in increasing the quality of events and festivals in the region or a company.

There are many models of awards an organisation can use to base their 'Excellence in Events' awards. One of the most comprehensive is the European Foundation for Quality Management (EFQM) Awards. The EFQM Awards are strongly linked to their quality model. This means that the EFQM Awards are a tool to increase the quality of the industrial sector. EFQM Awards are part of an integrated programme to assist companies in assessing and developing quality.

The EFQM quality model is used:

1. As a framework which organisations can use to help them develop their vision and goals for the future in a tangible, measurable way.

2. As a framework which organisations can use to help them identify and understand the systemic nature of their business, the key linkages and cause and effect relationships.

3. As the basis for the EFQM Excellence Award, a process which allows Europe to recognise its most successful organisations and promote them as role models of excellence for others to learn from.

4. As a diagnostic tool for assessing the current health of the organisation. Through this process an organisation is better able to balance its priorities, allocate resources and generate realistic business plans.

Refer:http://www.efqm.org.

The criteria for the EFQM are derived from their quality model. The application process for the excellence awards refers to the EFQM quality model. In this way the process of applying for EFQM Award will assist a company in identifying their level of quality. This is an integrated system. The awards are part of an overall management strategy and not isolated from industry development.

The integrity of the award system is basic to its success. Any hint of undue influence or bias will invalidate the whole process and ultimately devalue the current and past awards. There is difficulty in choosing the judges. They should have experience in the industry and at the same time have no interest in the outcomes other than the objectives of the award. Ideally, the judging is achieved by events experts who have many years in the industry and near or at retirement. Therefore, they are beyond any bias or corruption. However, the dynamic nature of the industry is such that the older generation may be unable to judge newer developments. This can be partially overcome by a rigorous set of criteria for the awards. Another problem is the commercial in confidence nature of the information needed from the event companies. If the entrants feel their information is being given to their potential competitors they will not enter the awards.

Three examples are presented below. The first is for a national tourism authority, the second for a commercial organisation and the third for an international events association. Each one of these award systems is very successful. A comparison of them shows quite different objectives. They contribute to the feasibility and development of events. The event awards are both recognition of quality and a method to raise the standard of events.

An example is the NZAEP event awards system which began in 2006 and includes four categories, being: Best Emerging Event; Best Established Event; Best Marketing of Event and Best Partnership in an Event.

The awards aim to bolster excellent performance, best practice and continual improvement within the event industry. Entrants not only have the chance to be rewarded for their outstanding work, but also to gain considerable profile within the events industry on the strength of entering and potentially receiving an award.
**(Event Awards, 2009; http://www.nzaep.co.nz/nzaep_files/File/NZAEP%20Awards%
202006.pdf)**

The example of the Tourism Department awards illustrates how an award system can support the policy of the supporting organisation. By linking the criteria of the

---

EXHIBIT 6.2 TOURISM DEPARTMENT AWARDS

Vision
Each year the Tourism Department presents awards to events that occur within the preceding 12 months for excellence in the production of events and festivals within the country and meet the objectives of the Tourism Department. The excellence awards encourage the events and festivals to increase their quality by providing examples of high-quality events and by rewarding success with national recognition.

Objectives of the award
1. To recognise quality in the festivals and events
2. To influence the development of types and quality of events
3. To raise the awareness of the benefits of events and festivals to all event companies and suppliers in the region
4. To develop a database of events, event companies and suppliers that can be used by the department in assisting the event policy
5. Through the application and award process to raise the quality in events, event management, event training, sponsorship and event suppliers

(Continued)

EXHIBIT 6.2 TOURISM DEPARTMENT AWARDS—*Cont'd*

Award description. 'Three Awards' is an entry level award system and is based on the event awards in a number of countries. It is quick to set up and can be expanded over the years to include other awards. It is simple to manage and set up.

Three awards
1. *Major*: festivals and events
2. *Significant*: festivals and events
3. *Innovation*: event and festivals

These awards may be expanded to include Best Event and Festival Promotion and Best Sponsorship for Event and Festival. Also the awards can simply be part of larger Tourism Awards.

Award criteria. The criteria for the awards are based on the policy of the Tourism Department.

Major festivals and events: summary of the criteria
This category is open to hallmark festivals or events that (a) create substantial economic impact, (b) attract visitors from interregion and/or overseas, (c) generate national or international media profile and (d) positively promote the destination. They may be once only events or recurring events.

Significant festivals and events: summary of the criteria
This category is open to festivals or events that (a) create substantial economic impact within the local community, (b) attract visitors from region and/or interregion, (c) generate regional media profile and (d) positively promote the destination. They may be once only events or recurring events.

Innovation award: criteria
This category is open to festivals or events that (a) contain unique ideas in the event programme, (b) are highly efficient in management, (c) have the ability to franchise and develop the event concept and (d) demonstrate overall creativity.

---

awards to the objectives of event support, the supporting organisation influences the development of the events programme in their region.

The example of the Middle East Event Awards outlines a full system of awards particularly aimed at the private industry. It is complex to set up and requires more resources. It has a maximum impact in the industry and the region. The Middle East Event Awards are an interesting comparison to the two other award examples as they are focused on corporate or business events and production. They are presented by the Dubai-based database and publication organisation called SourceME. The awards stared with the conference and exhibition event company IIRME in Dubai as part of their events conference. The rapid development of Dubai and its exposure to the world credit crisis seem to have little effect on the popularity of the awards.

The peak body for the festivals and events around the world is the International Festivals and Events Association (IFEA). Their awards programme, the Pinnacle Awards, has been in existence since 1995. The 65 categories range from operations to sponsorship to event education. This is one of the longest running event award programmes in the world. Most of the aspects of an award programme such as criteria, judging process, fees and scheduling have been ironed out through the years.

EXHIBIT 6.3 MIDDLE EAST EVENT AWARDS

Awards

1. Best meeting or conference
2. Best incentive event
3. Best trade exhibition
4. Best meetings or event facilities within a hotel
5. Best purpose-built events venue
6. Best music event
7. Best arts and cultural event
8. Best sporting event
9. Best marketing campaign for an event
10. Best innovative entertainment
11. Best exhibition stand design
12. Best creative use of event lighting
13. Best event sound production
14. Best av/video solution for an event
15. Best event design
16. Outstanding event using a temporary venue/structure or space
17. Best corporate product or service launch
18. Outstanding production achievement
19. Green award
20. Young achiever of the year
21. Outstanding contribution to the Middle East event industry

---

It has matured and provides a case study for other nascent award programmes. The awards system is highly sophisticated and efficient and, yet, still keeps its personal and human elements.

The following interview with the Steven Wood Schmader, CFEE, President and CEO, illustrates the power of an event awards system to influence the development of the event industry and assist in the feasibility of future events and festivals.

The IFEA has moved one step further in event awards and introduced the FEA World Festival and Event City Award. The award aims to recognise the partner relationship between the communities in cities and their events.

EXHIBIT 6.4 INTERVIEW WITH THE CEO OF THE IFEA ON THEIR AWARDS

The awards are very important to participating festivals and events as they enable them to say they are an award winning event. It is important for future media coverage and to selling sponsorship packages. The media immediately pick this up.

The events that have taken advantage of publicising their award have built up credibility. BorderFest in Texas is a good example. The festival wins a number of our awards. It is so important to them that they ask the IFEA to fly down to Texas to re-present the awards at their own ceremony. This, in itself, is a big event with a dinner where they invite all their sponsors, volunteers, government officials, and other stakeholders.

(Continued)

EXHIBIT 6.4 INTERVIEW WITH THE CEO OF THE IFEA ON THEIR AWARDS—*Cont'd*

The IFEA encourages the events to put it on their press releases, on their marketing materials and on their websites. It is raises their prestige with their peers.

The awards help the event industry as it raises all boats and improves the quality across the Board. When people win we make sure there are displays of the winning entries for all events to see. The other events are looking at what the winning entries did and how did they do that. If they won for best volunteer program, for example, other events and festivals contact them to discover how they did their volunteer program. It's the same with the merchandising program or any of the other awards. It gives the event teams something to strive for. It is a quality standard they can understand and know that they can achieve.

The benefits for the event organisations are many as the awards serve as a rallying point. It's a way for the staff to get together. If, for example, the event wins an award for their merchandising program – this gives the person in charge of the merchandising program an opportunity to go up on the stage and accept the award. It is a nice way to recognise the members of the event staff. It makes them feel like their efforts are worthwhile.

The association is assisting the development of the industry by choosing the categories, identifying current best practice and the latest trends. We are now adding best social media marketing campaign and we were quick to recognise the importance of the environment. In this way we can steer the industry. Awards are a way of saying there is best practice among your peers. The IFEA sees trends quickly as we are immersed in the industry. When the media calls to ask for event examples we point them towards the award winners. It also is a way of nicely saying that some people are doing things well but not well enough without misunderstandings. It is a carrot not a stick.

The awards are so important to the festivals and events that some people fly in months before the entries are due to examine the previous year's entries to see how they were done. On the day of the deadline it is a very busy time as trucks with the entries are arriving all day.

The gradual introduction of event awards around the world is a further indication that the events sector, as diverse as it is, is still following the path of other professions and sectors.

6.3 EVENT MANUAL

An important tool of events development is the event manual. In every profession there is a 'how to' manual. It is fundamental for the development of the industry and to increase the abilities of management. The manual is used to assist the management of an event, often on a day-to-day basis. It can be the book (or file) that resides on the event manager's desk to help with the decisions.

In the text 'Corporate Event Project Management', O'Toole and Mikolaitis describe in detail the contents and use of the event manual. From an events development perspective, the event manual is part of the knowledge management for continuous improvement of an event and a guide to the management capability when deciding on the feasibility of an event. In most industries a manual usually concerns the operations. The scale and project nature of events require that the management and operations are closely intertwined. A manual that describes the method of managing and marketing an event will often have operational level checklists.

A guide is essential for the development of an events portfolio. It is vital to understand the feasibility of an event. It must be useable and used. Manuals are often too technical, assume expert information or are bloated with information unnecessary for the task at hand. Many of the writers of the community events manuals realise this and produce a manual that fits into the theme of community celebration and have highly relevant information presented in way that is a pleasure to read.

The profusion of event manuals is confusing as the term is used loosely. This is due to the project nature of events and that event operations and management are not as separate as in other industries. To allow some order in this, the manuals can be divided into:

A. *Generic*: The textbook such as the 'Festival and Special Event Management' by Allen et al. and 'Event Production' by Sounder. These mix the management and marketing with the operational tips. These manuals are used in the training of event managers and staff. Often they are written in a textbook format so that they can be used in tertiary courses in events management.

B. *Category*: These manuals refer to a type of event such as fundraisers, folk festivals and conferences. Government, region, local authority, venue or city event guides such as Blue Mountains Festival Guide, the University of Melbourne Events Manual and Newcastle City Events Guide are examples.

C. *Specific*: The manual refers to a particular event such as the Hail Car Rally or the Science Festival.

D. *Instance*: Refers to an event at a specific date and place such as the Newcastle 2010 Celebrations in Civic Square.

E. Function manual that refers to an area of the event management such as a risk manual, disaster plan and accessibility. Examples include the 'Special Events Contingency Planning'; 'Federal Emergency Management Agency USA' and 'The Red Book: The Guide to Managing Health & Safety at Exhibitions and Events UK'. 'Accessible Events: A guide' for organisers in the meetings industry.

F. *Venue manual*: Concerns the management of an event within the venue. These are common in the exhibitions industry and outline the requirements. Many universities have an event manual with the rules and regulations of the University.

The categories can be subdivided into strategic, management and operations.

An example of a manual that is an instance and operational is the loose leaf manual given to the volunteers just before the events such as '2009 Singapore Science Festival Volunteers Guide — What to do at the event'.

These are not exclusive categories. The operations manual that is an instance or specific to an event on a particular day can provide the template for the next similar event. The specific event manual may be regarded as an 'instance' of the more general event guide.

Governments and local authorities are particularly concerned to ensure that events follow the local rules and regulations. Occupational Heath and Safety will be an important section in their event guides.

An event manual is essential to develop an events programme for a company or region. It enables the current event companies and organisers to understand what is expected of them. It can outline best practice in event management and improve the quality and sustainability of the events. It can show the event companies, individuals and organisations how to apply for sponsorship or other support. It is important for event companies coming from a different country or region as it can describe the rules and regulations pertaining to events in the region. In particular, it minimises the resources needed to approve support as most of the explanations and the FAQ are found in the event manual. The event manual helps to standardise the terminology and processes so that data can be collected, collated and used for quality improvements. Exhibit 6.5 provides an outline and tips for a regional events manual. It is aimed at the community level and must assist the potential event organiser to understand the complexity of developing an event without diminishing their enthusiasm.

EXHIBIT 6.5 SAMPLE OF RECOMMENDATIONS FOR AN EVENT MANUAL

An event guide for a public event may include the following information.
  Introduction; setting out the aims of the event guide such as

> *Events can be exhibitions, festivals, concerts, product launches, conferences, meetings, sports events, and much more. Our Events Unit is here to help you put on your event. This support may take the form of advice, facilitation or, if you meet our strict criteria, sponsorship. What ever level of support, we want to help you. On our website and in this guide is how you apply for our assistance. It is a step by step process. It is the same for most countries of the world. It is simple if you take a bit of time to read through it. It will save you a lot of time and help you make efficient use of your resources.*

Before you begin

A series of general questions to ensure that the event organisation understands the scope of the event and their management. It would contain these questions:

Have you organised an event before? If so this is just a checklist to make sure you know the reasons. If you haven't then please take the time out to read this carefully and have answers to all these questions:

  Why are you organising this event?
  Where are you going to hold it?
  How many people do you expect?

When and for how long?

Do you want to do it annually?

Do you know anyone who has done a similar event that could help you?

What can go wrong?

What do you need to get this event happening? Make a list of these resources.

How much will it cost?

Where will you get the money from?

How will people know about your event?

What plans will you need to put together?

Important organisations and people

A list of organisations in the region that interact with events would include the local authority or directorate responsible for the government agencies such as police and army and insurance companies.

Safety and security

This section must emphasise that the event manager has the ultimate responsibility for the safety and security of the attendees and staff. They need to produce a risk management plan. The flow-on effects of an incident need to be emphasised using examples, such as

> These safety risks may come from a number of areas. If the electricity stops, the lights and sound system may go out. Without the sounds system there is no way to tell the crowd what is going on. They can panic and surge towards the exit. People can easily be killed in such a crowd crush. All of this could be the result of you forgetting to check the electricity.

Food

The local rules and publications on catering, display and food handling are listed here. There may be a local requirement for food inspectors before and during the event.

Other headings for a public event guide

1. Water
2. Waste management
3. Toilet facilities
4. First aid
5. Noise
6. Traffic and transport issues including:
    a. Transport management plan
    b. Road closures
    c. Parking
    d. Public transport/taxis
7. Accessibility
8. Volunteers
9. Fundraising
10. Sponsorship
11. On the day
12. Evaluating your event

The guide is a communication tool. If the event organiser does not use the guide it has failed in its primary purpose. The event organisers are almost always busy as they are creating a unique event and making constant decisions. The event guide must show its value before it is read. The only way to do this is to have information in the manual important in the support or sponsorship process for the event. The event organiser must read the guide to gain any support from the host.

A manual on the web is a preferred method of delivery. It allows the filtering of the information on the web so it is more relevant to the user. By answering a number of simple questions, the relevant information can be delivered immediately to the event staff. A web manual can be linked to explanations of specialist terminology, similar events and other relevant information. It can be downloaded to a portable device or printed as a hardcopy. It can be accessed in almost all places and at all times when a web connection is available.

6.4 BUILDING COMPETENCY: EVENT EDUCATION AND TRAINING

Events are about people. They concern change and creativity. The fundamental resource for events development is human skills with knowledge. Event strategies that ignore the upskilling of a workforce are hamstrung. Too often an event strategy for events development is about physical capacity such as roads and beds, and the competency of the workforce is seen as secondary, if noticed at all.

A profession is made up of three areas: a body of knowledge; a proven and improvable methodology; and the rules of thumb or heuristics. The Event Management Body of Knowledge (EMBOK) represents a mixture of event experience, history and techniques taken from other disciplines. The EMBOK was a recent attempt by world experts to develop this body of knowledge. It is evidenced by the various books on the subject, websites and journals. A body of knowledge is not enough to describe a profession — just as owning a library of engineering books does not make a person an engineer. It has to be put to use by means of a methodology. The systematic method of planning comes from adaptation of project management. However in a fluid, ever changing industry such as events being able to plan is not enough. The professional event manager needs to constantly make decisions — often under pressure. The effects of decisions need to be thought out and their possible consequences evaluated. It is the combination of effective planning and the ability to make good decisions that gives the methodology to event management. It is the methodology that needs to be taught in courses and is the heart of any profession. The methodology is the transferable skill used to organise all types of events. However, a system and a body of knowledge is not enough as every event is special. Knowledge of heuristics or informal rules of thumb that apply to a particular event are vital to success of the event. Learning from these little tips and sayings can be the difference between event success and failure. In summary, an unskilled job concentrates on the heuristics, a trade concentrates on the body of knowledge, the heuristics and a little methodology and a profession requires all three, with the focus on the methodology.

A number of countries realise the importance of the skilled workforce. South Africa has taken this a step further and uses events, such as the World Cup, to upskill their workforce. Now event management is recognised in the National Qualifications Framework (NQF) in a number of countries. This enables the certificates in event management to be recognised countrywide.

In the event environment the management and the operations of an event are often so closely intertwined that it is impossible to separate them as different levels of competency. Being knowledgeable about event management does not mean a person can manage an event. This is a problem for anyone studying event management at a tertiary level. It has been solved by Don Getz when he renamed the field 'event studies' instead of event management. A course called event management implies that the graduate can originate, plan, implement, direct, control and improve an event. This implies far more than knowledge 'of' the discipline as it implied the ability to 'do' the discipline.

Knowledge is understanding and concepts. It is only one dimension of being competent. The other dimensions are skills and attitude. Skills include the practical application of knowledge. It is about performance and practical application. Attitude, although hard to define, is important to functioning effectively in the work environment. A simple way to understand the importance of these three aspects is to consider whether a doctor or an engineer is competent if they only read a book on their discipline. It is obvious that these professions need practical experience and the application of their knowledge in the physical world to be declared as competent. In both these fields the practical application of knowledge is performed as the person is learning.

A large part of the work in events is dealing with experts in their own field, such as sound engineers, lighting experts, structural workers and publicity agents. The ability to get the best work from a group of specialist subcontractors in the time necessary requires these three dimensions of competency. It also requires some knowledge of the terminology and skills used by the subcontractors. It helps if the event organiser has some practical experience in their field. Some knowledge and skill in publicity will assist the event manager in working with a public relations expert. It is the same for all the subcontractors. Table 6.1 shows the levels of competency when applied to events management. They are similar to the maturity models described in Chapter 8. The proof of competency level requires evidence in the three dimensions of knowledge, skills and attitude.

Once these levels of competencies are established the event staff can compare their level to the standards. For this reason the development of the International Event Management Standard (IEMS) is essential to the development of the events industry worldwide. Exhibit 6.7 briefly describes the IEMS. With an international standard based on competency there is the ability to recognise and certify current event professionals. It is important to the credibility of the competency standard as

Table 6.1 Competency Table for Event Management

Competency	Aware	Informed	Involved	Competent	Best Practice
Context					
Stakeholder management	Understand the concept of the event stakeholder Able to identify the major stakeholders of any event	Able to identify all the stakeholder in an event and their primary influence	Able to prepare a stakeholder management plan for an event	Able to identify limitations or gaps in a stakeholder management plan	Develop improvements to the overall stakeholder management plan. Able to adjust aspects of the event that are affected by stakeholder changes
Marketing	Understand the importance of marketing to events and the use of events in marketing Able to identify the marketing function of event management	Able to identify and describe the elements of marketing and how it related to events	Able to apply the principles of marketing to an event and create a marketing plan	Able to assess and improve a marketing plan for an event	Able to change the marketing plan and the event as there are changes in the event environment
Cost–benefit analysis (CBA)	Understand the basic idea of CBA Able to identify the obvious costs and benefits of any event	Apply the principles of CBA to an event	Apply a detailed CBA to any event	Able to identify gaps and improve a CBA of an event	Adjust the CBA to suit the changes of the event environment. Can assess the suitability of the CBA
Project					
Project management	Understand the knowledge areas of project management Able to identify these knowledge areas in any event	Can describe an event in terms of the project management knowledge areas	Able to create a management plan based on project management for an event	Able to identify the limitations of project management areas to events and suggest changes	Able to fully assess the ability of project management areas of knowledge to describe event management

Risk management	Understand the process of risk management and how it would apply to events	Can identify the risk management process in an event Can identify the major risks to an event	Able to create a risk management plan for an event	Able to apply the risk management process to an event risk management plan Able to integrate all the event plans under the risk management plan	Able to identify limitations of a risk management process to event management. Able to adjust the risk plans according to the changes in the event environment
Contract management	Understand the process of contract management Able to identify where contract management is used in events	Can describe the contract management process in an event	Able to create a contract management plan for an event	Able to monitor and control an event contract management plan	Able to identify gaps in the contract management process of any event and suggest improvements
Systems	Understand the concept of systems Able to identify elements of an event as a system	Can describe the event in terms of a system	Able to create a systems description of an event	Able to identify gaps in the event system and suggest changes	Establish a systems approach to event management. Adjust current system and compare with other disciplines
Specific Site selection/ design	Understand the importance of site selection and design Identify the various event sites	Able to identify the elements of site selection and design of any event	Can identify the constraints and opportunities afforded by a site/venue when matched to any event	Able to create a site selection and design checklist for any event	Manage the site selection and design for a specific event Undertake post-event reviews and improve the site selection layout and design

(Continued)

Table 6.1 Competency Table for Event Management *Continued*

Competency	Aware	Informed	Involved	Competent	Best Practice
Staging	Understand and identify the element of staging	Can describe the elements of staging and their relationship in any event	Can set up a draft stage plan for an event	Can identify the gaps in a stage plan for a specific event	Manage the staging of an event Undertake post-event review and improve staging
Volunteers	Understand the importance of volunteers to events	Can describe the application of volunteer management in any event	Can create a management plan of the volunteers of an event	Monitor and control the volunteer plan	Manage the volunteers of an event Undertake post-event reviews and improve volunteer management
Deadline management	Understand the concept of the deadline and how it applies to events	Can describe the influence of the deadline in any of the project management areas of any event	Can identify the problems and change a management plan of an event according to the importance of the deadline	Monitor and control the overall event management in terms of the deadline	Identify the areas of any event that are on the critical path and suggest workable changes so that the deadline is met. Compare these adjustments with historical data

it demonstrates that the standard is realistic and based on practical and current skills. The process of comparing exiting competency with the standard is named Recognition of Prior Learning. It allows the system to encompass existing expertise in the events field. The current practitioners in events can be assessed and certified. Also it can assist in identifying any area of competency that is missing. In the recent past the competency of risk management has been missing.

The event associations around the world offer a variety of certificates. As stated in Section 6.1, they tend to accredit one type of event management such as festival, special events or conferences. Many event teams cross all of these types of events. This implies that there are core or generic skills. The IEMS is the most recent attempt to cross-over all these types of events. Each type of event would build upon certain competencies.

By focusing on competencies for event management rather than on knowledge, the standard solves the problem of management courses described by Mintzberg and others after the collapse of major companies and institutions in the USA. This was bluntly put by Harry Markopolos in referring to tertiary management courses:

Half the stuff is out of date in five years and the other half is untrue.

The industry is dynamic and developing at a rapid rate and therefore the practitioner is essential in any teaching of event management. The body of knowledge that is taught in medicine or engineering has only just started in events. It would be unthinkable and possibly negligent to train a medical worker or engineer without operational or practical experience as part of the course. Therefore, any event management courses must be closely aligned to the industry. Even the case study method of teaching has its limitation in event management courses as the case studies quickly go out of date. A further limitation to the traditional lecture-based teaching by an academic professional is a result of the operations being so closely aligned with the management and strategy in the event field. Knowledge and experience in event operations is essential. The management cannot be separated out from the day-to-day operations. Interestingly, the close link between operations and management is increasingly being realised in other fields such as finance as evidenced by the collapse of Barings Bank. It has also been pointed for military command by the counterinsurgency expert David Kilcullen.

Events are an international industry. Just like accounting, engineering and plumbing, the competency is similar in every country. Hence, an important aspect of the IEMS is international portability. Event companies such as Jack Morton Worldwide, Maxxam International or Reed Exhibitions work around the world. Apple product launches or Red Bull's air shows are as likely to take place in China as they are to take place in London. An event management competency standard must reflect the reality of an international industry.

The various associations have their own certification. They focus on one area of the event industry such as the Meeting Professionals International Certification in Meeting Management (CMM) or the International Special Events Society's

Certified Special Events Professional (CSEP). In many countries the event professional will work on different types of events. A corporate event staff member may manage a conference, a VIP dinner and be involved in the planning of a product launch and a community awareness festival. There are certain skills that are common to all these types of events. Project and risk management competencies such as scheduling and resource planning are fundamental to event management regardless of the type of event.

Now that the event industry has globalised and matured, the competency standards need to be part of a national education framework. Currently, each tertiary institution has its own standards and courses.

There are a variety of measures used to introduce event training into a developing country. It can be accomplished gradually by first upskilling the current event professionals. When comparing this to other industries the pathway to training and education is as follows:

1. Upskilling professionals through short training at industry forums
2. Running short courses in specialist areas such as sponsorship and project management
3. Tertiary institutions develop short courses that provide a pathway into degree courses
4. Degree courses in event management are developed using the expertise identified by the short courses

---

EXHIBIT 6.6 SAMPLE OF RECOMMENDATIONS TO A DEVELOPING COUNTRY ON EVENT TRAINING AND EDUCATION

To enable the development of the training of events sector the lessons of other countries show that there is an optimal pathway.

Course development

There are two entry level courses that can be offered.

1. Professional training with a non-degree award such as a certificate
2. An optional undergraduate course of one semester within a Marketing or Management degree or diploma

Both of these will test the interest of the students in the course. The professional training will allow the college or University to identify successful event organisers. These people can be asked to assist in developing the Undergraduate courses and teaching.

Certify success

It is recommended that the Vocational Colleges and the Universities develop professional training courses.

This may have to be part of a larger qualification framework. But at this time there is enough standards that can be used to recognise the current event organisers.

Professional training courses are quick to set up and do not have the problem of approvals from academic boards. They recognise the success (and possibility of growth) of current events and they develop a pool of expertise.

National qualification framework

The government should now consolidate the work that has been done. It needs now to work with the National Qualification Framework to ensure that there are competency levels for event organisers.

The main conference on qualification standards and training in the event industry (and the Tourism Sector) will take place soon and it is recommended that the government send a representative.

EXHIBIT 6.7 INTERNATIONAL EVENT MANAGEMENT COMPETENCY STANDARDS

For the last 10 years there have been a number of competency standards developed in event management. Their creation demonstrates the maturing and recognition of the events industry. The Canadian Tourism Human Resource Council (CTHRC) has developed the most comprehensive standard. Their work is driven by the need for Canada to develop their workforce. The CTHRC began its project in 2008. The steps involved the collating and the analysis of competency standards around the world such as South Africa, UK, and Australia as well as the work of the International Event Management Body of Knowledge. They included detailed analysis of event management descriptions such as textbooks, journals, websites and courses. It was a huge project and involved event expertise from over 20 countries as well as developing and validating the standard.

The development of an international standard is important to the overall development of the events industry. The standard enables the industry to improve by developing training programmes, assessing events and creating job descriptions. It helps event professionals to move around the world to work. As has been demonstrated by many event disasters, the lack of competency of the management is too often the cause. The standard will assist in the legal and regulatory environment for event management particularly in negligence cases and future regulations.

The standard is divided into the following areas of competencies:

A. Strategic planning
B. Project management
C. Risk management
D. Financial management
E. Administration
F. Human resources
G. Stakeholder management
H. Event design
I. Site management
J. Marketing
K. Professionalism
L. Communication

SECTION 1: CONCLUSION

The feasibility and development of an events programme or portfolio of events is essential in the modern world for private and public organisations. Events can no longer be regarded as individual projects. They are an asset that has a solid return on the investment. The returns are commercial, social and goodwill. A way to maximise this return is to develop a strategy to direct the development. The strategy must be grounded on the policy of the organisation. The first step is to understand how events help the organisation to reach its objectives. Next is to construct a decision table with clearly defined criteria. The decision table forms the core of the implementation of the strategy and directs the organisation. Once the regulatory environment, capacity and capabilities from the event perspective are understood, the strategy selects from a number of tools and techniques. A regional authority, a city, state or nation will use all of them in planning and implementing their event development strategy. These are as follows:

1. Stakeholder engagement and consultation
2. An event support system including event classification, levels of support and development strategy
3. Event bidding system
4. Creation of an event office, desk or unit to implement and direct the strategy
5. Event forum and event awards for excellence
6. An event manual
7. Competency-based training path
8. Flagship event programme
9. An association to represent the profession
10. Event precincts embedded in future construction plans
11. An integrated country promotion

Many of these tools and techniques have been tried and tested around the world over the last 10 years. They are successful in UK, Australia, Singapore, Korea, New Zealand, Saudi Arabia and many more regions, cities and countries. Many countries are at various stages of development of strategy. Companies and semi-private organisations will use a subset of this list such as the decision criteria and the event support or sponsorship system to develop their strategy.

DISCUSSION TOPICS

There are numerous professional associations around the world. Compare the IFEA, MPI and ISES (International Special Events Society) to these associations. Research their awards and training systems.

Event manuals are often delivered and accessed via the web. What are the advantages and disadvantages to this method?

Using the two competency-based models in this chapter assess your own competency. What proof can you supply to support your claim? What areas need improving and how would you achieve this?

Steve Schmader, IFEA, at the Event 360 Conference, Dubai. Photo William O'Toole

Queen's Baton Relay 2010, Gambia. Photo courtesy of Maxxam International

Commonwealth Games Baton underwater, Australia. Photo courtesy of Maxxam International

Management feasibility and development

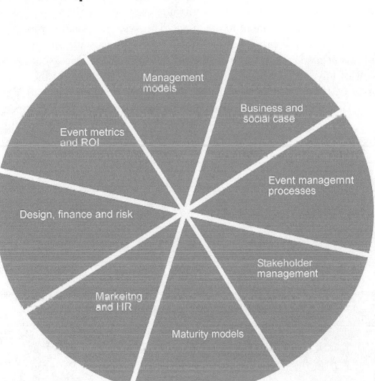

The second section of the book concerns the feasibility and development of the management of an event. It presents a model of the event management environment. Unlike the day-to-day administration management, event management is forever changing. It evolves over a short time of the project which is reflected in the rapid change of staff numbers, short-term logistics and temporary resources. The number of stakeholders and the intangible outcomes of an event create complexity of tasks and decisions and uncertainty in outcomes. The event may start with a clear business case or it may arise from an idea or from a social case. It is very common for people to assume that organising an event is the same as organising a small party. One of the major risks faced by the industry is the inability of governments and major clients to understand the professionalism needed for event management. The number of disasters, including deaths, at events resulting from this misconception is enormous. Event management needs a theoretical underpinning to demonstrate it is a highly sophisticated management system working in a complex operationally based environment.

Within this complexity there are a number of activities that interweave over time leading up to the event, during the event and after it has finished. The feasibility of an event and an events portfolio is dependent on the expertise of the event management. The management must have a well thought out systematic method if the events are to be sustainable and accountable to the client. The system is made up of interwoven threads of tasks called processes. This section introduces the method of process mapping event management to describe the system. The processes are common to any event of any size. Their relative importance may change and they may not be recognised by the event management, but they are present. Over time after managing a number of events the event team matures and becomes more competent. The section concludes with the all-important concept of the return on investment and event metrics.

PHOTO 1

Function for UNESCO delegation in Al Ulla, Saudi Arabia. Photo William O'Toole

Management models and the business case

7

INTRODUCTION

The feasibility and development of events must be based on a practical description of event management. The description must extract the essential processes in order to construct a model. As has been found by many event stakeholders, the event management environment is not the same as the ongoing management environment found in standard administration. In many cases it is characterised as turbulent, in constant change with quick decisions, creative ideas and constantly minimising problems and searching for opportunities. Leadership and teamwork take on an importance not found in other industries. Ultimately, the event management decisions have an effect on hundreds of thousands of people and the operational risks are enormous. Combining this with the absolute deadline produces a management environment like no other.

No strategic development of events can take place without understanding this model. The model presented in this chapter is a simplification and an abstraction. That is the nature of a model. It must capture the essence of the management and it needs to ignore so much more. A practicing event manager immersed in the day-to-day problems may find this either obvious or irrelevant. However, as the saying goes, the 'fish are the last to know about water'. A profession must be able to describe the essential processes that are used. This is what forms the framework to competency and, ultimately, a successful and ongoing events programme.

The chapter finishes with a description of the business case for events and a detailed case study.

7.1 A MODEL, PROCESSES, SYSTEM OR A BODY OF KNOWLEDGE

The management model for the dynamic environment of event management is best described by a group of interdependent management processes. The high-level process called 'event management' is illustrated in Fig. 7.1.

The objective of a management model is to support management to reach its objectives. It is both a descriptive or explanatory and prescriptive model. It describes and explains the entities and relationships found in all events regardless of size or type and is invariant. It is prescriptive in the sense that it shows management the efficient and effective processes that are currently hidden. This optimisation of management decisions is expected by event stakeholders. As set out by Williams

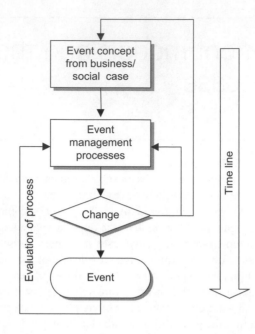

FIGURE 7.1

Event management process

> *A Model represents or describes perceptions of a real system, simplified, using formal, theoretically based language of concepts and their relationships (that enables the manipulation of these entities) in order to facilitate management, control, or understanding of that system.*

> **(Williams, 2002, p. 34)**

Mapping the features of good model to the corresponding characteristics of the dynamic model of event management produces Table 7.1.

The schemas presented in this section are not flowcharts in the engineering sense, but tend towards concept diagrams, cognitive maps or process maps. They capture the major processes and are related to the data flow diagrams of structured analysis. They lay the basis for information flow diagrams and a dynamic system model of event management. It is important to establish at the beginning that event management is a purposeful activity rather than a mechanical or computer system independent of people's individual decisions. A soft systems methodology can be used to describe such a system. Furthermore, such a model can be used as an intervention tool to assist the event management process. Therefore, it is a prescriptive model. The graphical display of the processes is essential in this intervention as it enables the process to be broken down into individual elements illustrating the logical relationships between the elements over time. Such a description enables a better understanding of what is involved in organising

Table 7.1 Model Quality	
Features that measure the quality of the model	Characteristics of the process model of event management
Empirically based	Primary source event documents and recent texts of best practice
Theoretically sound	Based on PMBOK™, EMBOK and the IEMS
Coherent	A series of interlinked processes
Simplified for the purpose	Process diagrams, process mapping
Addresses the complexity	The substance of the thesis
Adds value	Allows development and improvement in the management system
Impacts decisions	Makes overt the processes to assist in decision optimisation and improves future decision by gathering data in a structured manner

events and therefore enables the event team to improve their management of each event.

The high-level process is illustrated in Fig. 7.1. It is a simple representation of event management as a process working from the business or social case for an event to the delivery of the event and the fulfilment of the event objectives. However, there are two aspects that are not usually found in such a diagram. The process is subject to absolute time constraints. The process has a fundamental element of change.

7.2 THE EVENT MANAGEMENT ENVIRONMENT: COMPLEXITY AND UNCERTAINTY

The closest management model for events comes from two streams

1. Project complexity
2. Uncertainty and product innovation

Project complexity can be defined as a large number and size of tasks, subtasks and their interactions. The definition suffers from the need to know when the task analysis needs to stop. That is, the granularity of the tasks or the level of the Work Breakdown Structure. It implies that the complexity of a project is related to unfamiliarity of the management with the type of project. Given that novelty and innovation are part of the product, therefore, ipso facto, most events are complex.

Using Williams' division into structure complexity and product complexity, the product of event management — the event itself — is complex. In particular, it is a result of the intangible nature of event outcomes and the multiobjectives of the event, introduced by the numerous stakeholders. It is reflected back and contributes to the structure complexity of the event management. Structural complexity is measured by the number of reciprocal dependencies and the number of stakeholders.

The characteristics of project complexity are as follows:

1. Number of stakeholders
2. Number of reciprocal dependencies
3. Multiobjectives
4. Number of changes or modifications to both the product and the project
5. Uncertainty of goals
6. Uncertainty of methods

Each one of these characteristics is mentioned by the major event textbooks, such as Silvers, Getz and Allen on event management as part of the standard event management environment. A summary of the factors that contribute to the complexity of the process of event management and the strategies recommended by the event texts are shown in Fig. 7.2

The product innovation has similar problems faced by events when trying to capture the product and process. In particular, novelty corresponds to the Wow factor in events or innovation in event design. It is an essential component that differentiates each event and becomes the Unique Selling Point (USP) for the marketing of the event. It is a result of a creative process, such as brainstorming and storyboarding. The complexity of the product, i.e. the event itself is often an attraction for the attendees. Figure 7.3 illustrates some of the aspects of the event management environment that contribute to this complexity.

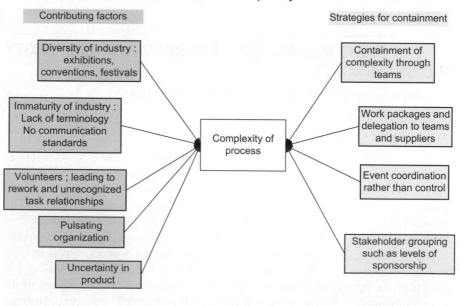

FIGURE 7.2

Process complexity

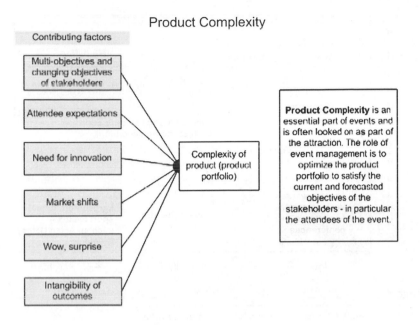

Product Complexity

Contributing factors

- Multi-objectives and changing objectives of stakeholders
- Attendee expectations
- Need for innovation
- Market shifts
- Wow, surprise
- Intangibility of outcomes

Complexity of product (product portfolio)

Product Complexity is an essential part of events and is often looked on as part of the attraction. The role of event management is to optimize the product portfolio to satisfy the current and forecasted objectives of the stakeholders - in particular the attendees of the event.

FIGURE 7.3

Product complexity

Combining project complexity characterised by 'multiobjectives' with Checkland's necessity of ambiguity in ill-defined objectives produces a general description of the event environment as uncertain. In such an uncertain environment, the event management must be flexible. Shone uses the two dimensions of complexity and uncertainty to provide a classification framework for events.

Their taxonomy of events divides them into:

- Individual
- Group
- Organisational
- Multiorganisational
- National
- International (Shone, 2004)

Figure 7.4 is a map of types of events according to their complexity and uncertainty. The events that have low uncertainty are the ones that seem to be able to use traditional management tools and techniques.

Special events, one-off or unique events, are highly uncertain in many areas of management, such as finance, marketability and sponsorship commitment. The financial risk involved in this uncertainty is also their attraction for entrepreneurs and promoters as the risk gives a higher return and keeps out competitors. Annual

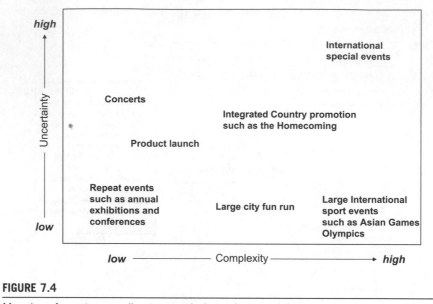

FIGURE 7.4

Mapping of events according to complexity and uncertainty

(after Shone, 2001)

events that have little or no changes in suppliers, finance, stakeholders or venue have low uncertainty and low complexity. In a sense they are similar to theatre productions that can refine the production and its management over the years.

An international one-off or special celebration, such as the East Timor Handover celebrations or the Reenactment of the Battle of Trafalgar, involves multiagencies from many countries, a short timeframe, intangible outcomes and a unique programme. Such an event has many areas of uncertainty and is highly complex.

The map (Fig. 7.4) corresponds to the applicability of current event management software to an event or festival. Events with comparatively low uncertainty and low complexity, such as conferences and exhibitions, have many commercial software packages to manage the event available to them. Events with low uncertainty and high complexity, such as the Olympics, Asian Games and International Grand Prix, use event or project management software. However, the applicability of event or project management software diminishes rapidly with the events in the upper region of the graph. It is difficult to program in uncertainty into a software program when the level of uncertainty is changing.

The complexity and uncertainty found in event management can be characterised by the model as a dynamic system. Such a system has the characteristics of:

• Dynamic — change in many levels
• Tightly coupled — changes in one area of the management will quickly affect other areas

- Governed by feedback — any action will have a result that will influence other similar actions
- Non-linear — effect and cause are rarely proportional
- History dependent — actions are mostly irreversible
- Self-organising — semi-autonomous groups or teams
- Adaptive — can quickly respond to changes to minimise their negative impact
- Counterintuitive — difficult to exactly predict
- Policy resistive — difficult to comprehend and therefore control using linear methods
- Characterised by tradeoffs — the effects of a decision in one area of event management will be traded against the results in other areas

The model for event management can therefore be described as a dynamic system made up of interlocking processes. The applicability of traditional management theory, such as project management, to describe this system is determined by its degree of uncertainty and complexity.

7.3 PHASES OF EVENT MANAGEMENT AND THE EVENT LIFE CYCLE

Project management theory recognises the different models for the project life cycle according to the industry to which it is applied. The phases are as follows:

1. Idea — concept development
2. Feasibility
3. Planning
4. Implementation
   a. Setup
   b. Event
   c. Shutdown

These phases have been simplified and adopted by the Event Management Body of Knowledge (EMBOK) as the basis of its three-dimensional description of event management. This is a simplification of the actual processes. The planning and implementation of the plan is often happening at the same time and the plan is adjusted accordingly. The marketing may be well planned at the start of the project. However, if more sponsors commit to the event this will significantly change the marketing. There are two ways to regard this fluid aspect of planning. One is to see the plan itself as a guide document and therefore more a statement of intention. The other is to incrementally plan. These problems have surfaced in other types of projects such as software development and implementation projects. A theory of project management called Agile attempts to encompass the reality of constant changes. Whichever theory is correct, the reality is dependent on the competency of the team and the leadership qualities of senior management.

There is no handover of a tangible asset such as a building or a piece of software at the end of the event management. The intangible asset is a result of the event experience, the event itself is seen as a separate phase. During the event the team is doing work unlike the tasks in the proceeding phases. Hence, it should be seen as a different phase. In some events, such as a New Year Eve fireworks, a new management configuration is created, with a stage or production manager having complete control once the event starts. The new staff will include production staff, volunteers in large numbers, operations or logistics staff and subcontractors. The occupational health and safety (OHS) issues are different on an event site to the office of the event team leading up to the event.

International multivenue sports events such as the Olympics prepared for this by restructuring their management from function or department based to venue based.

During the seven phases the event team is carrying out quite different tasks.

There is another more humorous version of the phases of event management:

1. *Despair*: no work, empty horizon
2. *Enthusiasm*: awarded a contract
3. *Disillusionment*: realised the full amount of work involved
4. *Confusion*: desperately seeking suppliers, venues…
5. *Panic*: ran out of time, money, friends and hoping the event is working
6. *Evaluate*: sacrifice of the innocent and promotion of the non-participant

7.4 INTANGIBILITY OF OUTCOMES

The inability to simply measure the event outcomes is a major limitation to a strict engineering or MBA approach to event management. In particular, events for celebrations have highly intangible objectives.

For many types of events artistic expression and creativity are regarded as essential. The sustainability of a festival, conference and exhibitions is sometimes dependent on the constant innovation in the programme elements. Innovation and creativity are related to the creation of the 'Wow' factor. The serendipity or surprise element of an event is a key driver for festival attendance.

Intangible outcomes are common across all types of events. The Auditor General's report on the V8 car races makes the observation that benefits of publicity value and civic pride claimed by the proponents of the V8 races is 'necessarily speculative and involves assumptions that are difficult to verify objectively' (ACT Auditor General, 2002, p. 22).

The lack of a direct measure of event outcomes and therefore the inability to set realistic measurable objectives led one experienced event manager Dr Joe Goldblatt to propose the term Return on Event (ROE). He links the ability to measure return on event with the ability to forecast. The ROE is made up of:

- Measure of financial return through advertising impression and through capita spending. The latter is related to the multipliers used to assess economic impact

- Measure of PR through various metrics used in public relations
- Measure of word of mouth advertising using focus groups
- Measure success of meeting attendee's expectation through comparative survey

The ROE is a parametric method rather than a direct method of indicating event outcomes.

O'Toole and Mikolaitis in their cost—benefit survey results list the metrics as suggested by practicing event managers. These range from lack of public complaints for community events to product awareness. The authors note the importance of measurable results in decision optimisation, using an overseas trade exhibition as an example.

> *Once the parameters that contribute to the cost—benefit of the event have been identified, then a look at the boundaries will provide an estimate of the cost benefit effect of a small change in one of the parameters. If more work (cost) is put into attracting higher-level contacts in the host community, will this additional work (cost) significantly contribute to the benefits, and if so, by how much?*
>
> **(O'Toole and Mikolaitis, 2002, p. 255)**

Perhaps, the most useful measure is called the Return on Objectives (ROO). This assumes that the objectives are clearly stated and agreed upon. It still begs the question on how to measure the ROO so that all the parties are in agreement. It must be noted that objectives change and fixing the objectives may create inflexibility and too strong a focus on the objectives by the staff and not the event. The search for measurable event objectives is found in most of the event literature. However, there is a warning that the measurable objective, due to its ability to be communicated simply, may obscure the far more important intangible goals. There is further discussion on Return on Investment (ROI) in chapter 11.

7.5 THE BUSINESS CASE

The business case is the justification to proceed with an event from a business point of view. It is generally a document or file sent to senior management to facilitate approval for the event. As any corporate event manager knows, the event funding rests on the business case for the event. The 'business case' is a justification for the company to support an event. The event unit within a company or large organisation has to create a reasoned argument for the event to be supported. In private companies, ROI will be uppermost in the minds of the managers who assess the business case. The business event is an expense and the return on the investment may take many years to be realised. For other organisations, the benefit of an event will be linked to the objectives of the organisations. The business case is most often in template form so it can be compared with other events and other projects that compete for the resources. The business case outlines the advantages of using the company resources for the event.

As it is used by senior management, it is a succinct document which directly addresses each heading.

A template for a business case will include the headings:

Date:	Event:

Purpose:
Event description
Target audience
Company participation and staffing
Required resources
Costs
Company benefits: direct
Company benefits: indirect
Action recommended

An example of a business case for a department to develop a seminar in a larger agricultural exhibition is shown in Exhibit 7.1. The exhibition is chosen as it draws the right target market for the software. The events desk of the government department will manage this event.

EXHIBIT 7.1 THE BUSINESS CASE FOR AGRIBUSINESS SEMINAR

Agribusiness seminar: rural business efficiency

Summary
Agribusiness seminar
Length: one day

Purpose
To provide the latest in Agribusiness software and business systems for farmers and other rural small-to-medium business in the region, during the agricultural exhibition.

Summary
The event will be made up of our staff and outside experts demonstrating the latest in technology and business systems. Our event will take advantage of the agricultural equipment exhibition taking place in the same town. We will liaise with the exhibition organisers to find mutual advantages. This is a unique and cost-effective opportunity to demonstrate rural business efficiencies to our target market. This event may provide a model for future events associated with rural shows and exhibitions.

Action required
Approval or rejection by the first of next month, as it will take at least 3 months to organise and promote.

Event
Our seminar/workshop titled: 'Rural Business Efficiency' will have the following advantages:

1. Improve the image of the department in the region at a time of rural recession
2. Enable our past clients to reengage with our services

3. Source new clients through direct interaction
4. Collect first-hand data on the current rural situation and the needs of the small-to-medium enterprises (SMEs) in the region

   Over the last 5 years, the economy in this part of the country has been consolidating. In this current rural situation, the SMEs will be on the look out for efficiencies in their work.
   The nearby AgriExhibtion has:

1. Nationwide recognition
2. The largest exhibition of agricultural machinery
3. Attracts over 200,000 visitors
4. Has 400 exhibitors

Target market
1. The market will be similar to the market for the AgriExhibition. The rural industries of the surrounding region include Dairy, Wine, Wool and Grains.
2. The business structures range from franchise, sole traders, partnerships and small companies.
3. The seminar is expected to attract at least 200 business owners and staff.
4. The catchment areas are seven regions surrounding the town.

Staffing and responsibilities
It is estimated that the staffing needed to market and manage the event will be 3 staff member at 10 part-time per week each over 3 months. We will call on the marketing and communication division to assist with the promotion. The legal division will assist with contracting, insurance and OHS issues.
   There will be two guest speakers presenting their use of the department products.
   Our tasks for the event are as follows:

- Event coordination
- Liaising with AgriExhibtion and other key stakeholders
- Contracting speakers and suppliers
- Promotion with the Marketing and Communication division
- Staffing including rosters, working hours, contact, evaluation training and briefing
- Logistics including venue and catering booking, transport and parking
- Onsite management:
  - Staffing
  - Venue layout and design
  - Shutdown and pack up
  - Delegate arrival, badging and information/sample distribution
  - Mini exhibition product display
- Data collection including design and distribution of forms and capturing enquiries/comments
- Data analysis and recommendations for future events
- Final report and accounts

Costs
The estimated direct costs to the Department of Rural Development are as follows:

Venue hire and catering	$5000
Promotion	$2000
Attendee	$4000
Speakers	$2500
Production	$3000
General	$2000
Total	$18,000

(Continued)

EXHIBIT 7.1 THE BUSINESS CASE FOR AGRIBUSINESS SEMINAR—*Cont'd*

Notes
1. Costs are estimated using past seminars and based on a per head cost for the catering and attendee costs
2. Indirect and overhead costs to the department include
   - Travel of staff, allowances, airfares and vehicle charges
   - Promotion costs absorbed by the Marketing and Communication division
   - Staff wages

Department objectives
The seminar meets three core objectives of the Department of Rural Development.

1. Increasing the efficiency in the rural sector
2. Maintain close contact with the developments in the regions
3. Be regarded by the constituency as a Government Department that responds quickly to their needs and uses resources to assist the industry development

The event presents a unique and highly effective way to reach our target audience. The seminar will demonstrate the use of our rural business systems to improve efficiency. At the same time there will be introductory, intermediate and advanced workshops. The personal interaction with our market allows the staff to elicit information that may otherwise not be found. The seminar is a two-way communication, as the staff can ascertain the response to the business systems including their ease of use and attractiveness. The seminar gives a human face to a large government organisation. It demonstrates the concern the department has with the state of the rural economy.

The success of the seminar will be measured by:

1. Number of responses to the promotion and invitation
2. Evaluation of the seminar by the participants
3. Follow up leads generated
4. Amount and quality of the feedback

Feedback: intelligence
The seminar will have a sophisticated system to capture and analyse feedback and other data arising before, during and after the seminar. The system will comprise:

1. Log of all enquiries prior to the event. The staff will be encouraged to ask specific questions, to assist the analysis of these data
2. Evaluation sheets handed out to the attendees with an incentive to fill them in
3. Questions and enquires logged during the event
4. Follow up communication to selected companies in 6 months after the event

The type of intelligence gathered will be:

1. Perception of the DRD in the field
2. Core issues with rural business
3. Trends and how they affect the rural business
4. Gaps in the provision of business services and products
5. Quality of the current services and how they can be improved

The business case is a common justification of event investment in the public sphere as well as the corporate. Many government organisations are being restructured to imitate the corporate model. This is seen as a way to improve efficiency, measure effectiveness and limit the growth of burgeoning bureaucracies. The Taxation Office in some countries, for example, has a number of event staff who develop and manage their events. Events are an effective way to achieve their objectives. In particular events allow the Taxation Department to:

1. Target specific industry groups
2. Gather statistics
3. Present the Taxation Department in a positive way by interacting directly with the public
4. Gather data through enquiries at the event

Their primary objective is to improve taxation compliance. The highly targeted nature of an event is a cost-effective communication channel to that sector. An exhibition of farm equipment, for example, will have a number of small businesses in the rural industry attending. The Taxation Department can produce a seminar or a mini conference at this exhibition.

For larger events, the list of costs and benefits in a business case should be subject to a best case, worst case and most likely test. Scenarios can be described that give the client or host a chance to understand the flexibility of the business case. For example, what if the full cost of the event is not recovered? What if the sponsors are not forthcoming? This 'stress testing' is part of the feasibility of the event. They are described in later chapters in this text. Case study 7.1 is a comprehensive business plan for a Country Fair. The level of detail in this plan illustrates the mix of operations, management and strategic aspects that is necessary in the development of an event.

CASE STUDY 7.1 COMMUNITY FESTIVAL: CREATING THE BUSINESS PLAN

COUNTRY FAIR

BUSINESS AND OPERATIONS PLAN

Created by: Country Fair Committee

and

Tracey Hull, THA Consulting

Bill O'Toole, EPMS

Version no.	Plan date:	File location:

1 Event history and achievements

The Country Fair is conducted during the first weekend of November during a time that traditionally has increased visitor numbers passing through and staying in the township.

The Fair is held at and around the Visitor Information Centre. It consists of market stalls, a bottle fair, kids games, bands, a monster garage sale, forest tours, pace painting, cemetery tours and heritage walks and a range of other activities.

The Fair is conducted by a voluntary committee with assistance from the local Shire Council.

(Continued)

CASE STUDY 7.1 COMMUNITY FESTIVAL: CREATING THE BUSINESS PLAN—*Cont'd*

2 Event Strengths, Weaknesses, Opportunities, and Threats (SWOT) analysis

Plans will be developed to maximise strengths and opportunities and overcome or minimise weaknesses and threats.

Strengths

- Community involvement
- Draws from surrounding area
- Opportunity to raise funds
- Showcases skills and local produce
- Fun and enjoyable
- Provides something for entire community
- Grown in numbers – activities and attendance
- Held on holiday weekend (lot of visitors)
- Main attraction at Fair each year
- Ideal location on highway (drive past visitors)
- Strong and committed committee
- Low cost activities for all the family
- Lot of activities for all ages
- Promoting the area and the attributes

To build on our strength we will

1. Cross promote with other long weekend events

Weaknesses

- Community involvement – lack of young parents and youth involvement
- Better allocation of jobs required – action plan, specific tasks
- Support from local businesses
- Keeping people for the whole weekend (morning only perception)
- Keeping up with new ideas with same committee members
- More leaders and doers, subcommittees
- Businesses criticise the event

To minimise our weaknesses we will

1. Approach selected young parents with specific tasks
2. Target businesses to become involved

Opportunities

- Forest and rivers, birdlife
- Bushwalk, cook-up, music in forest
- Wood chopping display
- Old time ball
- Garden tours
- Music night
- Pony rides (insurance an issue)
- Move activities to the Saturday afternoon
- BBQ breakfast on Sunday
- Packaged weekends
- Fishing competition
- Cocktail party for sponsors

To maximise our opportunities we will

1. Build an event focused on the forest and river
2. Invite a bird expert to host bird tours

Threats

- Insurance
- Parking and traffic management
- Other Easter Fairs and long weekend events
- Wet, windy, hot weather

To minimise our threats we will

1. Approach Council for support with parking and traffic management

3 Event issues and ideas

- Include schools (primary and secondary) in the Fair
  - Encourage schools to do something special for the event, e.g. build artwork, a performance (music, dance), competition, exhibition, choir
  - Get schools to make/develop something over the full weekend
- Get local businesses to embrace the Fair and become involved
  - Discuss an involvement one on one with two businesses (select key businesses which may be able to influence others)
  - Determine why they don't get involved and what they would like to do
- Developing new ideas
  - Bushwalk – in conjunction with the development of a new walking trail
  - Old time ball (pre-event dance lessons)
- Young people (young families)
  - Determine how they could be involved (tasks they could do)
  - Approach specific people in the community with the skills required (each committee member to be allocated 2–3 people to approach in the next month)

4 Event vision, mission and values

1. Vision:
   What we want the event/organisation to become?
2. Mission:
   Why the event/organisation exists?
3. Values:
   The way we want the organisation to operate and what is important to the organisation.

5 Key event objectives and strategies

The key goals of the Country Fair are to provide business activity and assist in the development of the region as a tourism destination.

1. Event objectives and strategies

   Objective 1: To promote the region as a place to visit
   Strategies:
   - Develop an event which will appeal to visitors
   - Determine the key target markets to attract to the event
   - Develop a marketing plan to attract the target visitors
   - Work with tourism authorities and operators to promote the event to visitors
   - Ensure visitors to the event have incentives to return at other times of the year

   Objective 2: To provide an opportunity for community groups to conduct fundraising activities and strengthen the community
   Strategies:
   - Invite all community groups (clubs, etc.) to become involved
   - Develop and coordinate the opportunities for groups to become involved

   Objective 3: To increase spend in the town and improve business activity
   Strategies:
   - Develop a specific marketing plan to attract visitors
   - Work with the businesses to have a special offer weekend during the event
   - Invite local businesses (retail and smaller businesses) to become involved directly in the Fair or in volunteer capacity

(Continued)

Objective 4: Operate a safe, successful and financially viable event

Strategies:

- Develop a risk management plan for the event
- Develop an event budget and manage budget
- Determine level of funding and sponsorship required and develop a strategy to achieve this
- Ensure the event complies will all relevant laws
- Develop an events action plan (monthly checklist) and an event evaluation process
- Ensure the experience of being on the committee is enjoyable
- Establish a database of volunteers

6 Stakeholder analysis

(Who are the key stakeholders? Who has an interest in the event?)

Stakeholder	Expectations	Communication	Who Will Do It?
Council	<ul><li>Safe event</li><li>Use of grounds</li><li>Info Centre shown off to community and others</li><li>Self-funding</li><li>Increased promotion of Shire</li><li>Inflow in income to town</li><li>Positive exposure</li></ul>	Officers 2. × report to Council	Event President – monthly
Visitor Information and Business Centre	<ul><li>Visitation</li><li>Promotion of the centre</li><li>Safe event</li></ul>	Ongoing	
Stallholders	<ul><li>Clear pre-communications</li><li>Safe and appropriate event sites</li><li>Post-event follow up</li><li>Power, water</li></ul>	Letter of invite Coordinator to liaise with	
Community groups - Sporting - Special interest - Schools - Kinda	<ul><li>Fundraising opportunity</li><li>Involvement</li></ul>	6 months pre-event 3 months pre-event 1 -month pre-event	Community subcommittee

Stakeholder	Expectations	Communication	Who Will Do It?
Local businesses	• Increased spending by visitors • Exposure • Return visitation • Sponsorship benefits	As above	Sponsorship subcommittee
Tourists	• Quality event • Uniqueness • Enjoyment and friendly experience • Ease of information		Marketing subcommittee
Local community	To know what is going on • Promotion of town • Pride • Recognition • Safe event	Monthly community newsletter	Marketing subcommittee

Suppliers:
- Music
- Stallholders
- Show Ducks -
  Chamber of
  Commerce
- Apex Club
	• Promotion
	• Good organisation and communications prior, during, after event
	• Good attendance at event
	• Supply of power, water, etc.
		6 months prior – letters of agreement	Programme subcommittee

Insurance companies	• No claims • Safe event	Annually	Finance subcommittee
Media	• News stories; photo ops • Advertising	8 weeks pre-event time	Marketing subcommittee
Sponsors	• Good exposure • Recognition • Speaking opportunity	Throughout year	Sponsorship subcommittee

7 Event management structure

Objective: Ensure the effective governance, management and operation of the Country Fair

Strategies:

1. Ensure compliance with all statutory obligations and requirements
2. Ensure the effective operation of the committee
3. Retain and recruit committee members
4. Establish procedures for effective event management

(Continued)

CASE STUDY 7.1 COMMUNITY FESTIVAL: CREATING THE BUSINESS PLAN—*Cont'd*

Committee structure:

Position	Person/s	Responsibilities
Chairperson		
Secretary		
Treasurer		
Subcommittee Chairs		
Finance		Develop event budget
		Ensure compliance with event budget
		Develop funding/sponsorship target
		Ensure accounts are paid
		Ensure invoices are issued
Marketing/sponsorship		Develop marketing plan
		Implement marketing plan
		Liaise with tourism operators
		Approach sponsors
		Develop funding applications
Site		Develop site plan
		Ensure compliance with OHS requirements
Programme development		Develop 'ideal' programme content
		Recruit entertainment, etc.

Meeting dates:

Meeting and decision-making procedures:

Event operations

Task	Responsibility	By When	Status
Site preparation			
Site set up; site clean up			
Develop site plan			
Power and lights			
Water supply			
Toilets			
Develop waste management plan			
- Organise bins (and emptying)			
- Organise for people to pick up rubbish during day			
Signage			
Determine type of signs – promotional, on site, directional			

Task	Responsibility	By When	Status
Design and production			
Quotes/approval in budget			
Determine location of signs			
Putting up, pulling down			
Organise for storage			
Traffic and parking			
Develop traffic plan			
Obtain council approval			
Obtain signage, bunting, barricades, etc.			
Erect signs			
Dismantle signs and return to depot			
Organise parking attendants			
Stallholder liaison			
Food and beverage:			
- Selection			
Permits and agreements			
- Site plan			
Develop criteria for involvement			
Send out invite letter			
Take registrations and check compliance with requirements (e.g. insurance)			
Send confirmation to stallholders (with site plan)			
Wine tasting			
Organise liquor licence, waiters			
Organise wine, suppliers, glasses			
Entertainment			
Confirm performers and details			
Meet on day			
Accessibility			
Assess site and promotional material to ensure accessibility			
Communications			
Obtain radios and PA system			
Develop communications list			
First aid			
Develop first aid plan and book provider			
Children's activities			
Organise farmyard			
Organise kids corner			

(Continued)

Task	Responsibility	By When	Status
Raffle			
Secure prizes			
Obtain permits			
Organise raffle books, barrel and sellers			
Organise for draw			
BBQ			
Organise BBQ			
Obtain health permits			
Garage sale			
Take registrations and collect fees			
Develop map of garage sale locations			
Risk and safety			
Develop risk management plan			
OHS supervisor for site set up, conduct on day, pack up			
Ensure all insurances are in place (event and stallholders)			
Develop checklist of all permits and licences required – ensure compliance			
Develop system to manage cash on day			

What to take with on the day of the event:

- Pencils and paper
- Phone
- Tape
- Scissors
- Blue tack
- First aid kit
- Tool box
- Contact list
- Clipboard
- Camera
- Screwdrivers
- Credit cards, cash
- Food
- Water bottle

8 Finance and administration

Objectives and strategies:

Objective 1: Plan and manage the finances to ensure the event is staged within budget

(a) Achieve a minimum of $x surplus at the conclusion of event (for ongoing operating expenses)

(b) Aim for a minimum of $x raised for the community

(c) Develop and monitor budget and report and correct any variances

(d) Aim to achieve sponsorship and funding to the value of $x

Objective 2: Ensure the event complies with legal requirements

(a) Ensure compliance with Associations Act

(b) Ensure appropriate insurances are in place and up to date

(c) Ensure all permits and permissions are obtained

(d) Recruit accountant to committee

Objective 3: Identify possible funding and sponsorship sources

(a) Work with marketing subcommittee to identify and seek funding and sponsorship

Objective 4: Ensure the event has adequate policies and procedures in place for all staff, contractors and volunteers

(a) Develop training programmes and policies for volunteers and contractors

Objective 5: Develop a succession plan for the events continuity

(a) Develop information systems and record keeping procedures

(b) Recruit others to the committee and undertake training in specific roles

Specific tasks and actions

- ☐ Finance policies (e.g. quotes, money handling)
- ☐ Sponsorship policy
- ☐ Budget approval process (approving accounts)
- ☐ Invoice procedures
- ☐ Budget monitoring process and cash flow strategy

Financial details

- ☐ Insert source of revenue, tasks, target amounts and who is responsible
- ☐ Identify the benefits offered and available to sponsors
- ☐ Sponsors approached and outcomes

9 Human resource plan

- ☐ Document volunteer policy
- ☐ Identify human resources – staff, volunteers, contractors
- ☐ Recruitment of volunteers
- ☐ Insurance
- ☐ Training and induction details
- ☐ Position descriptions
- ☐ Reward/recognition
- ☐ Equipment, tools, food/beverage, etc., required for volunteers/staff

10 Marketing plan

Objectives

1. Involve the local community in the event
2. Attract visitors from surrounding regions
3. Attract visitors travelling to/from other locations over the weekend and staying in the region

(Continued)

CASE STUDY 7.1 COMMUNITY FESTIVAL: CREATING THE BUSINESS PLAN—*Cont'd*

Target markets

1. Families with young children
2. Older adults
3. People in surrounding areas
   - ☐ *Marketing material*: Designer: Printer:
   - ☐ *Website developer*:
   - ☐ *Distribution strategy (of fliers, etc.)*:
   - ☐ *Process to evaluate marketing*:

Website listings

Organisation	Website	Who	When	Status

Marketing plan summary

Marketing Activity	When	Who	Cost	Notes
Available budget			$	
Launch {How will event be launched, who will be invited (media and others)}				
Ticketing {How tickets will be sold and distributed}				
Marketing material {E.g. list fliers, posters, programme, video, etc. Develop distribution strategy aimed at target audience}				
Direct mail/letter drops {Collate database for target audience; organise flier drops}				
Notice boards {Notices on public notice boards}				
Media releases {Insert topics, dates, distribution strategy}				
Television {Sponsor, community service announcements, paid ads, news stories}				
Radio {Sponsor, community service announcements, paid ads, prize giveaways, news stories, interviews}				
Newspapers {Identify newspapers to advertise or send media releases to, potential sponsor, prize giveaways}				
Newsletters {Identify newsletters, dates}				
Magazines				

Marketing Activity	When	Who	Cost	Notes
{Identify magazines, trade publications, etc., for media releases or advertising}				
Websites				
{Development of event website and list on as many websites as possible}				
Event listings				
{Distribute event dates/details to event lists, e.g. regional newspapers}				
Signage				
{Signs on town entrances, other locations, venue}				
Public relations				
{E.g. Distribute fliers at other events, invite journalists, presentation at forums, meetings, etc.}				
Tourism				
{Identify tourism opportunities, advertising, tour operators, etc.}				
Co-promoters				
{Identify potential partners to promote event – e.g. sponsors, local businesses}				
Photographer				
{Recruit a photographer for next year's marketing, organise permission form}				
Database development				
{Collect address details – address and email, from as many people as possible at event and from other sources}				
Market research				
{Develop market research form/process to evaluate event}				
Media clippings				
{Collate media details for use of the following year and to evaluate marketing plan}				
Total budget				

Flier distribution strategy:

Distribution to:	Number	By When	Who
Visitor Info Centre			
Regional list			
Local shops			
Regional galleries			
Databases			
Accommodation – e.g. Caravan parks, motels in region			
Rate notices to publicise the event (free postage)			
Get a database together			

(Continued)

11 Event evaluation plan

☐ Establish criteria used to evaluate the event
☐ Identify information required to evaluate the event
☐ Event de-brief –

Date: Time: Venue: Agenda:

☐ Responsibility for compilation of final evaluations

12 Key contact

Contact	Name	Address	Phone/Fax	Email/Website

DISCUSSION TOPICS

Research the meaning of uncertainty. Does it relate to the term "unfamiliarity"? Therefore does the knowledge an event manager possesses reduce the risk and the uncertainty of entrepreneurial events?

Are events complex or is it just that we do not see the simple pattern?

One of the famous quotes attributed to Lord Kelvin is 'If you can't measure it, you can't improve it' Is that true for events?

Using the Country Fair business case as a template prepare a business case for:

1. Bicycle ride
2. A product launch
3. A regional chess competition

Discuss the ability of this template to describe a major event. What items in the temple need to be 'scaled up'? What items need to be added?

Setting up the management system

INTRODUCTION

Once the business or social case for the event has been established, the event team must draft their management system to deliver the event. This chapter begins the tasks to establish the management system. The project management methodology is briefly discussed and illustrated in detail with a spreadsheet system for events. The spreadsheets assess the feasibility of the event and at the same time create the foundation to the management of the event. As the years go by many events will grow in size. There is a pathway for this development and this is explored. Also the event organisations mature and the chapter ends with a discussion of the maturity model.

8.1 EVENT PROJECT METHODOLOGY

The most applicable existing system for the development and delivery of an event is found in the methodology of project management. Numerous authors have pointed out the limitations of the current project management tools and techniques if they are applied without understanding the event management environment. The complexity and uncertainty of events, particularly found with special events and large public events, impose significant limitations. The need for constant asset redesign and innovation in many events is a major limitation to the employment of project management. The management system set out in this section takes into account these limitations.

The term 'management framework' refers to an outline of the management system used to deliver the event. A framework can be set up as part of the event feasibility and is gradually filled in to create the useable system. It provides the support to the thinking and at the same time limits the scope, so that the event team can come to terms with the complexity of event planning. During the feasibility stage, the management system must have two characteristics: flexibility and scalability. At the early stage of event development, most aspects of the project and the event are estimated. The event itself is vague or to use a mathematical term, fuzzy. The event programme becomes more defined as the project progresses towards the event deadline. This is an important point in the event management environment as many novices to events industry assume that the event is very well defined. Even major annual events, such as the Asian Games or the Olympics, have changes over the project. The interview with Di Henry describes how a major change occurred only weeks before the Torch Relay for the Doha Games. The conclusion is that the

Events Feasibility and Development. DOI: 10.1016/B978-0-7506-6640-4.10008-1

event management framework must be able to manage the uncertainty. As the project progresses, the management framework is adapted and gradually filled in to become a comprehensive system.

The event project, archive and review system (EPARS) is a graphical summary of the process of event management. Figure 8.1 shows the framework and explains the sections.

Each section of the EPARS management framework is treated separately in the following chapters. The framework is the core of the feasibility and the event development. Without a systematic way to manage all events, there can be little improvement in the management or the development of an event. That is not to say the event will always be a success. However, at least the failure will be understood and the mistakes will help the event management system become more resilient.

The event management framework will assist the client or sponsors and other stakeholders understand the methodology employed by the event company. There are many textbooks and websites with information on how to organise an event. However, most of this information is needed after the event is approved. Before it is approved the event company will be asked about their management framework or methodology.

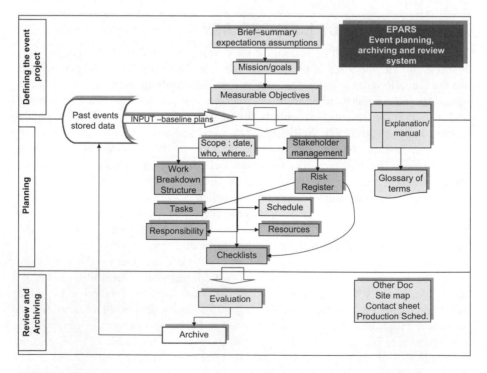

FIGURE 8.1

Event planning methodology

The framework is build from two perspectives:

1. *Scoping the management*: to assist in assessing the feasibility of proposed event by understanding what is involved in the management of the proposed event. Scoping enables the event team to understand the boundaries and limitations of the event management.
2. Drafting the management to create a starting point for the management of the event. Allowing the event to develop in way that is accountable and efficient. Drafting enables the event team to establish the system that will be used to deliver the event.

From the client's point of view, it is essential to know that the event company is competent. A framework allows the event company to demonstrate their abilities and thoroughness to the client. It answers the question 'what methodology will the event company use in creating the event?' This type of question is becoming more common in the requests for tender in the event industry. It is quite common in other industries. In the UK the project management methodology PRINCE, an acronym for Projects in Controlled Environments, has been adopted by a number of government departments as the de facto standard for IT development. It is now used in all areas of project management and PRINCE accreditation is often required for contracts.

8.2 MANAGEMENT FRAMEWORK AS A SPREADSHEET

There are a variety of software products available for events. Their quality and number are developing every year. In an informal survey of over 1000 public and special events, the author found that the spreadsheet and work processor are, in 95% of the cases, the most common software used for events. The humble spreadsheet is flexible and scalable. These are the characteristics needed to establish the event management system. The spreadsheet is the most powerful of the software tools as it is not far removed from the actual workings of a computer. The cells in a spreadsheet correspond to the fields in a database. The functions performed by the spreadsheet are close to the programming language, which means less can go wrong. This is an important consideration when purchasing software. The effect of a glitch in the software when organising an event is magnified by the deadline. An event team generally does not have the time to fix the software. This is often glossed over by the marketing of event software. A spreadsheet is basic to the working of a computer and the data can generally be exported to other software. In the future if the event company decides to use a specialist software package, it will be compatible with the spreadsheets used in the past.

The framework for the management system is constructed from a group of worksheets. By following the step-by-step process, the event team will minimise the amount of work that is done. At the same time, the worksheets provide a template for the feasibility and development of future events. It provides the event team with a system that can be shown to the client and sponsors to prove the competency of the event company. The management framework assists the teamwork and introduces a common language and work discipline to the team. It requires little or no training as the spreadsheet is a common tool in the workplace. The cut and paste feature of the software enables the event organisation to copy the material from one sheet to another. The simple delete feature means that once the framework is developed, it can easily be adapted for each event. The management framework can be created quickly as part of the feasibility phase. If the decision is to go ahead with the event, the framework will do its job and provide the actual basis of the event management system. If the decision is not to go ahead with the event, the framework can be adapted to the next event.

The management framework illustrated in coming paragraphs can be of use for training purposes. Any event's feasibility plan can be constructed in this way. At the same time, it allows the trainee or student to become familiar with the terminology and the inherent 'interconnectedness' of all aspects of event management. Various scenarios can be tested and the event management can be stress tested and its sensitivity to change can be ascertained.

The worksheets include:

- Scope
- Stakeholder
- Work breakdown structure
- Resources
- Finance/budget
- Schedule
- Contact list
- Risk register
- Checklists
- Event programme

Depending on the type of event and its complexity, other worksheets can be added including:

- Event development ideas
- Site or venue map
- Organisation chart
- Objectives/ROI/evaluation
- Target market

8.2.1 Contents page

In the spreadsheet, the first worksheet should show the contents. The cells are hyperlinked to the individual worksheets. In the worksheet, some of the cells can be 'bookmarked' on the contents page that allows easy navigation through the framework. It is essential that the navigation and the clarity of the framework be well thought out. The words that are used, the placement of the data, the worksheet names and the version control all enable the free flow of information. Once the feasibility stage is completed and planning/implementation stage moves forward, more staff will be engaged. As time goes by this basic framework will be filling out and very difficult to change. The words that are used will become the language of the management of the event. Exhibit 8.1 shows a sample of a contents page.

EXHIBIT 8.1 CONTENTS PAGE OF THE SPREADSHEET SYSTEM

EVENT PROJECT PLAN CONTENTS		
Scope		
Org Struct		
WBS		
Schedule	Milestones	
	Timeline	
	Production schedule	
	Running sheet	
Stakeholders		
Contacts		
Task Resp		
Resources		
Budget		
Program		
Risk Register		
Site map		
Checklists	Event Manual	Transport
	Operations Manual	Promotion
	Queuing	Entertainers
	Talent	Signage
	Tickets/invites	Media on site
	Site Issues	Sponsors
	Finance	On the day
	Shutdown	Exhibitors
	Toolkit	

8.2.2 **The scope**

The scope worksheet contains the objectives of the event as well as the major responsibilities and assumptions. The objectives can be goals or aims. Measurable objectives are useful for communication purposes. All parties understand a measurable objective such as positive invitation response of 30% or an attendance figure of 10,000. This is far clearer compared with a goal such as a successful event. As mentioned elsewhere in this book, the measurable objectives must be 'taken with a grain of salt'. They can imply that the event is only about measurable objectives. In most cases measurable objectives are a tool for communication with other parties and an indicator of success.

Exhibit 8.2 is a sample of a typical worksheet showing the scope of the event for an end of year corporate party. It is not exact, as the details have to be confirmed once the event is approved.

EXHIBIT 8.2 EVENT SCOPE

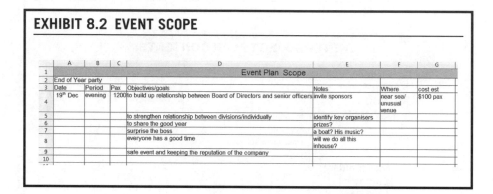

	A	B	C	D	E	F	G
1				Event Plan Scope			
2	End of Year party						
3	Date	Period	Pax	Objectives/goals	Notes	Where	cost est
4	19th Dec	evening	1200	to build up relationship between Board of Directors and senior officers	invite sponsors	near sea/ unusual venue	$100 pax
5				to strengthen relationship between divisions/individually	identify key organisers		
6				to share the good year	prizes?		
7				surprise the boss	a boat? His music?		
8				everyone has a good time	will we do all this inhouse?		
9				safe event and keeping the reputation of the company			
10							

8.2.3 The organisation structure

All events have a temporary organisation structure that is time-based. This means that the structure could be one person during the feasibility and concept phase, it can then grow to a company structure with a director and various divisions such as marketing and finance. The next step could be the growth of subcommittees or subdivisions. If the event is large, such as the Olympics or World Cup, these divisions are then devolved to each of the venues. The logistics department, for example, would subdivide so that each venue will have its own logistics division. During the event the organisation structure goes more into an operational pattern. Onsite management takes over and the suppliers need coordinating. Finally after the event, the organisation structure may return to a small company. This organisational flux needs to be flexible from the very start. The organisation structure is often derived from the work breakdown structure (WBS) as the areas of work are mapped against the staff or subdivisions. Exhibit 8.3 is an example of using the spreadsheet to accomplish the mapping process. The dark cells represent full authority and sign off. The light cells imply consultation. The event coordinator's role is to integrate all the work of all the committee and will have authority on programming and speaker engagement.

EXHIBIT 8.3 MAPPING THE WORK BREAKDOWN STRUCTURE TO COMMITTEES

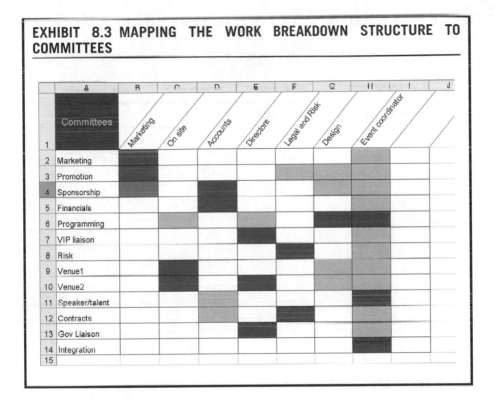

	Marketing	On site	Accounts	Directors	Legal and Risk	Design	Event coordinator		
Committees	B	C	D	E	F	G	H	I	J
2 Marketing	■				■		■		
3 Promotion					■		■		
4 Sponsorship	■		■			■	■		
5 Financials			■						
6 Programming		■				■	■		
7 VIP liaison				■					
8 Risk					■				
9 Venue1		■		■		■			
10 Venue2		■		■		■			
11 Speaker/talent			■				■		
12 Contracts					■				
13 Gov Liaison				■					
14 Integration							■		
15									

8.2.4 The stakeholder list

One aspect of public events that stands out from other types of events is the number of event stakeholders. Even corporate events, these days, involve a lot of departments within a company and may involve government agencies, if the event impinges on the public sphere. A stakeholder is defined as any individual or organisation that has an interest in the event. Setting up a viable stakeholder management system is essential to the development of event. It may be hidden in other areas of the management such as sponsorship or client relations. It amounts to the same process: identification, engagement, requirement analysis, planning, implementation, control and evaluation. Although this process seems straightforward it can be very complex and take up a large number of resources. It never seems to be finished as any change in the event programme or the event project can influence the relationship between the event team and the stakeholders. Change in the stakeholder relationships can arise as a result of internal developments such as a growth in the number of expected attendees or a decrease in available funds and external developments such as changes in legislation. The first task in creating a stakeholder plan during the feasibility stage is the identification of who and what has an interest in the event.

Exhibit 8.4 is an example of the worksheet set out to identify and manage the stakeholders.

The process used in stakeholder management is set out in the section on event management processes.

EXHIBIT 8.4 STAKEHOLDER WORKSHEET

	B	C	D	E	F	G	H	I	J
			Stakeholders reporting plan						
	New Years Eve Celebration in Shopping Mall								
			jan	feb	mar	apr	may	jun	jul
	Stakeholders	reporting plan							
	Public								
	Shop owners								
	Landlord								
	Security								
	Building management								
	event organisers								
	Police								
	Ambulance service								
	Service Staff								
	Volunteers								

8.2.5 Work breakdown structure

To decide on the feasibility of an event or its development, it is necessary to have a technique to describe all work that needs to be performed to deliver the event. This is WBS or 'a process of decomposition whereby a complex project is broken up into smaller units of work that can be easily managed' (O'Toole & Mikolaitis 2002:27). The advantage of using a WBS is that it can start as a 'coarse' level description and will be refined as the event becomes more defined. The WBS can follow the planning and implementation of the event project over time. The WBS can be created from the 'top down' by dividing the event project into departments such as Marketing, Administration, Logistics, Stakeholders, Finance, Onsite and Venue. If we assume that the name of the event is a level one heading then these may be called the level two headings. Note that these are similar to departments or divisions in any industry. The WBS for the event is temporary and must allow for growth, consolidation and the possible reduction of the scope of work. For public events such as festivals, the categories of the WBS often correspond to the various committees set up to run the event. As illustrated Exhibit 8.3 it can be mapped to the organisation structure of the event. Different types of events will use slightly different level two headings. Sports events may add 'Accreditation'; corporate events may have 'Client Relations' and 'Hospitality' and public events may have 'Entertainment' and 'Volunteers'. Different countries and cultures will have slightly different headings. In the Gulf countries, for example, 'Protocol' and 'Security' are high-level headings. The point is that the WBS is flexible and at the right level of definition to describe the event and its management. During the feasibility stage, the WBS enables the event management company and the client to understand the scope of the undertaking. Each of the headings will direct questions as to its viability and the capacity of the event company to manage them. A good capacity and capability analysis can only flow from a well thought out WBS. As the event develops, the WBS is used as the complete description of the scope of work.

Exhibit 8.5 is an example of a WBS of a proposed event. Note the use of the outlining or data grouping feature to help with the clarity of the information.

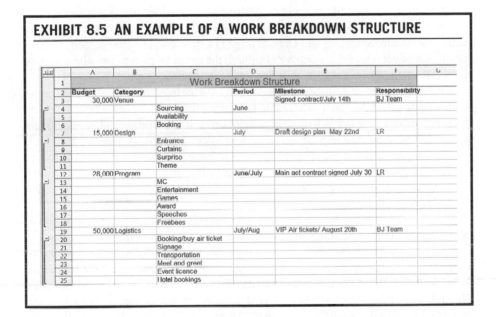

EXHIBIT 8.5 AN EXAMPLE OF A WORK BREAKDOWN STRUCTURE

	A	B	C	D	E	F	G
1			Work Breakdown Structure				
2	Budget	Category		Period	Milestone	Responsibility	
3	30,000	Venue			Signed contract/July 14th	BJ Team	
4			Sourcing	June			
5			Availability				
6			Booking				
7	15,000	Design		July	Draft design plan May 22nd	LR	
8			Entrance				
9			Curtains				
10			Surprise				
11			Theme				
12	28,000	Program		June/July	Main act contract signed July 30	LR	
13			MC				
14			Entertainment				
15			Games				
16			Award				
17			Speeches				
18			Freebees				
19	50,000	Logistics		July/Aug	VIP Air tickets/ August 20th	BJ Team	
20			Booking/buy air ticket				
21			Signage				
22			Transportation				
23			Meet and greet				
24			Event licence				
25			Hotel bookings				

8.2.6 The schedule: milestones

The next step in developing the management framework is to decide on the milestones for each of the level two headings or categories. Milestones are dates that mark the conclusion of an important task. The most efficient technique to decide on the milestones is to use the concept of deliverables. A deliverable, in the management framework, is a file or document that passes from one group to another and is the culmination of a series of tasks. An example is the site map or venue layout map of the event. To create a site map a number of tasks have to be performed. These include decide on location, have input from the programming, designing the onsite logistics and positioning of all the suppliers and vendors. The site map, once completed, represents all of these tasks. The 'site map' or 'venue layout' may be a milestone for heading 'Venue' or 'Onsite'.

The example shown in Exhibit 8.5 has the milestones for each of the management divisions.

By using milestone planning, the event team can decide to delegate key areas of the event project once the event has been approved. The site map, for example, can be delegated to a group or a person within the team. The ability to delegate tasks and areas of management is essential to event development. The team is given the deliverable as the major task such as 'create the site map'. The event management knows exactly when it is completed as the site map will be sent to the event team. The deliverable is a proof that all the tasks have been completed.

To further illustrate the concept of deliverables, consider the management area with the heading 'Entertainment'. The subheading or level three headings may include Sourcing, Selecting and Contracting. The deliverable is the signed contract for the major act. Once this contract is signed, the event team can 'breathe a sigh of relief'. If this is given a date then it becomes a milestone.

Deciding on the milestones and describing the deliverables creates the framework for the schedule. Each deliverable is a mini project. The person or team given the responsibility for the deliverable can create their own project plan. The event project can be described as a cluster of mini projects. It is a fractal model as there is a large project made up of mini projects. For large events, the mini projects are themselves made up of even smaller projects. The fractal nature of this model implies that the process is exactly the same and allows for expansion and contraction of the framework.

A further example will help the reader understand this fundamental principle of event management. The stage set up for an event includes a number of tasks. For a large event the responsibility for stage set up would be allocated to a team or a separate company. A milestone for the stage set up is the delivery of the stage plan for approval by the event director. This may include lighting or audio–visual plan. The delivery of the stage plan to the event director allows the director to know that many tasks associated with the stage set up have been completed. The event manager may not be an expert in stage set up. Therefore, the stage plan is proof that the design has been completed.

The 'deliverable' method is not a perfect system and there are many risks. However, it is the only way to manage a group of people in this situation and allow for future growth. The alternative is complete control by the event manager or living in hope that tasks will be completed. A result of micromanaging is 'burnout' of the manager. They cannot physically or mentally control everything. In the experience of the author this is one of the most common risks in growth of an event. The management model employed when the event is young is retained as the event grows. The event manager is doing 'everything' and delegating very little. The manager complains they cannot trust the volunteers or new staff with the responsibility. With a result the event manager leaves the event. The event organising committee realises all the knowledge of the event has left. To prevent this loss a system for delegation needs to be part of the every day management and needs to allow the event organisation to keep the knowledge. For the future development of events and festivals there must be a system for delegation.

Each milestone and its deliverable is a mini project. Once these are placed on a schedule, such as a Gantt Chart, the rest of the schedule can be filled in. Some of the deliverables may be outsourced to specialist companies. The tasks necessary to create the deliverable will be internal to the outsourced company and of little concern to the event organisation.

At the same time as setting up the milestone plan, a progress reporting time can be determined. Although this will be 'firmed up' once the event is approved, the feasibility stage is a good time to consider how the progress reports will be done. When a large number of tasks are delegated to a team, the event manager will need to know 'how they are going'. The fixed deadline of event means any changes in the deliverables will affect the scope. If the deliverables are late the event management team will have to put more resources into making sure this does not affect the event deadline. It is essential that the management team knows any of these risks as they may have to put pressure on those delegated with the tasks. An example will illustrate this vital point in the organisation of events. The site planning team has the deliverable as the site map. A completed site map is needed by other members of the event team so they can continue their work. The logistics people need to know where the stages and utilities will be delivered onsite. The marketing team needs to know where the sponsorship signs will be placed. The signage team needs to know what should be on the signs and where to put them. There is a lot of the event organising dependent on the deliverable from the site design team. If their deliverable is late it will mean that the other teams will have to work harder as they will have less time to complete their tasks. In the terminology of project management, the lack of time means that cost or quality will be sacrificed. If these two variables are to remain constant, then the time must be taken from other areas of management.

8.2.7 The resources

The WBS can be used to develop a list of resources. Exhibit 8.6 is a sample of a list of resources on a worksheet. The headings in row 2 are filled in as the resources are discussed in a team meeting. The worksheet is the deliverable of the meeting and a way to frame the discussion. The heading WBS refers to the categories of the work breakdown structure. The WBS is used to identify the resources needed. The outsource/in-house and make/buy/hire decisions can be recorded here. The quotes are recorded as is the status of the contract.

The procurement process, including sourcing, comparison, calling for quotes and contract management, is involved in the development of this worksheet. This worksheet can be improved with every event as it evolves into a resource master list. For an inaugural event, the event team often has to source equipment and services from new suppliers. The correct description of these can be a problem. This system of specification or description is outlined in the section on procurement.

EXHIBIT 8.6 RESOURCE LIST

	A	B	C	D	E	F	G	H	I	J
1					Resources					
2	WBS	Resources	Inhouse	Make	Hire	Buy	Quote	Quote	Contacts	Contract status
3										
4	Admin	IT equip				Yes – laptops, PDAs				
5	a	Office space	yes							
6	a	Office stationery	yes							
7	Marketing	Creative Agency	yes					Office space		
8	m	Ad Agency	yes					Office stationery		
9	m	Printing	yes							
10	m	Brochures and collateral		yes						
11	m	Vouchers		yes						
12	m	Designer	yes							
13	m	Web design				yes				
14	m	Graphics	yes							
15	Logistics	Valet			yes					
16	l	Couriers			yes					
17	l	Transport			yes					
18	l	Shuttle bus	yes							
19	l	Travel agents	yes							
20	l	Limo			yes					
21	l	Taxis			yes					
22										

8.2.8 The budget

Using the WBS as the master document, the budget worksheet can be created. The term budget is used in a variety of ways in international event management. It is a monetary plan of the event. Sometimes the term used to mean the total amount of money available for the event. Exhibit 8.5 shows how the WBS can be used to draft a budget

8.2.9 The programme

This is the ultimate deliverable of all the processes. It is easily set out in a worksheet and can be sorted according to the times or programme items.

8.2.10 The risk register

The ultimate and constant deliverable of the risk management process is the worksheet called the risk register. Sometimes it is called an issues log. It is here that the possible problems and their management are recorded. The spreadsheet is a good tool for the risk register as it can be updated easily and it is adjacent to all the other worksheet to enable cross-checking. The risk register can be open at all meetings and accessed as webpage so the team can keep an eye on the problems and their responsibilities. It will feed into the task and responsibility sheet. Exhibit 8.7 is a sample of a risk register for the feasibility of the launch of a new building. The WBS is used as a code and sorting tool as well as being consulted to analyse any risks. At the feasibility stage the risks are given a more general description such as 'lack of supplier'. The *Result* column describes what will happen if the risk occurs. This is an important part of the risk management process as the event team must understand why something is a risk. It is a common mistake to only superficially look at a risk. The traffic problem with rain can easily be overlooked if the members of the event staff have never experienced it. In some countries the rain will stop traffic as they are not used to it and the drivers cannot see the potholes in the roads. In other countries the people are more than used to rain but would be confused by a sand storm. Exhibit 8.7 is the type of template recommended by various risk standards and codes around the world. Note that the event in the exhibit is an example and should not be used as an actual risk register. Every event organisation needs to create its unique risk register by consulting with the event team and other interested parties.

EXHIBIT 8.7 RISK REGISTER

	A	B	C	D	E	F	G	H	I
1						Risk Register			
2	**WBS**	**Risk**	**Result**	**Lik**	**Con**	**Level**	**Treatment options**	**Responsibility**	**Deadline**
3	Site	Building not ready	Launch delayed	pos	maj	Extreme	Change scope (date)		
4			Event scope changed						
5	Finance	Cut in Budget	Scope changes	pos	mod	High	Sign contract well in advance		
6			Lack of resources				Cancellation/postponement clause		
7			Different priorities						
8	Resources	Lack of Supplier	Show details change	unlik	minor	Moderate	Invite international tenders		
9			Budget increase - change						
10	Legal	Civil Aviation permission not happening	No flying in of VIPs to site	rare	minor	Low	Make government part of the event		
11							Have alternative e.g. luxury yacht		
12	Site	Rain during the event	Guests get wet	lik	mod	High	Plan alternative		
13			Equipment damage				Local and experienced suppliers		
14			Traffic problems				Discuss with traffic police		
15	Contracts/re sources	Performers do not turn up	Gap in entertainment program	lik	minor	Moderate	Bring them early		
16							Flag possibility with other performers		
17									

8.2.11 The site map

The worksheet contains the drawings of the site or venue set up. It is the deliverable of the event design process. For complex events, this worksheet will link to other software that contains the map. However, a simple .jpeg version can be kept here for reference. By having it as one of the worksheets the teams using the risk register and WBS can easily have access to the map.

During the feasibility phase, a draft map or a mud map can be constructed to see what fits where and the viability of the placement of the facilities, exhibitors, vendors and staging. The flow of the audience and other movements at all times must be considered in drawing the sketch map.

Figure 8.2 illustrates a simple example of a staging map for a firework and fountain display. The original was drawn quickly using pencil and paper. It is not meant to be accurate. It is to assist with the design of the site, the logistics and the risks. If the event is approved an accurate site map will be drawn.

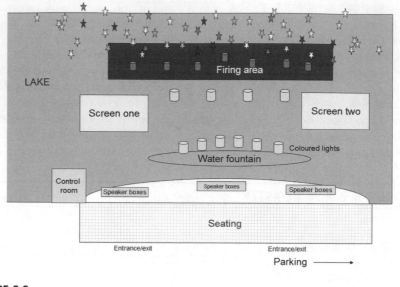

LAKE

Firing area

Screen one

Screen two

Water fountain

Coloured lights

Control room

Speaker boxes

Speaker boxes

Speaker boxes

Seating

Entrance/exit

Entrance/exit

Parking

FIGURE 8.2

Sketch map of an event

8.2.12 **The event checklist**

The checklist is a fundamental tool for the on-the-ground and at-the-moment event management. It is essential in the dynamic management environment. By having a worksheet containing checklists and a navigational aid to find them quickly, the members of event team have access to an important resource. The checklist can be created straight away from a meeting of the event staff. They can be adapted from other events, downloaded off the web and refined with every event. They should be started from the first meeting and recorded. By using the worksheet and placing it on the Intranet or web, all team members can have access whenever they are connected to the net. With the use of mobile phones, the checklist can be accessed wherever there is a connection. The numbered checklist is important to delegating tasks as it allows the delegated person or team to give efficient progress reports.

The importance of checklist has recently been studied and tested by people working in high-pressure environments including pilots, surgery staff and emergency teams. The evaluation expert Michael Shriven describes how the checklist reduces the 'halo effect'. This is the tendency of staff to only see one important item and ignore the rest or regard them as trivial. In some cases they are so focused on the one task that they completely miss the other tasks. A checklist forces the staff to review all the items. According to Shriven, it also reduces the Rorschach effect. That is the tendency to see a pattern in group data or tasks. Any task that does not fit into this pattern is ignored. Using a checklist ensures that the items are treated individually.

Event staff use checklists constantly and their use indicates how important operational tasks are to minimising problems and to the success of the event. An oversight made during the operations of an event can quickly lead to a disaster. This is due to the importance of timeliness of actions combined with complexity of tasks and impact of the tasks on the event. While the event is occurring, the tasks are highly coupled. They are linked to each other so that if a task is missed or not completed, the effect can be amplified. The saying 'for want of a nail the war was lost' is a reality on the site of many festivals and large events. For example, a missing chair on stage for a performer can lead the performer refusing to go on. This can lead to delays which are amplified as the event programme progresses to cause a crowd management issue at the end of the event and possible booking of venue to go over time. This causes extra financial payments for the event going over time. Ric Birch, the international event producer gives many amusing examples of these problems in his book 'Master of Ceremonies'.

There can be no greater endorsement of the value of checklists than the work of the general surgeon Atul Gawande who introduced the simple checklist to hospital surgery. The operational importance of doing everything quickly and thoroughly in the operating theatre is similar to an event environment. His work has made a large impact by preventing mistakes in the operating theatre and reducing the deaths as a result of surgery. The importance of timeliness and making sure seemingly small tasks are completed is similar to the event operational environment. He studied the similarity to the checklists used by pilots for takeoff and the efficiency of the project management process in complex building construction and civil engineering. In all these situations, a simple task that is forgotten can cause a disaster.

> *...under conditions of complexity, not only are checklists a help, they are required for success. There must always be room for judgement, but judgement aided and even enhanced — by procedure.*
>
> **(Gawande, 2010, p. 79)**

8.3 THE DEVELOPING EVENT: A MATURITY MODEL

The maturity model refers to the level of organisational excellence of the event company, committee or organisation such as the event office within a larger company. While an industry develops and grows the individual components change and mature. As with the competency model, the maturity model provides both a description of the current situation and the gaps needed to fill to become more efficient and effective. For this reason the model is part of the strategic planning for the industry. There are a number of maturity models that may be examined for their application to event organisations. The Capability Maturity Model developed by the Software Engineering Institute has been adapted to other industries. As well, the Project Management Institute (PMI) is developing organisational maturity models.

Over time, a maturity model maps the changes in an event organisation. These are similar to a phase change in science whereby a product's basic structure undergoes transformation. One can track event companies across these levels of maturity. Many event companies start by being entrepreneurial, dependent on the personality of the owner, full of ideas and brashness. As the company grows, so does the complexity of its management, formal systems are introduced. At this level the management is accountable for the actions both within the company and to the stakeholders. At their height, the event company has all of the above plus a method of learning and improving for each event.

This phase development is not confined to the corporate world. It is demonstrated in the area of public celebrations. Many annual festivals started with just a group of friends. People with similar interest attended the event and the celebration grows. In this way community or small celebrations become major festivals. Figure 8.3 illustrates the growth of the local event. At the same time the event management or committee needs to grow and change. In particular, there is a major phase change when 'outsiders' are attracted to the festival. Authorities become interested in the festival and it now needs to be documented and accountable. Insurance, bank loans, sponsors, legal requirements mean that the organisation has to be properly managed. In the long term, to survive in such a complex environment, it also needs have the ability to assess its management, think strategically, look for new ideas and adapt to internal and external changes.

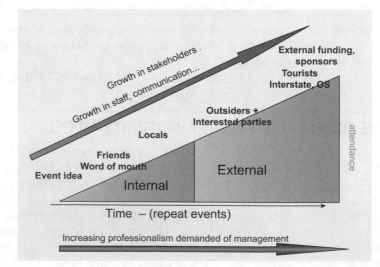

FIGURE 8.3

Growth of an annual public event

At this stage in the early development of the event industry it is difficult to compile an exact maturity model. The model outlined is based on the author's research while working on a variety of events around the world.

The first phase is the Initial or Informal. It is characterised by the lack of any formal processes, an ad hoc approach and often disorganised. The success of the event will directly depend on the personality of the event manager. There is no or little documentation and it is impossible to repeat the event. Planning, if any, is done on the run. The next phase is the Formal. Some of the management processes are recognised and they able to be repeated for the next event. Some of the events are overorganised and others lack any detail in their management. There is some documentation and reporting. Risk management is done from a safety point of view. Historical information is used and the work is scoped. The client brief or statement of work is recognised as the major document. The event company would be a member of an association. During the Managed or Accountable phase the event company has written plans and monitors these plans with techniques such as regular reports and milestones. The plans are based on templates created from previous events. The risk management is integrated into the whole managing process. Staff are trained in the terminology and methodology of project and risk management. Forecasting techniques such as cost–benefit analysis are performed for events. Event feasibility is an essential aspect of the process of choosing the event. There is an event manual. Stakeholder analysis is undertaken.

Optimised or Adaptable and Improvable is the highest phase. The event management, organisation or company has a strategic plan for their events and can adapt these plans to changing conditions. The individual events are regarded as a way to test the management system. Scenarios are developed and there is flexibility in response to unforeseen risk creating resilience in the organisation. Past events are archived and their management can be compared to future events. Cost–benefit analysis and sensitivity analysis are used both at the event level and at the strategic level. The management of the event is continually improving using management tools and techniques adapted from other industries such as information technology, engineering and the military and disciplines such as systems analysis and logistics. The event organisation provides training for their staff and therefore a career path within the company, within the industry and in related industries. Finally, the event company or team has a keen sense of the value of the event to the client and their contribution to creating this value.

If these categories are used as the heading of a matrix and the areas of event management are listed down the side, a table such as Table 8.1 can be produced. This table can then be used by the event organisation to map their competencies.

Table 8.1 represents the beginning of a maturity model for event management. At this stage in the development of the industry there is not enough data to test this model. The construction of a valid and acceptable event organisation maturity model can only be achieved with input and assessment from event managers around the world. The PMI is currently conducting such a world workshop called the OPM3 programme through their website.

Table 8.1 Maturity Table for Event Management

Explanation of levels:

- Informal level – where the event is organised on an ad hoc basis, little is written down
- Formal level – the event has structured management with delegation
- Accountable level – this includes the competencies of the formal level and the event and the management can account for their management and decisions
- Adaptable level – this includes the accountable competencies and means the event management, although a formal system can respond positively to change and improve for each event

Area	Informal	Formal	Accountable	Adaptable and improvable
Management system	Depended on one personality	A management structure in place	Structure identified and documents with work areas	Ability to change management and assess its effectiveness
HR – staff and volunteer	Group of friends. All event staff are known personally to the event manager	Uses volunteers/staff outside of organisation, uses some training or briefing	Defined and written positions with event responsibilities, tasks and schedules	Formal debriefing with volunteer and staff assessment
Risk management	Responds to problems as they occur	Has a safety risk strategy, uses a risk standard. Has incident report sheets and a method for reporting risks	Uses a full risk management plan across all event areas	Employs a method to change the risk management plans and assess effective of plan

Financial system	Cash in cash out accounting	Book keeping system with commitment accounting	Accounting system integrated with other areas of event management, has a financial plan for capital growth	Financial plan integrated across all event areas with a CBA used. Plan is able to change with changing conditions and continually assessed
Decision making	Decision left to event manager – sole authority	Delegations, i.e. decisions allowed according to level of position in event	Approval method implemented for decisions, all major decision documented	Major decision and communication assessed and improvements suggested
Logistics	Event manager is responsible. Based on verbal agreements	There is a schedule for logistics. Contacts are dealt with on a need basis	Logistics is well documented and includes sourcing contract managements and scheduling	Logistics is optimised and monitored for improvements. Each event is regarded as a way to improve the event logistics
Staging	Staging is ad hoc and often confused	Staging is scheduled and themed	Using stage plan, schedules, and integrates into overall event schedule	Staging uses a combination of advanced scheduling and theming to produce a high impact and creative result
Stakeholder relations	Can list the stakeholders	Creates a list of stakeholder and a management plan	Detailed stakeholder management plan (SMP) integrated with risk management plan	Able to assess the SMP and change it during the course of the event
Sponsorship	Sponsorship sought	Sponsorship gained and monitored	Levels of sponsorship Documented sponsorship plan	Sponsorship continually monitored for improvements

CONCLUSION

To create a sustainable portfolio of events the management system of the event needs to be defined and described. It is no longer enough to go from organising one event to another without understanding the underlying system. This chapter demonstrated the system through the use of spreadsheets and project management methodology. Project management enables the event team to assess the feasibility of each event using a standard methodology. If the event is approved, the methodology can be employed and expanded. By using the spreadsheets the event team is using familiar and straightforward software which can be exported into any event management software or just used as is. Recognising the management system is an example of a measure of the maturity of an organisation. The maturity model can be adapted to the event industry to demonstrate the pathway event organisations or an event can take in order to develop. The next chapters describe a model of interweaving management processes comprising professional event management.

DISCUSSION TOPICS

Research the project management methodology and its application to events. Compare the types of events and their use of project management.

Download the free Openproj and use this to draft a project plan for an event. Discuss the problems of using this type of software.

Research the work of the PMI in the development of a maturity model for project organizations and compare this to event companies and long term repeat events.

Aqaba Festival, Jordan. Photo courtesy of the Events Unit, Aqaba

Event management
processes

INTRODUCTION

The next two chapters propose a process model for event management. The event management body of knowledge (EMBOK) is combined with the project management to construct a series of flowcharts. The first chapter describes the processes involved in scope, stakeholder, sponsorship, design, marketing and financial management.

9.1 FROM DOMAINS TO A PROCESS MODEL

This section concerns the description of event management as a group of interconnecting processes. Most of the event texts, the EMBOK and the current event courses divide event management into knowledge domains or subjects. This text takes a different approach as it describes events management from the perspective of change and development. The dynamic nature of event management weaves a number of processes together. The advantage of a process model is that it emphasises time in every aspect of the model. A subject or domain model is a composite of snapshots of the event management. The process model shows event management as constantly changing priorities while the processes are called into play and interact with each other.

A process is series of step-by-step tasks or activities repeated in the management of an event. These actions can be regarded as the components in the overall process to deliver the event. Each action contributes towards the completion of a main task. Processes may be illustrated by a flowchart. In engineering terms, there are inputs, the process, tools and techniques and outputs. Of course, this is a simplification of the complexity of organising an event. Unlike a classification system of the subjects of event management, the process model describes the actions. The actions are part of a series of other actions that produce a thread that weaves together to produce event management.

The model put forward by the EMBOK committee has two major dimensions. The first dimension comprises the knowledge domains of Design, Marketing, Administration, Risk and Operations. These can be subdivided, as most textbooks do, into chapters or topics. The second dimension is the phases. It was an important step to recognise that the event management passes through the various stages from the initiation to the planning and implementation. The third dimension to event management comprises various processes. Risk management, for example, is a process. It is a step-by-step task used to recognise risk and deal with them.

Events Feasibility and Development. DOI: 10.1016/B978-0-7506-6640-4.10009-3

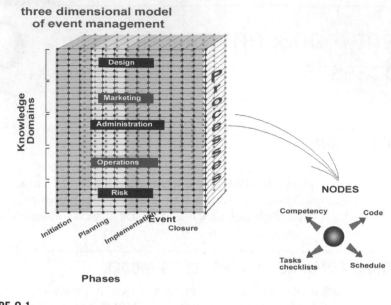

three dimensional model of event management

FIGURE 9.1

Three-dimension mode of event management

Figure 9.1 shows the model proposed that includes the numerous processes. Each cell or node in the cube is described by its:

1. Domain
2. Phase
3. Processes that are employed

The processes can be specific to the node or they may be a generic process. Each node will have checklists associated with it as well as schedules and tasks. The nodes will have quality control and they can be used in the assessment of competency of the event management.

Each node can be described by filling Table 9.1. This is the analysis of event management. All these parts fit together to describe the management. It is held together by the integration of all the processes or workflows described in this chapter.

To illustrate this process model, we can take any cell in the three-dimension model and describe it using Table 9.1. One area in the domain of Marketing, for example, is 'promotion' during the implementation phase. The processes involved will include risk management, financial management and communication management. There is a level of knowledge, skill and the right attitude necessary to undertake the promotion during the implementation phase. This is the competency needed. There is a certain standard perhaps to do with professional behaviour and environmental codes that must be maintained. There is a series of tasks that must be completed on schedule. These are all related to checklists.

Table 9.1 Identifying Each Node

Descriptor		
Cell (Matrix Model) or Node (Array model)		
Knowledge Domain		
Descriptor	Sub Class	
	Phase	
	Processes	
Micro Dimensions		
Characteristics	Competency	
	Code/Standard	
	Tasks	
	Schedule	

Every aspect of event management can be captured in this approach.

The profession of a mature industry, such as engineering or accounting, recognises the common processes or workflows that produce the services or goods. By recognising these processes the industry can develop. The development of the profession and the event industry needs a description of the event management process. The recognition and the efficient application of the processes are fundamental to a sustainable event programme.

The processes of event management can be grouped under the following headings:

- Scope: the integration and control of all the workflows
- Stakeholders including sponsorship management
- Design
- Marketing
- Finance
- Time
- Risk

- Communication
- Procurement
- Human resources

Each of the processes listed draws on other disciplines. Design, for example, draws on the extensive knowledge of staging and theatre. Event finance processes include the standard accounting techniques and adapt them to the event environment.

The priority or relative importance of the processes will depend on an array of internal and external factors. Perhaps, the most important is the type of event. A new exhibition, for example, will place greater emphasis on marketing than a yearly conference of an association when they are compared. The team organising a special event will emphasis risk management more than when organising the same event next year. It is the relative importance of the processes that gives the event management its differences for different types of events. The human resource management will take a large part of the time of the event team for a new public event such as a festival with a large number of new volunteers compared to a corporate event in a hotel with paid staff. Event companies that move across the spectrum of events understand that the processes are the same and their relative importance is different.

Two universal subprocesses act on all of the above: Trend Forecasting and Deadline Analysis.

Forecasting trends is essential in a dynamic profession sensitive to time. *When* the tasks are carried out is as important as the task itself. The outsourcing/in-house policy of an organisation is an example of a trend in the event field. A number of event companies have commented that it is like a pendulum. At one time a client will outsource all their events and at other times they prefer to hire permanent event staff and do it all in-house. The credit crises, the swine flu, the collapse of Enron, the disaster at the Love Parade, increase in the spread of international terrorism and the rise and fall of the Gulf city and estate building boom had significant affect on the event industry. There are internal trends in other industries that influence events. The rise of experiential marketing has made inroads into most commercial events such as product launches. The increase in universities and the need for academic publishing to advance in the profession have led to a huge number of academic conferences around the world. The professional licensing requirement to accumulate continuing medical education (CME) points has fuelled the medical conference industry.

All the processes described in this section are subject to trends. The event management team as well as the key stakeholders such as the government and clients must be aware of the event industry's exposure to external trends.

The other process that acts on all areas of the management is the deadline analysis. This is discussed in detail further in this book.

Some of the processes may be the responsibility of a division of the events team. HR and marketing are examples. These may be the responsibility of a committee. Other processes are found throughout the event management, such as risk and time management. The next level in the process description of event management is to describe the subprocesses. At this level the tasks that can be automated or partially completed by the use of software are identified. The scheduling process is an example of this. This can be completed using project management software. At this level the process descriptions become part of the modern science of business process modelling.

9.2 SCOPE MANAGEMENT

The scope of the event is made up of all the tasks, resources and time necessary to organise and close the event. It is an important term as too many people assume that the work done during the event is all the work necessary. It is common for the work leading up to the day of the event to be hidden. The core of scope management process is managing all the other processes described in this section. It is the integration of the processes so they are working towards the success of the event. An easy way to describe this is to examine a festival organised by a committee. The committee will be made of subcommittees. There may be a marketing, finance, operations and volunteer/HR subcommittees. All of these will need to be coordinated so they work for the event. It is easy for a subcommittee to loose sight of the big picture and become too concerned with their own area of immediate responsibility. This is referred to as *siloing* in most management textbooks. The scope management process, illustrated by Figure 9.2, ensures that all the subcommittees work for the good of the event.

Scope management includes defining the scale and time of the event. It includes date, the objectives, how long the event will go for and how many attendees and any other factors that will limit the resources and tasks. During the initiation stage the definition may have to be estimated, such as the expected number of attendees. It is vital to the validity of the feasibility study that the scope is defined.

The description of the work necessary to put on the event is also called the scope of work. This is described by means of the work breakdown structure (WBS). Although the WBS is a foreign term to many event practitioners, they all must breakdown the work into management units. This is the definition of WBS. It is the heart of the event scope as it allows the event management team to estimate the amount of work to be done and control this work. Any changes that occur will affect the scope and directing these changes to the benefit of the event is a central task of the event team. Examples of scope and WBS are found in the section on *the management framework as a spreadsheet* in Chapter 8.

9.3 STAKEHOLDER MANAGEMENT

The management of stakeholders is essential to the success of any project. It is not a simple matter of aligning the event with the objectives of the customers, stakeholders or clients. The customer for events is a complex entity. The event, such as a festival or a conference is a portfolio of products, made up of the numerous

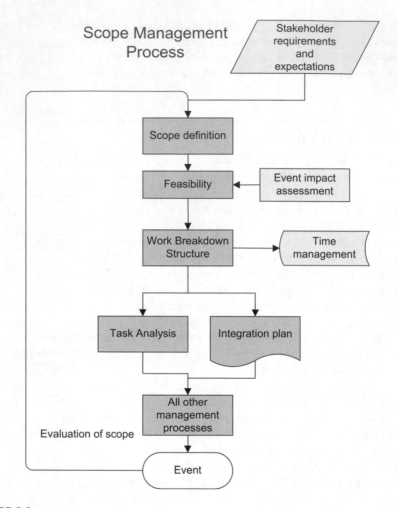

FIGURE 9.2

Scope management process

sponsors as well as the attendees and the client. Each customer may have different objectives, which may change over the course of the management of the event and conflict with other customers. The marketing process is a management tool to allow the clustering of similar interests of the stakeholders so they can be managed.

Stakeholder management is rarely treated with any detail in the textbooks on events. Therefore, this text will go into some detail. It is vital for the feasibility of an event that the management can identify and ultimately manage the varied interests of the stakeholders. The team must use a well-honed methodology. This chapter adapts the stakeholder management used in project management to the event environment. The development and management of sponsors is an example of the highly sophisticated stakeholder management used by event teams. Understanding the stakeholder management process is essential for the creation and continuation of events and an events strategy. A robust stakeholder management process underlies the longevity of a repeat event such as a yearly conference, festival or sports meeting. Thorough researching of the stakeholders is essential to event feasibility.

Most of the risks in events are directly related to the stakeholders. The stakeholder's tolerance to risk will define many aspects of the levels of risk that can be accepted by the event, that is, the event's tolerance to risk. For example, an investor in the event will be interested in the financial risk, the exposure they have as a result of their investment. They expect to make a profit. The level of this profit will set the tolerance of the financial risk of the event. This tolerance is a major input into the risk management process for an event. The fact that it may be difficult to measure should not mean it is ignored. Sponsors of a cultural event such as an art exhibition may not want certain types of art works exhibited as it may reflect badly on their image. If their requirements are ignored the event could be cancelled. For some extreme sporting events the risk will be well known and accepted by the competitors. However, if the risk goes beyond a certain limit they will not take part in the event.

Ideally the stakeholders are obvious and discovered at the beginning of the event planning. They would have straightforward needs and the event team could measure the feasibility of the event with these needs. For the event to have a good return on investment (ROI) it would be a simple matter satisfying the stakeholder's requirements. As expected the reality of event management is far from this ideal situation.

9.3.1 Definition

A large part of the standard event literature deals with the role of the stakeholders. It tends to be used in a specific sense of the type of stakeholder. On the surface, the process of stakeholder management is generally distributed between:

1. Sponsorship
2. Suppliers
3. Audience
4. Legal issues

From a festival point of view the stakeholders are often classified into:

- Host organisation
- Host community
- Sponsors
- Media
- Coworkers
- Participants and spectators

This classification only identifies the primary stakeholders. Secondary stakeholders, such as government agencies and licensing bodies, who have an interest in the event, can easily be forgotten. Recognition that the event stakeholders are more than those organisations directly involved in the event management is further proof of the maturing of the event industry around the world.

The stakeholder of an event is any individual or organisation with an interest in the event. This is a vague definition; however, it does make sure that no one is left out. Basically, the stakeholder is someone who can influence the event in a significant way. With the growth of the event industry and its influence on other organisations, it is to be expected that these organisations have a growing interest in events. A small local agricultural exhibition will have the following as stakeholders:

- Roads and Traffic Authority
- Local Police
- State Emergency Service
- Fire Service
- Local Council
- Nearby residents
- Local business — as suppliers and those affected by the event
- Farmers and their cooperatives
- Agricultural services
- Community groups and services
- Event participants — sports groups, exhibitors, vendors, entertainers
- As well as the public attending the event.

Forgetting to pay attention to any one of these groups can threaten the success of the event.

One National Day celebration that included a civic ceremony and a parade identified over 70 stakeholders including Government Departments, competing events, Defence Forces, Friends of local Zoo and Opera venue.

To the event management each stakeholder represents a cluster of risks and opportunities. Within some of the stakeholder organisations there will be further risks. The Local Council for a community event will include the risk arising from the various departments with their own agenda for events. Add to these clusters, the problems arising from the combination of stakeholders. It can be both from a one to one relationship and in various configurations over time. The result is an exponential increase in risks related to events in the public sphere. One of the attractions of managing private and corporate events is the low number of stakeholders when compared to public events. Hence, this chapter may seem like too much analysis for those event managers who only deal in business events. The process is scalable and comes into its own when used for international events.

As illustrated by the flowchart shown in Figure 9.3, stakeholder management process includes the following:

1. Identifying the stakeholders
2. Identifying and analysing their interest in the event
3. Assess their possible impact on the event
4. Identifying trends that may change their interest, including internal and external trends

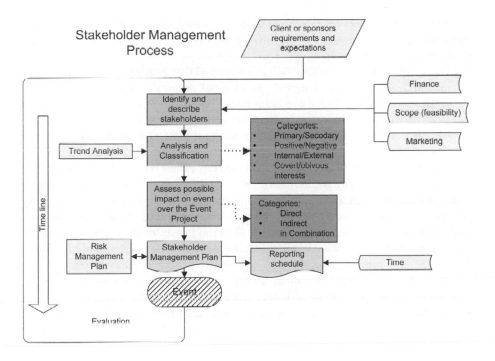

FIGURE 9.3

Stakeholder management process

5. Creating a stakeholder management plan
6. Inputting the results of the stakeholder analysis into the risk management plan

Analysis and classification are important to the understanding of most aspects of developing and managing a portfolio of events. Particularly for large and international events when the team is communicating with many parties and across cultures. A robust classification enhances the ability to communicate and manage. The classification system used here is adapted from project management. The event stakeholders can be categorised in a number of ways:

Primary stakeholders — those who are very focused on the success or otherwise of the event such as the attendees or a sponsor. These stakeholders will require constant management, reporting or other communication.

Secondary stakeholders — those who will only be interested in the event if it passes a threshold of importance such as the local police.

Internal stakeholders — those that are involved in the event planning and implementation of the plan such as the event committee.

External stakeholders — those who are not directly part of the event but still have a strong interest in it, such as the local residence, the banks or sponsors.

They can be further classified by the affect of the event on the stakeholder into *positive* such as the sponsors or *negative* such as events held at the same time that could attract the same market.

These are not mutually exclusive categories and they may change as the event is planned and as the event is repeated. An external primary stakeholder such as the Road Traffic Authority can move from being positively affected by the event to negative very quickly if a proper monitoring and communication is not used.

Also it is important to understand the resistance the stakeholder may have to aspects of the event. This may be difficult to ascertain. However, identifying resistance is essential to the correct management of the stakeholders. Resistance may not be stated overtly but may need more subtle methods for the event manager to bring them out. Often this is the reason for need of cultural understanding. 'Loss of face', for example, is an essential cultural characteristic of some Asian countries and misunderstandings in this area can lead to the failure of the event. Barbara W. Tuchman's 'Sand Against the Wind: Stilwell and the American Experience in China, 1911−45' is a valuable exposition of the results of two cultures trying to work together on a major event (Tuchman, 1970).

The key personnel in the stakeholder organisation should be identified. They are the people who make the decisions that directly affect the event. If possible they need to be engaged early in the planning stage or the feasibility stage so that there are clear communication channels when needed.

9.3.2 **Priority and action**

Once the covert and obvious interests of the stakeholders are discovered, the next step is to prioritise the stakeholders and establish how the relationship may change over the event planning cycle. What are the costs and benefits to the event and to the stakeholder? For example, a sponsor may not be a benefit to an event if the cost of servicing the sponsor is greater than the benefit of having one.

Table 9.2 shows a standard project management tool used to analyse the various stakeholders. These types of tables are used at a meeting with the management team as

Table 9.2 Sample of a Stakeholder Classification Table

Stakeholder	Primary or Secondary	Influence on Event	Importance	Stk. Expectations	Impact + or −
Commercial sponsor	Primary/ external	*** 3/5	***** 5/5	• Product placement	+
				• Maximum onsite exposure	+
				• Keeping out competition	−
				• Maximum print PR	+

a way of structuring the discussion and producing a document of the results and the actions required. In other words this is one of the deliverables of the meeting. During the discussion the influence of the stakeholders on the event and importance can be given a five-star score. Their impact may change over the event planning and implementation (this is the *event project life cycle*). It can go from positive to negative with the changes as the event planning and implementation proceeds.

Once the stakeholders have been identified it is necessary to devise a strategy to manage them. This will develop over the life cycle. Some of the stakeholders will require only to be informed, whereas others may need to be included in a partnership with the event — such as the major suppliers. Putting together an action matrix such as Table 9.3 will assist in this process. The event management team can:

Inform — Let the stakeholder know what is happening. It implies little or no input from the stakeholder except where it goes beyond their tolerance level.

Consult — Expect some input from the stakeholder. This may be only in one area of the event management. To consult implies good two-way communication with timely replies. It may mean attendance at meetings.

Partnership — Implies active communication and decision making between the event and the stakeholder. They will be involved in all major decisions and attend all important meetings.

Control — the suppliers will need a different strategy than any of the above. Their involvement needs specification and monitoring. The event staff will also need control.

Stakeholder reviews are an integral part of the ongoing planning. For large or complex events it may be necessary to decide on dates for stakeholder reviews and produce a review document to be sent to the whole event team. These dates may be prior to times of important event decisions, such as the go-no-go decision after the feasibility study. For large events a stakeholder communication plan may be necessary. The plan may include the following:

- Types of reports required — status reports, project review reports and work in progress (WIP)
- When communication is necessary — weekly meeting, core meetings and which groups will attend
- Preferred method of communication — email, telephone, face to face

Table 9.3 Stakeholder Action Matrix

Action Matrix	Inform	Consult	Partnership	Control
Initiation				
Planning				
Implementation				
During event				
Shutdown				

Further analysis can be done using weighted tables whereby the impact on resources and success is quantified. They can also be scored on the degree of difficulty, risks and possible conflicts. A useful figure is found by quantifying the interest the stakeholder has in the event (from -10 to $+10$) and multiplying this by the impact they could have on the event (from 0 to 10). The resultant table of stakeholders enables the event management to have a priority list and develop strategies for management accordingly. Of course, this is unnecessary for many small events. However, it is a useful tool for the large international events.

Table 9.3 helps with the relationship of the event team to the numerous stakeholders. However, one aspect of stakeholder analysis not shown is the *interrelationship* between the stakeholders and how that will impinge on the event. An obvious interrelationship that affects the event is the clash of sponsors. The sponsor of the venue, for example, is in direct competition with the sponsor of the sporting team. Issues, such as stakeholder conflict, can only come to the fore and be pre-empted when the management team understands the attributes of the stakeholders such as their business, trends, competitors and corporate culture. The sponsorship issue is of such great importance for many events it is seen as separate from the management of the other stakeholders.

9.3.3 Stakeholder expectations

Part of the management of the stakeholders is the management of their expectations of the event in the minds of the stakeholders. This may change over time. Setting performance indicators is a method of managing their expectations. They must know what the event sets out to achieve in clear concise objectives. For most events these can be measurable objectives, such as audience numbers, brand exposure, keeping to a budget and economic impact. Some events may have more intangible objectives such as community goodwill or objectives that will not be realised for many years, such as saving an environment or creating a sense of place. Those objective that can be measured must have in place a method of measuring them.

Therefore, the stakeholder management plan has a major influence on the evaluation methodology of the event. How and when the event is evaluated will have to be integrated with the stakeholder reporting plan.

The following question should be asked *what are the costs and benefits to the stakeholder*. This may need research into the interests and trends that will influence the stakeholder. For example, it may be in the political interests for a local council to support the event to show their involvement with the community. Such research will affect how the event management deals with the stakeholder as it will contribute to predicting their behaviour when there are the inevitable changes.

The event team should have a system to identify and control any changes in expectation of the stakeholders. It is not enough to expect the stakeholders to remain dormant once the event starts being organised. This can be called scope change control. There should be a clear mechanism or procedure to make the stakeholders aware that any change may create a large change in the scope of work.

Changes originating from the stakeholders should go through a review system so that the implication of the change is understood by all the parties. For large events such as the Olympics, the World Cup and the World Expo this change control is an essential part of good event management.

The Strengths, Weaknesses, Opportunities and Threats (SWOT) analysis can be used to assess the mutual influence of the stakeholders and the event. The SWOT analysis is used to assist the event management in assessing and forecasting the influence of the stakeholders on the event. External trends — such as the drop in the value of the US dollar or new government tax regulations — could have a significant influence on some of the stakeholders with a flow-on to the event itself.

The largest group of stakeholders for most events is the attendees. They can be variously described as spectators, attendees, the public, participants, audience, ticket holders, or guests depending on the type of event. The management of this group of stakeholders is complex and takes a large part of the event's budget. However, they are often the primary source of the revenue for many events. The stakeholder management used for attendees is proactive. It seeks to manipulate expectation of the attendees prior to the event. This is further explored in the section on marketing. The ability to change expectations and perceptions of the stakeholders is an essential tool in event management.

In a detailed project plan for the east Timor Handover Ceremony, Johnson identified 20 primary stakeholders (Johnson, 2002). These include a large number of international organisations such as the UN, International News Media and Catholic Church. The analysis grouped the numerous sponsors of the ceremony under one category, International Companies. There are only five identified secondary stakeholders — those which will be interested in the event if it passes a threshold of importance. However, these include large complex organisations such as the Indonesian Government and the US Department of State. A large part of the risk in stakeholder management arises from the involvement of vastly different organisational and social cultures. These range from the subsidence farming economy with little infrastructure to the highly technical requirements of the international media companies.

The Olympics is an example of complex stakeholder management handled in a coordinated and systematic way. There are a number of techniques used. The first is to group the stakeholders by their common interests. Forums are set up for the various interest groups such as the media, operations, other events, local authorities and major venues. This fits under a special division called the Stakeholder Coordination. Communication, forums and discussion are vital to this huge undertaking. Issues can be discussed from various angles than just the one stakeholder's impression. Establishing a feeling of team effort and cohesiveness among the stakeholders was regarded as one of the reason for the success of the Olympics.

The grouping of stakeholders can be initiated by the stakeholders as well as by the event team. It can be a strategic management decision by major organisations to create a standard process in order to manage their relationship with a multitude of events. Understanding these processes, codes of conduct or local rules is essential in the feasibility and development of events. The rules and regulations regarding the use of public roads means that the stakeholders for a public event may include the following:

- Local Government Authority
- Insurance Agent
- Police Service
- Road and Traffic Authority

The complexity of the relationships leads the Road and Traffic Authority in a number of countries to publish a traffic management guide for events. The US Department of Transportation manual describes in detail its relationship to the events held within its jurisdiction. The manuals assist the event team with the planning of the events. They start by classifying the event according to its affect on traffic flow. As stated in the introduction of one of the state authority manual:

> Western Australia's vast road network provides the opportunity for organisations and community groups to stage events on roads for the benefit of the public at large. Such events need to be managed in a way that ensures safety for all involved, and minimises disruptions to the normal daily usage and function of our road network.

(Traffic Management for Events Advisory Group, 2008)

Another initiative by primary or key stakeholders is to create the planning pro forma document for the event. Government authorities such as the Liquor Licensing Division produce a planning guide for event managers. These online booklets assist with the planning of the event and help the event team to comply with the requirements of the various legal stakeholders in the event.

National, regional and city governments have entered into this field. There are now numerous event guides available for the event companies. The development and contents of the event guides or event manuals are discussed in detail further in this book. They represent the key stakeholder's attempt to influence the management of the event so that it is a success from their point of view.

These primary resource documents illustrate that many of the stakeholders do not expect to play a passive role in the planning of events. Their requirements are complex and often involve the active participation in the event management decision making in all the phases of the event planning process.

The active involvement of key stakeholders in all phases of the event management leads Johnson to propose a procedure for change during the phases of the East Timor project. He used this as a way to control the numerous changes. The control flowchart is illustrated in Fig. 9.4. However, it is important to note that Johnson mentions that the signoff procedure became too unwieldy when there were any changes. The deadline of the event did not allow this process to be followed as it

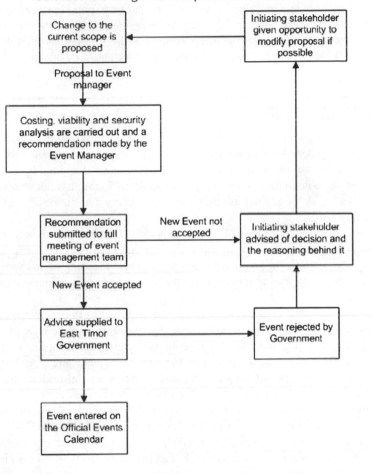

Johnson's change control process for East Timor

FIGURE 9.4

Change control process

neared. As Johnson states in his analysis of the Independence Day Event in East Timor:

> *The UN in general and UNATET itself are highly bureaucratic with a very hierarchical responsibility adverse structure …. On the other hand, an event requires creativity and flexibility*

(Johnson, 2002, p. 1)

In outlining the formal methods of stakeholder management in a complex environment governed by a fixed deadline, informal processes are essential. Too many misunderstandings arise when communication is all done by email and template documents.

Events are unlike many projects in that they can include an enormous number of stakeholders. This is particularly the case with public events. Fortunately in some countries stakeholders, such as the emergency services, traffic authorities and local councils, have got together to make it easier for the event management team to comply with the complexity and ever-changing rules and regulations.

9.4 SPONSORSHIP

A highly developed stakeholder management process description is found in the numerous articles and books on the event sponsors. It represents the most sophisticated example of the current application of process mapping to events. For this reason there is no need to describe it in the detail found in other event manuals and textbooks. A large part of these texts concerns the feasibility of gaining sponsorship.

There are many definitions of an event sponsor. In some countries it means the same as a project sponsor — the organisation that owns the asset, initiates the project and hires the company to produce the asset. A broader meaning of an event sponsor is any investor in the event. In many cases it is used specifically to mean commercial transaction.

The sponsors who provide the finance or defray the costs by providing in-kind services are seen as primary stakeholders. Sponsorship management includes an element of risk management to minimise the uncertainty of event finance.

The number of sponsors for even the smallest event may be huge when compared to other types of projects. A small event in a rural region, the summer games, lists 93 minor sponsors and 12 major sponsors. The latter had in-kind or cash contribution of over $1000. Using the stakeholder classification matrix all these sponsors can be designated as external and primary. They can exert a positive or negative influence on an event. The likelihood of business change occurring to such a large number of sponsors is high and therefore leads to an uncertainty in event finance. Their strategy for risk minimisation is to spread the risk by increasing the number of sponsors.

An important function of event management is the job of seeking and developing sponsorship. Sponsors are often the initiator and client of the event. The event is a part of the marketing strategy of the sponsor. This adds an essential task to the stakeholder flowchart — the development of a sponsorship invitation or proposal. Figure 9.5 illustrates the process involved in this aspect of stakeholder management. Of necessity this is a simplified diagram. Sponsorship management is a highly refined part of event management for some types of events and each one of the boxes in the flowchart calls in numerous tools and techniques.

The monitoring and controlling of the sponsors is the same process in both stakeholder management and sponsor management. One technique employed by event management is to set up levels of sponsorship. This establishes a standard and therefore assists controlling the relationship between the sponsor and the

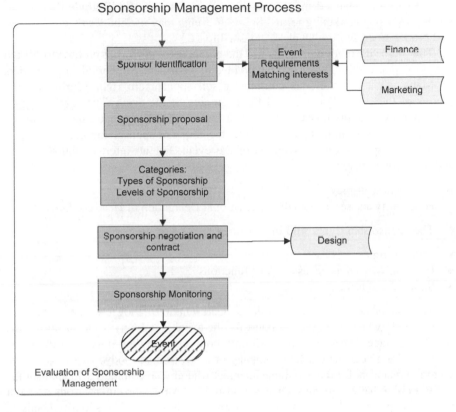

Sponsorship Management Process

FIGURE 9.5

Sponsorship management process

event. The levels of sponsorship are related to the types of sponsorship. The level can be:

- *Naming sponsor* — whose name or logo is used in the event title
- *Programme sponsor* — investing in a part of the event programme, a stage or an act
- *Cosponsor* — shares sponsorship of an area of the event
- *Media sponsor* — generally this is in exchange for media exposure
- *In-kind sponsor* — used to offset the costs of the event

The levels are often set up as part of the theme of the events. For example, the sponsors to a wool exhibition were named according to grades of merino wool such as Strong, Medium, Fine, Superfine and Ultrafine sponsor. The level of sponsorship enables the company to establish an initial commitment to the event while minimising their possible financial exposure. It allows the sponsor to change their level of sponsorship in a planned manner. In many cases the event will grade their sponsorship by using marketing terms. Sporting events may use the terms *gold, silver,* and *bronze* to signify the level of sponsorship.

The major international events use the competitive tendering process to fill the levels of sponsorship. They are often divided into Partners, Supported and Providers

Many event organisations continually sell sponsorship rights during all the phases of the event planning until the beginning of the event. The level of sponsorship allows the organisation to control the sometimes dramatic increase in the number of sponsors in this area. A further technique of sponsorship management is to offer the sponsorship of sections of the event. For an international event the sponsors were offered:

- Pyrotechnic display
- Hospitality and services to the International Delegation of Heads of Government

The sponsorship rights sold included:

- Naming rights
- Hospitality, such as access to VIP functions
- Signage and banners

Many sponsors will not commit to the event until they are sure it will be a success. In which case, their support for the event is unlikely to occur during the feasibility stage. Other sponsors will only commit once they have seen the event endorsed by a large established company or a government body. This leads to the common quandary for the event management whereby no company will sponsor the event until other companies have sponsored it. An endorsement from a major politician, prince, VIP or celebrity can provide the security a sponsor needs to become involved. It explains why an inordinate amount of time is spent by senior event managers courting politicians. Once they have endorsed the event, the sponsors will commit. There tends to be a last minute scramble for sponsorship when an event looks like it will work.

Partnering is the most involved form of sponsorship. Partnering has the advantage of employing the sponsor's resources, such as marketing, accounting and legal services as well as cash. It may imply that the partner will co-own the event. Media, loyalty programmes and telecommunication partners can significantly reduce the cost of promotion. Airline loyalty programmes, such as Skywards with over 4 million members, reach enormous number of potential customers. By partnering with a mobile phone provider a Short Message Service (SMS) campaign can be launched. If the sponsor is a large company or government organisation, the employees of the sponsor can make up a significant number of ticket sales.

The tools of partnering and establishing various levels of sponsorship can be regarded as a strategy to minimise uncertainty in finances. In most events there is no freeze on selling sponsorship. It continued throughout the event planning, during the event and, in some cases, sponsorship was sold after the events for the products of the event such as videos and mementoes.

Event management entails complex relationships with multiple stakeholders. The use of requirements analysis is not sufficient to establish a stable setting in which to deliver an event. The number of stakeholders will change over the project and the intangible nature of the product result in an ever changing and uncertain project environment. Even the simplest event will have multiple stakeholders. The influence of the stakeholders will be felt on the event throughout the phases of the project. Each event attendee is a stakeholder and their objectives and requirements may be unique, changing and intangible. Event management uses tools to reduce the resulting uncertainty. Marketing is used to group, influence and manage the changing requirements of the attendees. Event management has developed sophisticated tools to assist with the management of sponsors. These tools include sponsorship development, marketing, promotion and the manipulation of stakeholder requirements.

9.5 EVENT DESIGN

Event design is defined as purposeful arrangement of elements of an event to maximise the positive impression on the attendees and other key stakeholders. Therefore, it solely concerns the event itself. The term is generally used in conjunction with the object of the design process such as lighting design, décor design and site design. Design has artistic and creative inputs. The design process is illustrated in Fig. 9.6.

The areas of event management involved in the design process are as follows:

- Staging and production — including the elements of staging such as lighting, sound, catering
- Site/venue location and layout
- Theatrical considerations including the look of the event
- Event programme or content
- Wow factor — or unique experience by the attendees

The diagram is highly simplified. It shows the inputs to the design process coming primarily from the marketing and the stakeholder requirements and expectations. The outputs are the programme or schedule of the event, the site or venue plan and the production or staging plan. These will be inputs to the procurement process.

9.5.1 Site/venue location and layout

Site or venue choice and layout are essential elements in event success. It is as important as programming and the layout is integral to the 'wow' factor. The choice of the site crosses all the areas of event management. The site choice involves input from the stakeholders such as the sponsors. The site choice will be influenced by, and has an influence on, the risk management decisions and marketing. However, the site choice reflects one of the fixed deliverables of the event management process. Once the site has been selected it will remain fixed, in a similar way, the date is fixed. For

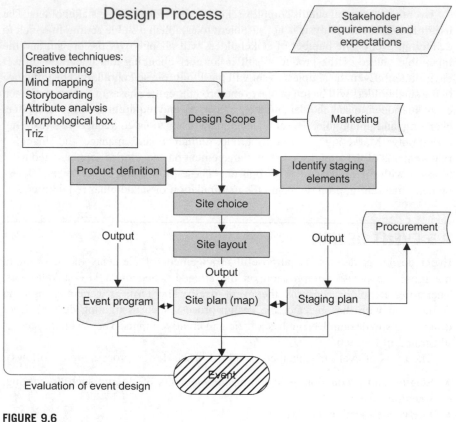

FIGURE 9.6

Event design process

this reason the constraints of the site are integral to any decision in other areas of event management. Some of the large events prefer to construct the site, in which case the event becomes part of a much larger project that includes construction and other aspects of civil engineering. The result is an interface of two projects. Figure 10.7 (Chapter 10) contains the site choice flowchart. Once the decision has been committed to, the design of the layout of the site becomes the major way to minimise risks. The site moves from a variable in the marketing mix to a parameter.

The changes in marketing will have a significant influence on the design of the layout of the event. The financial penalty for changing a venue is a major incentive to minimise any changes.

9.5.2 Programming and the programme

Programming is the core of the design process. It originates from the definition of the actual event. It is the creative process that blends many elements into an attractive event. The programme is the deliverable of the programming process. It is, according to Don Getz 'both the substance of the event and the way in which it is scheduled and produced' (Getz, 1997, p. 159). Therefore, the deliverable is the schedule of the event itself. It is an output of the product definition and lists what is on at the event and when it occurs. The programme includes arranging the elements to create maximum impact on the audience.

Design and its effect on the attendees illustrate the intangible and ephemeral nature of the core of the event. For many events the audience reaction of surprise or wonder is the goal of the event.

The problem with a high-level process chart such as Figure 9.6 is that it does not show the creative thought that goes into design. It is well to remember that the process mapping of competent event management is only a model — it is an approximation. Of necessity there are intangible aspects that are very important but cannot be simplified into a process diagram. Also there are microprocesses with a huge effect on the audience or attendees' experiences that are hidden in the master process diagram. For this reason this book does not attempt to describe creativity.

9.6 MARKETING PROCESS

A schema of the marketing process is illustrated in Fig. 9.7.

Marketing an event concerns increasing the probability of its success. In the first part a marketing strategy will assist in the feasibility of the event. Once it is decided to proceed with the event, marketing will assist in the ongoing development of the event. Marketing is not only list of tools and techniques adapted to the event environment but it also has input into the design of the event.

Unlike other areas of event development and management, marketing an event has a long list of studies, report and textbooks devoted to it. In part this is because many events and festivals are part of a marketing mix for a company, government or destination. It is one of the tools to assist in marketing a product. This section will overview some of the tools.

A large part of marketing an event is taken up with aligning the event experience with the needs and wishes of the attendees. This may be difficult when the events purpose may be to introduce a new experience to the attendees. The event experience is a combination of the programme, service and other elements of the event design. The simplified process illustrated in Fig. 9.7 is an outline of this. Marketing of some events can be highly complex. Many events are part of a more general marketing strategy of an organisation. Tourism events are often regarded as primarily a branding exercise.

The core of the marketing process is understanding the target market and it is fundamental to the event feasibility. Whether the event will work or not will depend on this. Hence, it is not uncommon to find events organised by a team who are part of that market segment. The World Cup, Grand Prix and music concerts are mostly managed by people who are immersed in their event. They know their target market

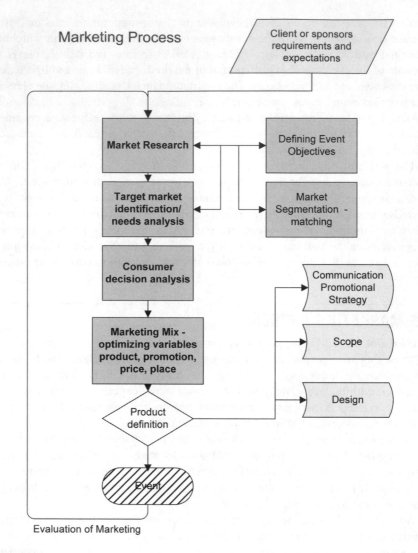

Marketing Process

Client or sponsors requirements and expectations

Market Research

Defining Event Objectives

Target market identification/ needs analysis

Market Segmentation - matching

Consumer decision analysis

Communication Promotional Strategy

Marketing Mix - optimizing variables product, promotion, price, place

Scope

Design

Product definition

Event

Evaluation of Marketing

FIGURE 9.7

Marketing process

as they are part of it and mix with them constantly. Their market research can often be asking their friends if they would attend the event and how can they develop it to make it more attractive. In an age of limitless surveys and feedback forms, there may be a major risk in planning an event based only on the results of market surveying. The difficulty in applying marketing theory to events is because the event is not experienced until the person attends the event. Unlike a product that can be tested or a theatre production that friends can try out, events are paid for and then experienced. The product has to be sold on its potential to give an intangible experience. It makes the marketing of some events highly important. The promotion side of the marketing can be the difference between success and failure. The name for an event managers/producer in the music industry was *promoter*. Much of their time was spent on this process with sophisticated feedback mechanism to make sure the promotion was working long before the event occurs. The quality of the brand of a repeat event and that of the event team is important in predicting the quality of the event for the stakeholders prior to the event.

The quality of the event as experienced by the attendees is essential to its development and sustainability. The expected quality of the programme and the service will be a function of the target market. The event team must be careful about applying the theory of needs analysis to events. It can be far too simplistic for event management. The stakeholder's needs are many, varied and may change over time. There may be a large number of people who attend the event and those who witness it through the media. Each attendee can have quite a different set of motivators for being attracted to the event. Once again the collection of characteristics constituting the market segmentation can assist in this process. The expectation of the event can influence the target market and change their motivation and expectations.

The alternative to using the needs analysis of the key stakeholders is to compare the quality of the event to an external standard. Currently, there are no government endorsed standards for the event industry. Some event industry associations have created certification programmes such as 'Certified Special Events Professional' of the International Special Events Society (ISES) and the 'Accredited Member MIAA' of the Meetings Industry Association of Australia (MIAA). As described elsewhere in this book there are industry awards programmes such as International Festivals & Events Association awards and ISES awards recognising excellence in their member's events and event-related products. Some governments have investigated licensing events and event companies to guarantee quality of the event.

Market segmentation involves discovering the needs and motivators of the customer and is the major focus of event marketing. For events that have a large customer base, such as public events, there are a number of tools to do this. Maslow's theory of a hierarchy of needs can be adapted to the event environment. Market research techniques are used to match the event product to the needs of the market. The event marketer should understand the motivational needs of the target market.

The research may be part of the event feasibility study and therefore performed during the initiation phase of the event project life cycle. In this way the marketing process begins in the initiation phase and forms part of the scope and product definition.

Market segmentation is the division of the potential market into groups with common characteristics and can be utilised in the event marketing. It facilitates the management of the event marketing through clustering of audience characteristics.

Market segmentation assessment results are transformed into the event objectives. It is recommended that these objectives be defined using the Specific, Measurable, Agreeable, Realistic and Time (SMART) criteria. The SMART objectives

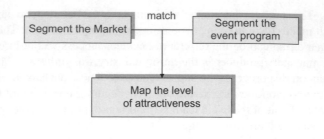

FIGURE 9.8

Matching segments

combined with the characteristics of the segments of the market may be used as a measure to assess the quality of the event. The SMART criteria may be seen as a method of reducing the uncertainty inherent in the needs analysis process in a complex environment. As stated many times in this book, the limitation of the *event management by objectives* is due to the changing event environment and the influence of the deadline. The changing event environment, such as extra sponsors, new opportunities for promotion, legislation, competition for other events and changes in the objectives of the stakeholders will reduce the efficacy of the original event objectives. The absolute deadline does not allow time for the whole needs assessment process to be repeated. Therefore, both these factors, which are common in event management, will result in the objectives becoming irrelevant to the new conditions.

There is a well-developed body of knowledge on the creation and development of products that can be employed in the event field. An analysis matrix is a good way to assess the attractiveness of each part of the event programme. The process to create it is illustrated in Fig. 9.8.

Table 9.4 shows a simple example of a water festival with many elements. It is very easy to get carried away with one aspect of the event and forget about the low profile aspects. According to one event company the success of their huge dance

Table 9.4 Sample of Matching Segments

	Canoe Race	Symposium	Concert	DINNER AND AWARDS	Dance	Water Circus
Academics		xxxxx		xx		
Youth	xxxx		xxx		xxxx	xx
Young families	xxx		xxx			xxxxx
VIP/ politicians	xxx	xxx		xxxxx		
Press	xxxxx	xx		xxx		xxx

parties was because they built a silence room where the people who did not want to hear music could go and relax. An international conference that ignores the accompanying persons programme will quickly loose their attendees. Table 9.4 rates the segment match for a public awareness event concerning the environmental health of a major river. It shows that the symposium is of major interest to the academics and of little or no interest to the youth. For large repeat events the table can be quite complex.

9.6.1 Marketing mix

An important tool in events feasibility and development is the marketing mix .The marketing mix is a group of marketing variables that can be altered and controlled so the event achieves its objectives. The aim of event marketing is to optimise these variables. The marketing variables included in most event texts are as follows:

- *Product* — all the elements that make up the event
- *Price* — the value of the event to the consumer
- *Promotion* — marketing communication between the consumers and the event
- *Place* — location of the event and the point of ticket purchase

Others identify further variables such as people, programming and partnerships.

The product, the event, is therefore a variable and part of the marketing mix. The event is both intangible and changing in response to marketing. The marketing mix will be optimised during the event planning. The event programme and design is a variable, created and developed by its own marketing. This degree of uncertainty means that the risk management model can be employed.

A number of marketing tools are used to reduce the product uncertainty. In particular, the Boston Consulting Group Matrix for product division is employed. The outcome is a product analysis of the event portfolio. The Ansoff matrix is utilised to create a strategy for marketing.

The marketing mix is a predictive control tool for event and management definition by reducing the uncertainty inherent in a changeable and intangible product. Marketing has primary inputs into the event design process. It is also a risk management technique to reduce the uncertainty related to sponsorship, financial management and stakeholder management. Marketing can also be viewed as a feedforward control mechanism, whereby the product is designed to fit into the results of the marketing process.

9.6.2 Promotion

The promotion variable of the marketing mix is a way to manipulate the customer's expectations. In part it is a risk management strategy so the expectations will be satisfied. This makes promotions a proactive tool in event management, rather than a responsive tool. It is used to create a desire and thrill for the event. Colloquially known as 'building the vibe'. The vibe is the feeling among the target market of the event as being an important experience and one 'not to miss'. It is a delicate concept and can quickly dissipate. The use of Twitter, Facebook groups, online banners and other Web 3 tools is an example of trying to create a vibe. Once again this demonstrates that creativity and innovation are at the heart of event management. The ability to build the vibe is highly creative. It rarely works if it is templated or copied from previous events.

Event promotions must be able to respond quickly to changing conditions and recognise promotional opportunities. There are deadlines within a promotion campaign. The promotion campaign becomes a subproject within the larger event planning with inputs into the event design.

Event evaluation is regarded as part of event marketing, as it primarily concerns itself with evaluating the customer experience. It is a feedback device and important part of continuous improvement for repeat events.

Event marketing is one of the key knowledge areas and a process carried out to align the event with the needs and motivators of the attendees. It is achieved by optimising the variables of the marketing mix of product, promotion, place and price. One of these variables concerns the ability to change the perceptions of the attendees through promotion. The marketing process then is a method to reduce the inherent uncertainty in events. It inputs into all other areas of event management and is a fundamental agent of change and development during the event project life cycle.

9.7 FINANCIAL PROCESS

Events are an expense. The outlay for some international events is measured in billions of dollars. It may be hidden by capital expenditure on infrastructure. For some events this spend of money is rapid and occurs long before the event and the incoming finance is not immediate. It gives a different set of priorities to the every day financial processes found in the day-to-day business of companies. For events, all incoming and expenses have a value that is dependent on time.

One of the important functions of event management is sourcing, monitoring and reporting on the event finance, i.e. revenue or in-kind cost reduction. The incoming finance may not be a fixed entity decided upon or agreed upon during the initiation phase. The event revenue may come from a constant stream such as ticket sales or in sudden spurts due to sponsors joining the event. Figure 9.9 illustrates the financial management process for events.

9.7.1 Revenue

The sources of revenue for an event are numerous including:

- Clients
- Ticket sales or related attendance fees
- Selling advertising

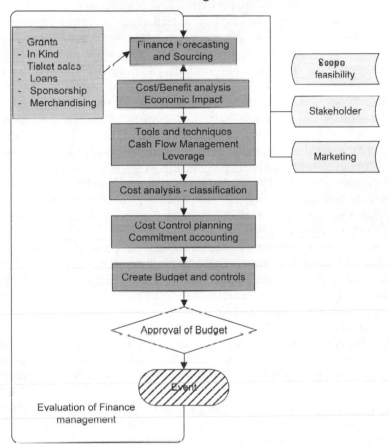

Financial Management Process

- Grants
- In Kind
- Ticket sales
- Loans
- Sponsorship
- Merchandising

Finance Forecasting and Sourcing

Cost/Benefit analysis Economic Impact

Tools and techniques Cash Flow Management Leverage

Cost analysis - classification

Cost Control planning Commitment accounting

Create Budget and controls

Approval of Budget

Event

Evaluation of Finance management

Scope feasibility

Stakeholder

Marketing

FIGURE 9.9

Financial management process

- Fundraising
- Sponsorship
- In-kind assistance
- Merchandising
- Selling exhibition space
- Food and beverage sales
- Government grants
- Broadcasting
- Other onsite revenue such as auctions and competitions

Some of these revenue sources such as ticket sales and merchandise are directly proportional to the number and type of the event demographic. A fact well known to fundraising events as they closely monitor their target market. Most of the other revenue sources are indirectly related to the level of attendance.

In many events, the revenue and cost reduction are sought by the event team during all the phases of the event management. This may include finance gained after the event has occurred, as part of the shutdown procedure and recouping costs from faulty suppliers. The uncertainty with the incoming is reflected in the uncertainty with the outgoing, that is, the cost of the event. Income is regarded as a variable by some of the events and for others it is a fixed budget. One of the advantages of working for a corporate client is often the budget is fixed and the arduous work of 'finding the money' is not necessary.

The tactic in finding finance is to estimate the core income and look for ancillary income. The event team needs to be constantly aware of methods to reduce costs should the necessity arise. The level of uncertainty needs to be established so that a dynamic costing system can be used. Incremental planning or taking it one step at a time, such as that recommended for software projects, is one solution to the problem of uncertainty in income.

For some types of events, such as fundraisers, the event itself is the main source of finance. The amount to spend on the event is fluid. The budget is used only as a guide. The importance of special events in fundraising is indicated by their cost–benefit ratio of 0.5. The benefits have to be estimated so that the scope of the event can reflect the ratio. This introduces the concept of value of the event to the participant/attendee.

The value of the event to the attendee must reflect the expected common value of the equivalent cost. In general, this implies that an increase in the number of attendees requires more of the incoming revenue to be spent on the event experience. The ability to forecast attendee numbers at many events is highly specialised and is discussed in the section on predicting crowd numbers further in this book. Predicting the number of people coming to an event is an essential part of revenue and cost estimation. In such a situation changes in the budget are inevitable.

9.7.2 **Pricing the ticket or entrance fee**

The revenue for some events will depend on the effectiveness of ticket pricing. The price is a variable of the marketing mix. The price of the tickets is difficult to set when the event is unique. The value of the event to the attendees is not evident until after the event is experienced. This leads to a situation of selling a product that cannot be described as it has not occurred. Just as giving away the plot of a thriller novel would defeat the purpose of reading it. Setting the price of the ticket is a highly skilled mix of science and art. The implications of a tiny mistake in the price are huge as it is caused by the amplification through large numbers. In other words if the ticket price is too low the event will make a loss and if it is too high the event will make a loss due to lack of sales.

At first it seems that the price of the ticket, conference registration or entry should be set to cover the cost of the event averaged over the number of tickets.

However, the costs of some events can vary or may not be completely confirmed until after the ticket price is set. The number of tickets sold can vary, which makes it impossible to average the cost. This is where experience in the industry counts. The number of variables is enormous and the event team cannot afford to make a mistake. To illustrate this consider a conference dinner with a number of keynote speakers and entertainment. If the *covering cost* model is used then it must be assumed that when the price of the ticket is set the event team knows all the costs as well as all the in-kind sponsorships and other incoming finances. The ticket price will have to be set before any publicity is sent out. This leads to the all too common problem of deadlines not being met. It is in the interest of the headline acts, for example, to delay signing the contract as 'something better may come up'. Also, in most cases, the event team would be foolish to stop looking for incoming finance just because the ticket price has been set. Covering the cost of the event is indeed one of the considerations when deciding the entry price — but it is only one.

The next theory of pricing says that the ticket price should be 'what the market will bear'. This is discovered by comparing the event with similar events and using the same ticket price. The target market should be clearly defined for this to occur. The ticket for a concert by a hip hop star would be priced according to what the target market will pay. The ticket price would be similar to comparable events for that type of audience. The problem with comparative pricing occurs when the event is unique and cannot really be compared with other events. For example, the event used in Table 9.4, a public awareness event about the importance of rivers to the national environment. The event includes a concert, a symposium and a canoe journey down a river. This event is unique and attractive. But it makes the price of the registration or ticket fee difficult to set. It is an important rule of thumb in events that the more unique the event, the more risky is the finance and yet the more the event can attract promotion. This problem is common with the release of highly secret innovative products such as a mobile phone with new features. The buyers cannot be sure of the value of the product until they have bought it. Experiential marketing is a response to the problem of selling innovative products. At an experiential marketing event, the attendee has an opportunity to try the product.

The event management team when pricing the ticket, registration or entry for events has a number of techniques to maximise the income. Many of these will depend on the target market. Some segments of the market will expect different types of pricing. Having only the one price ticket may actually reduce the sales.

Flat rate pricing is the fee paid for event entry or registration and includes all the extras such as food, accommodation, transport and all the entertainment. The product is bundled together and the one price is given for it all.

The unbundling of a price is a method of increasing income by charging for aspects of the event previously included in the entry price. The tolerance of the attendees to suddenly charging for what was once 'free' can be a problem. Charging for extra services, shows or areas within the event is a common method to obtain income.

It is common for some events to charge a ticket price so the crowd numbers can be controlled. This is not primarily as a source of income. One major public event, a firework display, decided to charge for entrance as the crowd numbers were unpredictable. The organisers erected fencing to control the entrance to the area and had ticket collectors and extra security. They decided to charge a minimal amount to cover the fencing and the overheads. They were widely criticised in the press for charging for public events. However, the event still attracted many thousands of people and made a large surplus. The surplus was then used to improve the quality of the event in the next year.

Exhibit 9.1 shows some ideas for generating extra income suggested by many event organisers around the world.

EXHIBIT 9.1 TIPS FROM THE FRONTLINE: FINDING EXTRA MONEY

Brochures – selling programme
Merchandise – caps T-shirts, glow sticks
Valet parking
VIP service – host and sitting area
Picnic hampers
Catering stands
Exotic services – henna, fortune telling
Massages
Bean bag rental
Charge for transport
Rights to CD/DVD
DVD of event – highlight
Selling database
Photo 'I was at the.....'
VIP/corporate boxes
Bid for best seats
Selling advertising on screen
Advertising on brochures
Charity auction – post-event
VIP dinner with main star
Raffle prizes
SMS campaign
SMS to screen at the event
Media rights
Running promotion before the event to make money
Scaling sponsorship
Advertisements in the bathrooms
Rented kiosks

Tickets scales – different price
Selling the land after the event
Selling the management system
Shisha corner
Kids corner
Rides and races – camel, horse, goat
Face painting
Gaming zones
Exhibition such as photography for sale
Paid workshops
Create special offers – spend a day with the star entertainer
Percentage of sales onsite
Stars can donate goods for sale or auction

The correct pricing for the ticket or registration is vital to many events. Too high and the audience does not buy, too low and there may be a loss. As pointed out by numerous studies summarised by William Poundstone in his book 'Pricing' (Poundstone, 2010), it is not the absolute amount that will determine if people will buy a ticket. He explains the concept of anchoring applied to a concert tickets, whereby people use the most expensively priced ticket to judge which level of ticket they will purchase. By changing different levels of price or scaling the tickets there was an increase in sale of the midrange-priced tickets.

Special events often use the implied fear of 'missing out' to sell tickets. If the event is highly innovative and the market is tentative about buying tickets, the event organisers will emphasise that anyone who does not buy a ticket will miss out on this unique event. This can influence the buying decision of the market. It illustrates that price is closely connected to promotion for many events.

A problem for the development of events in one country was a population who expects all public events to be free of charge. They expect the government to pay for everything. In the past, from car rally to public concerts, the audience never had to pay. These were a gift from the government to the people. One characteristic of money is that it indicates what people want. Money can be seen as a feedback mechanism. It allows the organisers to understand whether aspects of the event or the event itself are worth the expense. Without this information the spending of money provides, it is difficult to improve the quality of the event to fit the target market. In the country with free events, people travelled to other countries as their events were of higher quality. They were quite willing to pay for events in neighbouring countries. The solution was to gradually change the audience's expectation by introducing new higher quality elements to the events and charging an entrance fee to these elements. For example, at the car rally a VIP area was created with a ticket price. The extra money was used to improve this aspect of the event.

9.7.3 **Revenue and resources**

Resource planning will relate directly to revenue planning. The amount and timing of incoming revenue will be reflected in contracting the suppliers. In some cases the event will reduce the need for finance by offsetting cost through in-kind sponsorship. Sponsors will not be involved in the event until it has reached a level of importance and looks like being a success. Figure 9.10 illustrates the flow-on affect of the inability to estimate attendance numbers.

The uncertainty in the number of attendees will create an uncertainty in revenue. This will flow-on to the availability of funds for procurement and what facilities will be used for the event. Procurement uncertainty will affect the programme of event and the site layout. The marketing of the event may need to change to increase audience numbers.

This can be readily illustrated by a statement from the past Olympics. The Olympics is a highly refined event, repeated over many years, with numerous test events and complete government support. Even such a unique event has uncertainty with regard to revenue sources:

> *From early 2000, due to declining income projections, it was evident SOCOG would face substantial risks pending the early success of ticketing campaigns. By June 2000, it was evident that underwriting of SOCOG's budget would be necessary if the quality of the Games were to be maintained at the highest level.*
> **(SOCOG, 2001; Official Report of the XXVII Olympiad 2001, pg001778.htm)**

A further area of uncertainty in revenue and cost estimating arises when approximating the work of staff if they are volunteers. Without an extensive training session, such as provided by the Olympics and other major sporting events, the value of the work by volunteers is difficult to estimate. There is a different attitude with regard to finances as their motivation is not financial.

There are a variety of event management techniques to control the revenue. Such as:

1. Presales of tickets for public events, preregistration for conferences and exhibitions and ticket scaling

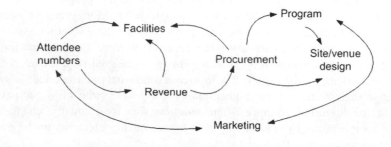

FIGURE 9.10

Influence of attendee numbers

2. Increasing number of sponsors and levels of sponsorship leverage of current sponsorship
3. Alternative onsite sources of revenue such as broadcast rights, merchandising
4. Sale of secondary event products, post-event auction
5. Consolidating all sales
6. Event programme sensitivity analysis to identify area of savings
7. Well-publicised public profile to attract further sponsorship

The last minute purchase of tickets, registering for a conference or accepting an invitation has become a major problem in recent years. As a result it is difficult to forecast tickets sales and therefore revenue. It is partially the result of a policy by some companies of cancelling the events such as seminars if the ticket sales have not reached a certain level by a specific date. Event companies, in the music industry, for example, will also put on extra events if the ticket are over sold or drop the price if it is undersold. The best strategy for the ticket buyer is to wait until the last minute to purchase the ticket. This is a positive loop and leads to more uncertainty of income.

Figure 9.11 illustrates a summary of the recommended process of event budgeting through financial management.

As mentioned in the section on stakeholders, there is an enormous body of work on sponsorship. An event sponsorship agreement can range from a detailed cost–benefit analysis prepared for the sponsor and presented at the right time in the sponsor's business cycle to a simple handshake over dinner. Despite that, it is the author's experience that many event managers regard sponsorship as 'free money'. As far as this section is concerned it is one of the inputs into the financial process. It is well to remember that most major sponsors have a highly in-tune marketing department constantly looking for suitable events to sponsor. The quality of the event, its longevity and the competency of the event organisers as well as the target market are important to most sponsors. The possible risks at an event due to

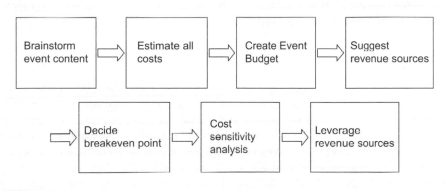

FIGURE 9.11

Budget process

incompetence of the management can be a large disincentive for a sponsor to be involved. Although sponsors would like their name associated with people celebrating, they do not want it associated with disasters.

The management of the sponsorship and the relationship between the event and the sponsor is an important part of financial management. The techniques range from distributing the risk, such as seeking a number of sponsors, to cash flow planning. Setting up levels of sponsorship, as described, is a technique for managing the sponsor—event relationship. It can be viewed as a risk management strategy to minimise the event exposure to financial risk.

The management of sponsors will have input from the other areas of event management. In particular, the marketing and stakeholder management will significantly interact with the sponsor management.

Raising the public profile of the event may be part of the event planning and will be developed while other areas of management are being implemented. The result is that sponsors can commit to the event at anytime.

9.7.4 Cash flow

The management of the cash flow is an essential skill in event management because money has a time value. As the project moves towards the deadline, cash is often used to speed up the tasks and patch up any problems. There may be multiple sources of income and the timing of the payments may be distributed over the whole planning and implementation. If the event income is directly dependent on a variable such as the attendees, commitment by sponsors or exhibition space sold, then the breakeven point must be established. Reaching the breakeven point becomes a milestone in the lead up to the event. The breakeven point has a time component. The breakeven point is an indicator for the event team of the success or otherwise of the promotion for an event. An exhibition, conference or concert that depends on the sale of tickets or registration will be focused on the date when they reach the breakeven point. On that date the event company starts to make a profit. Unlike the two-dimensional chart used in business, the breakeven chart for an event has three axes: amount, number of ticket sales and time.

9.7.5 Cost

Event cost is estimated through quotes and expert judgment. Zero-based budgets or 'starting with nothing' are common with special events. Estimation of the costs becomes more accurate as the event and the scope of work become more defined. The initial cost estimates can vary up to plus or minus 50% as the event may require special resources. Event cost estimation often uses parametric methods such as cost per head for conferences or cost per square metre for exhibitions. In this way the costs can be directly related to the essential event variable. The variable may also correspond to the event revenue. Thus revenue for a festival will increase with ticket sales, as will the cost.

Cost planning uses cost classification as a method of predicting, monitoring and controlling costs. Event costs are divided into direct or indirect, unique or standard, fixed or variable, onetime or recurring. This classification assist in forecasting costs as it helps dividing the costs according to their accuracy.

Due to the fixed deadline and possible changes in scope, the time of estimating will make a difference to the degree of accuracy of estimating. The cost of marketing to gain sponsorship is an example of this.

The intangible results of an event, such as marketing, raising awareness of issues, cultural enhancement and political impact can mean that the financial aspects of the event are secondary to these results. That is, the money can always be found. Hence, the strategic objectives of the event can have significant influence on the more measurable cost and income of the event. To emphasise the wider impact of events the term *triple bottom line* (*TBL*) has been used. It is important to include the social, environmental and the economic effects, the TBL leaves out the important measure for many events, the political effect.

9.7.6 **Pricing the event management services**

Part of the feasibility process is working on 'how much to charge' for the event management service. There are three pricing models:

- Fixed fee
- Incentive fee
- Percentage of cost fee

The fixed fee is an amount given to the event company to produce the event or after all the costs of the event are met by the client. In latter case it is called cost plus fixed fee. The client must be aware that the cost of the event should be monitored. There are many opportunities for the event company to obtain favours and kick backs from the suppliers. This practice is more widespread than is supposed and should be referred to in the engagement contract between the event company and the client. It is only with experience that an event team can work out a realistic fixed fee. They compare the event to similar ones they have managed in the past. They have a good idea of what factors significantly contribute to the cost of the event. Developing the draft project plan with its WBS, tasks and schedule, as demonstrated in the Chapter 8 on *the management framework as a spreadsheet*, will assist in estimating the fee.

The incentive fee is a variable amount based on the success of the event. For this to occur the success must be measurable. The number of tickets sold to the event is an example. The number and size of the exhibitions are another.

Percentage of cost is perhaps the most common for private event companies. The company is given a fixed amount, sometimes called the budget. Most companies will charge between 10 and 30% of the cost depending on their workload.

An event company new to the field will use *entry pricing*. They decide what the standard market price for an event management service is and charge less so they can gain the work and build a reputation in the industry. Other event companies use project pricing. It employs cost per hour and task analysis to estimate the cost. The more sophisticated companies will use the concept of added value as a way to estimate the fee. The event company estimates the value the event will give to the client. Using the asset management concept described in this text, the event is assessed on its potential ROI to the host or client. The ROI gives a measure to the value of the event to the client. For example, an experiential marketing event for a car that involves attendees driving the cars through a maze with prizes. If successful it will result in an increase in sales and brand recognition. If the outcome is estimated it gives the value of the event to the client. A percentage of the value to the client is charged as the fee for developing and managing the event. The advantage of this type of pricing the fee is that it begins the contract negotiation with the value to the client. Underpricing and overpricing lead to a series of problems. Underpricing ultimately results in too much work being done or a loss of quality and the loss of talented staff. Value pricing forces the event company to understand exactly what type of expertise they are selling.

As well as the three pricing models there is the reality of 'spending the lot'. If the event company is given a fixed amount they may set out spending it all on the event regardless of the other outcomes. The recent excesses of a number of international companies during the credit induced boom of the late 2000s produced a spate of extravagant events such as corporate parties and end of year functions. The types of events were reminiscent of the extravagance of the Roman Empire and interestingly the toga party was one of the themes of the corporate events. Such excessiveness comes under the term unjust enrichment. It occurs when the event company knows they are being paid far above the ethical fee.

CONCLUSION

Understanding and setting up a management framework is essential for the feasibility of an event, for the development of the event and ultimately the development of an events portfolio. The event industry around the world has matured to the level where we can establish a model for best practice. The model chosen by this book is the process model. Taken from the numerous theories and working models of business process management and workflows and combining this with the model proposed by the EMBOK, each of the areas of management can be described. This chapter summarized the processes involved in the areas of scope, stakeholder, marketing, design and finance. Some of these area, such as marketing and sponsorship are very well covered in numerous other textbooks. Other area such as stakeholder management and pricing are covered in more detail. The aim is to produce an over all process model and each of these processes must be summarized. The essential skill of creativity or innovation was not described as it is in doubt whether a textbook such as this can really do it justice. The next chapter continues with this process model.

DISCUSSION TOPICS

Research other models of management and discuss their applicability to events. For example the event management may be viewed from the perspective of risk management, project management or arts management.

Scope creep is a reality in event management. Find examples of this in major sporting events and discuss how it can be contained and if it can be used as an opportunity.

Stakeholder management even for the simplest events such as a wedding is a complex issue. Can it be achieved through requirement analysis? Are there other ways to minimise the management time spent on this process. Can leadership and ethical outcomes be employed to keep control of the stakeholders?

Sponsorship may be a cultural issue. Research the use of this term around the world. Does it mean the same in democratic countries as in socialist or guided economies?

The processes outlined in this chapter have different priorities according to the type of event. Design, for example, is essential to the corporate dinner. Using the typology of events discuss the relative importance of each of the processes.

Fashion Parade, Uganda. Courtesy of Peter Kagwa, Events Warehouse

2010 Queen's Baton Relay, Swaziland. Courtesy of Maxxam Events International

Event management processes — section two

INTRODUCTION

Continuing to map the processes in the event management model, this chapter explores the all important time management process. The deadline is one of the defining characteristics of event management and it influences every decision made by the event team. The process of risk management is so fundamental to events that it is only mentioned when looking at safety or finance. Risk management is performed on every aspect of the event planning and implementation. It is generally called making sure there are no problems. Event managers are excellent procurers. They have to source everything for lap laps to satellite dishes. Event managers are expert communicators as they are constantly talking, emailing or reporting. The communication process is essential because events are about people. They can be paid staff, volunteers, friends, truck drivers, IT engineers, cleaners, politicians, clients and attendees. This chapter investigates all of these, as an understanding of the processes is fundamental to decide if events are feasible and can be developed.

10.1 TIME MANAGEMENT PROCESS

Scheduling with the deadline in mind is a core to event management. All the processes including finance, marketing, logistics are dependent on time. This process and the risk management process directly touch on almost all areas of event management. It is made up of the tools and techniques of identification of activities and their optimal sequencing to produce and control the schedule. The management of time for events is one of emphasis and priorities and using the standard tools and techniques of scheduling in a dynamic and often uncertain setting. The scheduling of an event includes what occurs at the event in the form of the event programme and the production of the programme. The latter is represented by the production schedule comprising the supporting activities of the programme, such as the catering, audio—visual and security.

The fact of the immoveable deadline means the planning process must begin by setting the date of the event and work backwards to establish the timelines. The complexity of such formal time and task analysis means the weekly meetings and informal communication take on a special importance as it needs constant readjustment. It is rare that the scheduling can be simply set and all the tasks accomplished as per the schedule.

Figure 10.1 illustrates the time management process used in management of events.

Events Feasibility and Development. DOI: 10.1016/B978-0-7506-6640-4.10010-X

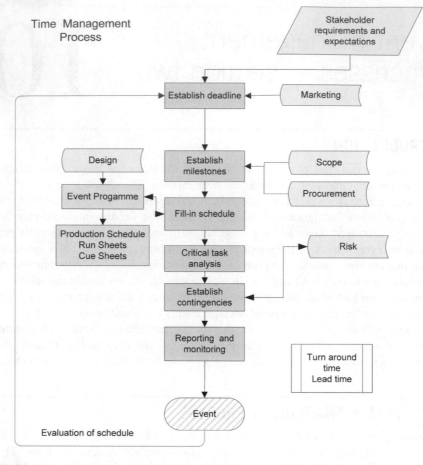

FIGURE 10.1

Time management process

The direct input to the process is from the stakeholder requirements, in particular, the client and the attendee expectations. Marketing will assist in the decision on the deadline date of the event. The scheduling of the tasks will be initially determined by the design of the event in particular the content of the event. There are inputs from the scope and procurement processes. The tasks will be scheduled back from the date of the event. Critical tasks are identified by combination of the inputs from scope and procurement with input from the risk process. The risk process will assist establishing the milestones and the time contingency such as buffers. When the changes occur, they will be assessed by the decisions concerning the deadline algorithm as illustrated in Fig. 10.2. Time management is performed over time and will be influenced by the external and internal trends in the other areas of the event management.

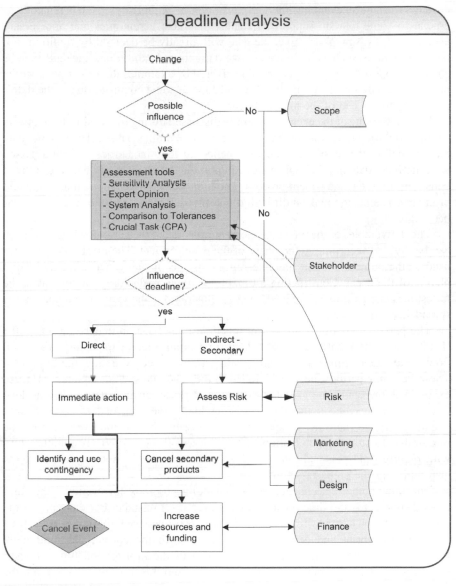

FIGURE 10.2

Deadline algorithm

10.1.1 Event date

In the strategic planning of an event or festival the choice of the date of the event is crucial to its success. The time of year for events whose objectives are to attract tourists to a region needs to be carefully thought out to maximise its impact. The decision to stage an event in either *off-peak* or *on-peak* tourism season is regarded as crucial to some tourism support strategies. For most ceremonies and anniversary events, such as New Year's Eve, the date will already be decided by tradition. For corporate events, such as conferences, award nights and exhibitions, the date must be chosen to optimise its commercial objectives. For example, there is a peak in the number of conferences during the May and June in some countries due to the date's proximity to the end of the financial year.

Hence, the date of the event is generally discussed during the feasibility stage and confirmed during the initiation phase of the event planning. The decision on the date may be before the feasibility stage and hence all the other processes are assessed with the fixed date in mind. Once agreed upon the date henceforth becomes a fixed constraint on the management process. The number of stakeholders, marketing and promotions campaign make it difficult if not impossible to move the date once it has been agreed.

The deliverables of the time management process are the various schedules. They can be divided according to the phase of the event project. The most common term used is the 'timeline'. The timeline represents the planning and implementation phases of the event. Constructing a timeline is done by deciding on key dates, the milestones and optimising the lead times as illustrated in the section on management spreadsheets in Chapter 8.

The person preparing a marketing schedule must have an understanding of the 'lead time': The identification of a lead time is an attempt to manage the work flow delay. Lead times are found in all aspects of coordinating the suppliers. These key time periods must be included in the schedule such as a Gantt chart. An example is the lead time to put a story into a glossy airline magazine. The lead time for this may be 6 months. The long lead time can lead to some absurd situations. If the main act or speaker has cancelled before the event, it may be impossible to stop the publication of the story in the glossy. The fabulous story with pictures and personal interviews is fixed and there is nothing to do except grin and bear the embarrassment.

The other important concept in the scheduling toolbox for events is the 'turn around time'. It is the time for a supplier to rectify a mistake. For example, if the printed invitation has the wrong date or the logo is printed back to front, it is the time for them to reprint and deliver the invitations with the correct date and logo. Experienced event managers have a good idea of the turn around time for their suppliers. Mistakes are quite common in printing and this must be factored into the feasibility of the event schedule.

Key event stakeholders, such as the road authorities and government agencies, often publish sample timelines and include the lead times or key dates that must be met.

These factors, the lead time, turn around time and other uncertainties mean that management software has to be flexible to work in this dynamic environment. Hence, the use of spreadsheets for many events. If these scheduling uncertainties are minor, such as in yearly association conferences, then the scheduling software such as project management works quite well.

The deliverables of the time management process for the event operations and staging are:

- Onsite/venue set up and breakdown
- Delivery schedule
- Programme
- Production schedule
- Run sheets
- Cue sheets

These are an output of the subprocess of staging in event design. Unlike the event planning timeline, the staging schedules are often critical down to the minute. They are used to coordinate the programme on the day of the event and involve a number of key contractors, such as the media broadcast company and the firework suppliers.

The production schedule for some events may include the tasks and times for the preparation of the venue on site. In this sense, the production schedule is employed as an operations manual. The complexity of tasks and times on the day of the event is illustrated by the system recommended by Sonder (2004, p. 123), when explaining how to decide on the preparation time:

> Subtract the time a task takes to accomplish from that time it needs to be finished to determine the time it should start. Then factor in other conflicting activities and adjust the schedule accordingly. Submit the schedule to all relevant parties and adjust as needed. Repeat this process until consensus is achieved. All involved should feel that they have sufficient time to complete their tasks in a manner that does justice to their skills and experience.

In this quote, Sonder recommends to the event manager that they work backward from the deadline, use quality control, allow expert opinion and, at the same time, enhance the work as a team.

10.1.2 Deadline management

The delivery of the event on time is the major priority and every task comprising the event management is assessed according to its possible affect on the deadline. The date of the event is regarded as a hard deadline. As the date closes in, it becomes increasingly difficult to change it. The risks involved in this are explored in the section on exposure profile. Each of the processes described in this section must undergo assessment according to this deadline. It is a simple process as illustrated by Fig. 10.2 and explained in Fig. 10.3.

With almost all events there will be changes. As explained in the section on uncertainty and complexity, the number of stakeholders and tasks make change inevitable. It may be a simple as the bride's mother deciding on a different colour for

Change

The change can be internal or external. The descriptor must contain its sources as well as an exact description.

Will it influence the deadline?

This decision may not be obvious at first and therefore may be a draft decision until the next stage is used.

No

Many changes will be a matter of adjusting aspects of the event and therefore adjusting the scope. They may not have any bearing on the event deadline.

Yes

Initially accepting the change will impinge on the deadline.

Assessment tools

These are a number of techniques to assess the consequence of the change and the strategy required to management it. These include:

- **Sensitivity analysis** - testing the affect on the event by a small change in a parameter.

- **Expert Opinion** - using the experience of event experts. The dynamic and unique nature of many events and the immaturity of the industry give value to experience in previous similar events.

- **Systems Analysis** - the interconnected nature of event management means that the tools of systems analysis such as fault trees and flow diagrams can be employed.

- **Crucial tasks and the critical path analysis (CPA)** - the critical, or more correctly crucial, tasks will be affected by any change.

Comparison to Tolerances - the tolerance of the stakeholders will be a significant part of the assessment of the change.

Direct - the change will have a direct influence on the deadline.

Indirect - the change will have a flow-on to the deadline. The strategy to deal with this comes from the risk management process.

Immediate action - the assessment calls for action to manage the change.

Identify and employ contingency - the assessment calls for the implementation of a contingency plan. This is occurs when the change was expected and allowed for in the risk management planning.

Cancel Event - the extreme solution to the change. Cancelling would require a variety of further tasks and is part of contingency planning arising from the risk management process.

Cancel secondary products - sections of the event are cancelled to allow continuation of the main product. This will have implications on Event Design and the Marketing of the event. Also there would be inputs form the Marketing in order to make the best decision on what parts of the event to cancel.

Extra resources/finance - extra resources area engaged to deal with the change. This is a common solution to changes and is a characteristic of the dynamic nature of event management.

FIGURE 10.3

Explanation of the deadline algorithm

the tablecloths to the arrival of warships on the day before a national celebration. Risk management is the formal system to handle the changes that can be foreseen. There will also be changes that can never be foreseen. The external changes such as sudden sandstorm or a drop in the US dollar or the major sponsor being upset by a comment of a volunteer to the press, can and do happen. The process described in the figure is a formal flowchart of what happens. In the field this may take a few seconds in the head of the event manager. If there is change, one of the major problems is if it affects the deadline. If it has no influence on the deadline, then it may be handled by simply altering the scope of the event. If it looks like it will change the deadline, the event team must analyse it to see what the effect will be and what remedial action can be taken. The tools of sensitivity analysis, expert opinion, systems analysis and crucial tasks listed in Figure 10.3 may sound too formal to the practicing event manager. However a moments reflection will show, indeed, this is what happens. For example if the client says they will drop the budget by 20%, the event management team will discuss this in terms of: How will it affect the event? What aspects of the event need to change? What new jobs do we now have? And finally does anyone know someone who has been through this before? The reason for using the terminology is to give expression to the problems and solutions outside of a specific event.

The time overruns experienced in other projects, such as the 30% of time overruns in software projects is an impossible situation for event management. The fact that the event must occur at the scheduled date is so implanted in event management that only the recent event texts bother to mention it.

The well-known project triangle comprising the three interrelated factors of cost, time and quality is applicable. In this case a change in time is analysed to determine what changes are needed in the cost of the event and if there needs to be changes in the quality of the event.

10.2 RISK MANAGEMENT PROCESS

In a similar way to time management process, the risk management is a cross-functional process. It is applied to all the other areas of event management. If risk is defined as possible problems, it can easily be seen that there are possible problems in all the parts of management. The term used in many of the world's risk standards is that risk management must be embedded in all areas of management.

The simplified schema of risk management as shown in Fig. 10.4 has a number of limitations. Some events have numerous objectives that can change. In some cases each stakeholders will have different objectives. Navigating such a field is difficult. As the planning progresses, the stakeholder objectives can change and they are influenced by other stakeholders.

There are some excellent textbooks written by practitioners such as Silvers and Berlonghi on risk management.

The risk management process takes time and therefore is subject to the time constraints under a deadline. In such a situation, the risks must be highly prioritised. In a dynamic system with uncertainty that characterises event management, this is a major risk in itself.

Risk Management
Process

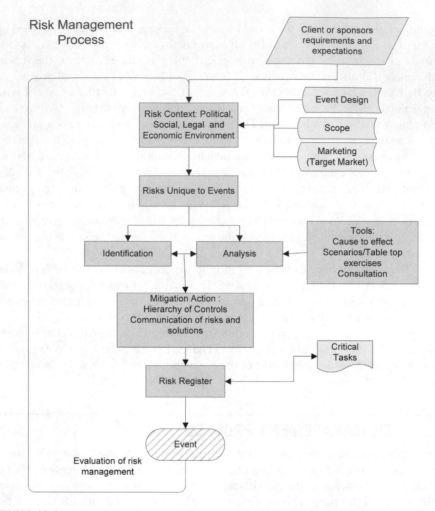

FIGURE 10.4

Risk management process

The inputs and outputs to other event management processes and knowledge areas are illustrated. In particular, the areas of marketing, scope and design have a strong influence on the risk event management.

Event risk management, in the past, has stressed the area of Occupational Health and Safety (OHS). There is a good reason for this. The other risks such as found in marketing and finance are dwarfed by the consequences of operational problems. When an incident occurs at an event it can involve very serious consequences for all those involved. This is illustrated by the number of deaths at events and the criminal charges brought against event managers in various countries. Many of the incidents during the event can be traced to competency in management. A simple marketing decision of having prizes for the first people to buy goods at a store, for example, can lead to a crowd crush. A decision by politicians with little or no experience in events to host a parade can lead to the death of many people. The tools illustrated in the process chart of Fig. 10.4 enable the event team to trace these risks back to their source.

10.2.1 Operational risk and upstream design

The importance of the operations to events cannot be overstressed. Unfortunately, there are many event courses that relegate event operations or onsite skill as a lesser priority to management and marketing theory. In a similar way to modern military teaching on counterinsurgency and banking, the operations are the front face of the organisation and it is here the hearts and minds of the people are won.

Quantitative methods of risk management have the allure of accuracy to many event stakeholders. A number of factors limit the comprehensive use of quantitative methods of risk assessment for events. The appearance of accuracy may diminish the risk awareness of the organisation through misplaced confidence. As has been amply illustrated by the recent world credit crisis, mathematics of risk can be so complicated to cause the wrong assumptions to be hidden.

Risk management awareness is one of the important factors in application of the process. Staff awareness of possible problems can be achieved by calling staff and volunteer risk assessment meetings. The meetings empower the staff and volunteers to take responsibility. It is part of the consultation process and the combined expertise and experience may spot risks that were unseen by the management. At the same time the meeting demonstrate a duty of care to the team. A tool that remains unstudied for events and yet is used very effectively by the armed forces and emergency services is the tabletop exercise.

The documentation of risk management process is an important part of reducing the flow on consequence of the risk as it provides proof of the process being used. The core of risk management is the management of change. It includes forecasting and setting up the conditions to monitor and control changes. Once the event concept is developed the feasibility of the event can be seen from the risk management perspective. It is looking for possible problems.

The most relevant perspective of risk management for event feasibility is the upstream model. It hypothesises that most event problems are an outcome of a mistake in event design. The upstream model is a useful way to view risk as it implies that the source of the risk can be discovered. This could turn into a circular argument where the proof that there are mistakes in design is the problems at the event. In other words the statement cannot be refuted. However, studying the history of event risk and the results of many coronial inquiries invariably shows that it was a management problem earlier in the event planning.

One of the current limitations of the risk management methodology is that not all countries use it. Although it is endorsed as an international standard in many industries, is part of the ISO 31000:2009 and a major part of the EMBOK and the

IEM, it has still to be adopted or at least endorsed by governments in a number of countries. It is the only system used in many countries and it provides a common methodology and clear terminology.

Other limitations of the formal risk management methodology is that it is inherently risk averse and may waste time that could be better spent organising the event.

Risk management is found in all areas of events. It is also used in the management of an events portfolio. As the world businesses are realising, operational risk can be as important as other kinds of risk. The various laws on corporate responsibility such as the Sarbanes—Oxley Act in the USA stresses that the organisation's operations are not at arms length from the board or the senior executives. Similarly, the legislation for corporate or industrial manslaughter, such as the Corporate Manslaughter and Corporate Homicide Act in the UK, can place the owners of a company or senior executives in an organisation on trial before a jury, if they are believed to have contributed to a person's death through gross failure.

The highest penalties are found in the management of people on the ground and on the day. The consequence of an operational mistake can be death and criminal proceedings. Hence, the operation of the event is the core to risk management. The results of mismanagement, negligence, misconduct, omissions and misleading marketing occur at the event itself. The consequence can be dire. Event risk management must show the results of mismanagement. It must trace the management mistake, no matter how small, to demonstrate how it grows to a major problem on the day of the event.

As listed in a number of fine books on event risk management, in particular the encyclopaedic Julia Rutherford Silvers, there are a number of tools and techniques to assist in the risk management. In the subtlety of a dynamic management there is no substitute for experience. An accomplished event team is always on the look out for people with experience in any new event or aspect of the event they will have to manage. Exhibits 10.1 and 10.2 are two examples of experience in risk management.

The many risk management standards understand the importance of team discussion and consultation as a way of bringing experience to the fore.

EXHIBIT 10.1 CORRUPTION AND RISK

Our major problem was that we had booths and exhibitors from a variety of countries and cultures. Some of them had no idea of health and safety compliance. They were not used to working in a regulated and enforced environment. Some of the countries had the regulations but did not bother to enforce them or they were made to go away with a quick payment to the local officials. Our only solution was to make sure they sent in their site plans and photos or drawings of any structural work they were going to do. At the same time we constantly stressed the importance of health and safety at all the meetings. This is definitely a work in progress for the next festival.

EXHIBIT 10.2 EXTRA SECURITY

We decided to include a major art exhibition as part of our event. This was not local art it was to be major works of art from Europe. The amount of security was enormous. It included:

- Specially trained security at all points along the transport route to and from the site
- Bullet proof vehicles with escorts
- Internal and external security cameras and operators
- Vibration sensors
- Infrared motion detectors
- Special control room to overlook the exhibition
- Visible presence of police

10.3 COMMUNICATION PROCESS

The temporary nature of the event management environment combined with rapidly changing staff numbers often from completely different work and social cultures gives the communication process a priority not found in other industries.

The communications involved in event management can be categorised as:

- Internal staff
  - Documentation/office
  - Administration manual
  - IT system
- Internal volunteers
  - Meetings, briefings
- Internal — during event:
  - Onsite communication systems
  - Operation manual
- External — stakeholders:
  - Progress reporting such as legal requirements
  - Promoting (audience)
  - Development (sponsors)

As well as these formal means there are informal means of communication made up of social networks. The informal communication channels provide mutual understanding, a common language and shared experience important in team development. Oral communication also provides an explanation of formal communication. It places the formal communication into context and clarifies issues. This is missing from many aspects of formal communication of reports and templates. The informal communication such as chats over a coffee provides the bedrock of common understanding to the event team and supports the formal reports.

Event management concerns timely and selective communications. The number of stakeholders in some events can easily exceed one hundred. It is a physical impossibility to include them in all the meetings. The buy-in or including all parties in the decision making is a common suggested solution to management problems.

However, there are many problems with including all the stakeholders in every phase. It needs to be traded off against the risks, such as the conflict of stakeholder requirements, as well as its affect on the deadline. New stakeholders will be introduced as the event project progresses through its phases. In particular, sponsors and the audience will, ideally, increase as the event nears. Having all parties involved is impossible for many types of events. With the ease of data flow afforded by information technology, too much data can be a risk. It diminishes the value of communication and leads to communication left unread. Unthinkingly forwarding and copying emails as a way of covering the sender's risk has no place in event management. Assuming an email is read and understood just because it is sent is a dangerous assumption. Timely and highly relevant to the receiver are the two characteristics of communication in the event environment.

Event manuals are important to the communication process. They provide the basic information and often include the terminology used for the event. Due to the transitory nature of events, they do not correspond to the operation or procedural manuals such as the ones recommended by the International Organisation for Standardisation. The manual is an important communication medium and different types are used extensively in events. As described in the section on strategy, event manuals can take many forms such as master event manual, report manual, operation/production manual and the staff manual.

The relevance of the information in the manual is time dependent. For some of the types of manuals, their life is over once the event has finished. However, they can still be used as a series of templates or headings for a similar event.

The event environment characterised by the deadline, complexity and uncertainty has been compared to the military environment when conducting a campaign. In such a situation of change, the concept of information inertia is useful to describe the characteristic of information's resistance to move in complex environments. Factors that contribute to the lack of dissemination of relevant information are as follows:

- Number of people or work units (teams) and related to the organisation structure set up for the event
- The staff/contractor experience in events
- Staff and subcontractor ability to work together
- The communication technology available and the staff/contractor competence
- The number of communication channels and their network ability
- The information's relevance and interconnectedness

All of these factors contribute to the delay in the relevant application of information.

Checklists or prompt lists are easily created and common to most work cultures. They are used as the most prolific form of management communication tool in event management. Almost all event manuals contain checklists. The characteristics of the checklist are as follows:

- They represent the combined experience and knowledge of the event team
- The checklist is the final output of the work breakdown structure and therefore is a tool of management integration

- They can represent mini milestones
- A checklist is easy to read by staff and volunteers
- They can be adapted to future events
- They are quick and simple to create
- They can be used in a variety of communication channels — paper and web

The checklist is a solution to the problem of 'information inertia' outlined above.

The emphasis is on the flexibility of the checklist. It therefore solves the problem of documentation being quickly out of date as the event internal and external environment changes.

10.3.1 External communication — promotion

Promotion of the event includes communicating information to the major stakeholders in the event — in particular the attendees and creating a favourable image of the event to influence stakeholder's decisions. Correctly delivered promotion influences the buying choice of the target market. Promotion can also be part of the cross-promotion for the sponsor, when the event is used as a tool of marketing.

The effectiveness of promotion is a result of optimising the allocation of resources to the variables in the communication mix. These variables are as follows:

- Advertising
- Sales and personal selling
- Public relations
- Cross-promotions
- Direct marketing and invitations
- Street promotions
- Online promotion

The inputs to the event promotion come from the marketing function.
The tools and techniques used include:

- Constructing a press campaign
- Media kit
- Press release
- Website and other online tools

The external communication process is illustrated in Fig. 10.5

The promotion of the event needs to be flexible so it can take advantage of opportunities as they are identified. Whereas the advertising mix can be planned with set media deadlines, the public relations campaign has to look for opportunities provided by occurrences outside the control of the event management. Promotion also will feed back to the event design thereby assisting in the development of the event programme. The involvement of the media can make large changes to the

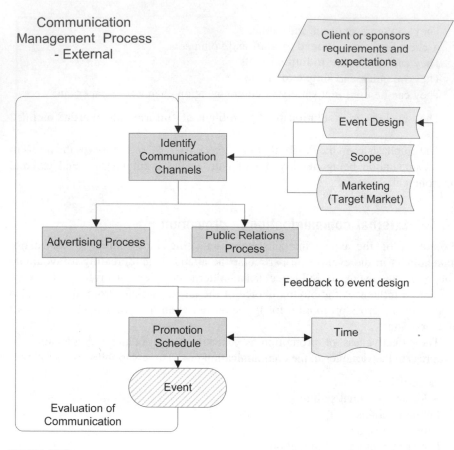

FIGURE 10.5

External communication management

financial management. In many events, the media will not make an early commitment to an event. This adds extra tasks to the already full list of activities and often results in confusion and bad last minute decisions.

As pointed out in the case study on predicting crowd number, the event finance will depend on the size and composition of the potential audience. The promotion campaign must be able to respond to the need for more or less promotion or a change in the promotional message.

The promotion campaign for a public festival or events is tightly coupled to the other event plans. It is an example of event management integration being embedded in each of the processes of event management. Exhibit 10.3 describes the use of an aspect of the social networking on the Internet to promote their services.

EXHIBIT 10.3 THE WEDDING VENUE

One venue is involved in planning and hosting many weddings. Fortunately, the young target market is highly web literate. To make sure the clients know about the service the company's Facebook page is used as their primary communication tool. On the first enquiry the prospective client is asked to join as a friend. The Facebook page has information about weddings and event checklists as well as recommended suppliers. The suppliers have joined as friends on the Facebook page. According to the event manager, in the highly competitive market of wedding receptions it is vital to build trust. It is not like buying a product. A consumer generally has an idea of the quality of a product. In the region where the venue is situated it is highly unlikely that the client hired a wedding reception before. The business relies on reputation and ultimately on trust. With Facebook the client can ask other clients about the quality of the service in real time. The regular websites have lost their trust as they are over used for promotion. The client's quotes on a website do not have the power to build the necessary trust. On Facebook the client can communicate with the venue management immediately and chat to previous clients. The previous client can also comment on the best decor, food and service. A wedding must be perfect as it is a highly emotional event and a milestone in the lives of many people.

10.3.2 Onsite communications (OSC)

All the event handbooks and event operations manual contain a section on onsite communication. This can be divided into:

- Onsite promotion and sponsor promotions
- Signage — directional, statutory, operational and facility
- Voice communication through radio, PA announcements, mobile telephones
- Event operation manual
- Digital communication through SMS, Twitter and web announcements
- Information booths
- Visual and audio cues
- Onsite briefings
- Print — programmes, leaflets, newssheets

In an industry subject to change, the ability to communicate changes in plan is essential for success. Part of the OSC function is to monitor the implementation of the design plan and communicate changes in the plan. For this reason the onsite communication can take a high priority. The onsite voice communication system is important for announcing last minute changes, directing crowds and during an emergency. The value of an efficient onsite communication strategy and the use of checklists is often only apparent when there is a crisis. It is not unusual for these tools to be ignored by inexperienced event organisers and there have been ample disasters around the world to prove this. Both tools are able to communicate quickly with the core event stakeholders — the staff and the attendees — and enable the event management to minimise the secondary risk resulting from any changes.

10.3.3 **Event documentation, filing and archiving**

The documents and files used to support the communication process and record the event management process include:

1. Budget
2. Tasks lists
3. Responsibility lists
4. Contracts
5. Schedules
6. Proof of compliance documents
7. Reports

Although the event textbooks list these documents, they are often under different names. This is to be expected in an immature industry lacking a standard terminology. For example, the output of the time management, the schedule, is called by a variety of names such as production schedule, run sheets, time sheets and cue sheets.

Many of these documents are outlined in the section on setting up the management system in Chapter 8. The digital storage allows the modern event to use a knowledge management system to archive, template and retrieve information. For smaller events a filing system is sufficient such as the one using the work breakdown structure as the folder names.

10.4 PROCUREMENT PROCESS

The concept of the event coordinator was central to the events industry. Generally, this meant organising the suppliers and coordinating their expert or specialist work. It illustrates the central role of the procurement process to many events. A wedding coordinator would find and hire the venue, flowers suppliers, caterers and the band. It was their core expertise. In some cases the venue did most of it and the wedding planner was there to take the stress away from the families. A concert promoter sourced and hired the band, the venue, a public relations company and an accountant.

Procurement can be defined as acquiring the needed goods and services for the event. It includes the fundamental decisions involved in sourcing these goods and services such as outsourcing and contract management. In a similar way to the risk management process it is found in most of the areas of managing an event.

The procurement management process used in most businesses is similar to that used in event management. However, due to the complexity of the event environment, the short time frames, a fixed deadline and the intangible end product, there are different priorities. The ability of the suppliers to accommodate change, for example, is important as the event develops. The required goods and services are found from the work breakdown structure. This is an input into the process. Procurement has to take place within the constraints of the stakeholders (Figs. 10.6 and 10.7).

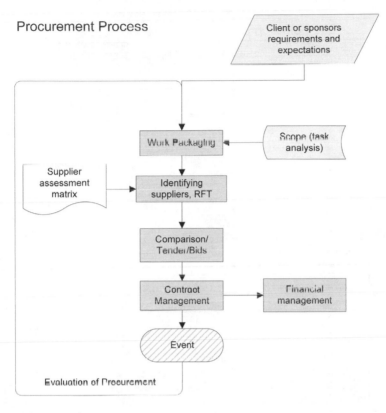

FIGURE 10.6

Procurement management process

10.4.1 Site/venue choice

The decision on the choice of the site or event venue is central to event management. It is part art and science. The site can become part of the event experience or it can be invisible to the attendees.

Once the event management is committed to the venue or site, it becomes a constraint to all other planning. It will influence all other areas of event management. Sponsorship of the event is one example. A specific company may sponsor the venue. This restricts the choice of event sponsorship. It is regarded as so important that the term 'clean site' is used to describe an event venue that has no sponsorship requirements.

As it becomes a constraint on all other event activities, it is essential to investigate the requirements and opportunities afforded by the venue. Detailed checklists are often used during the site inspection to ensure all aspects of the site planning are covered. The site or venue map is employed to design the event site and as the deliverable or output of the site planning/design process.

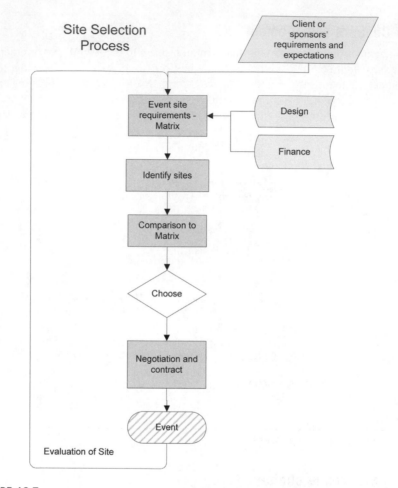

Site Selection Process

FIGURE 10.7

Site procurement process

The procurement of the site is, therefore, closely linked to the design process.

One of the site selection decisions made is whether to use a purpose-built venue or a venue that does not normally have events. A purpose-built venue offers the standard features to accommodate the event. It has been built with the consideration of the flow of attendees and equipment as well as facilities and staging. The familiarity of the venue to the target market can diminish the unique nature of the event. A unique site can be used but it may lack the event facilities. On the other hand it enables the event company to contract in all the food and beverage and staging and allows the event company to have complete control over the design. It is a good example of a decision made in the early part of the event planning that will have repercussions throughout the event.

10.4.2 **Contract management**

The management of the contracts is an essential process to the overall procurement. The standard contract management techniques are used such as assessing the requirements, matching these with suppliers, comparison of quotes, engaging the company, agreeing on terms, monitoring the contract and acquittal.

To minimise the problems that come with the dynamic management environment, the event team can use three ways to specify the supply of services and goods: their function to the event; a technical description and their performance at the event. It is recommended that the event team establish a relationship with the suppliers. The use of informal communication is a way to ensure clear understanding of specifications and minimising any disruption from changing circumstances. Not all aspects of the event can be described in a contract and a working understanding between the event team and the supplier is essential.

The deadline of the event is felt keenly in the contract management. Suppliers who are unfamiliar with events can be a problem as they do not understand that the time of the delivery for the goods or services can be as important as the quality.

There are many types of event contracts. They can range from the straightforward standard contract such as an entertainment contract for a band to the media contract that contains specialist terminology and long-term implications such as copyright and broadcast footprint.

Many contracts are made with suppliers whose core business is not necessarily to supply events. The event manager needs to have knowledge of a variety of non-event industry specific terms. The common example of this variety and uniqueness of contracts is provided by the *rider* on the entertainment contract. The rider is an extra sheet to the contract. It is unique to entertainment contracts and can cause significant financial loss to the event. It details the hospitality requirements of the artist and their accompanying personnel. These hospitality requirements may cost more than the original negotiated fee.

The intangible and transitory nature of the event outcomes is reflected in the procurement process. An important decision is the make, buy or hire the supplies and services. The contractor may supply goods that only need to last to the last day of the event. The short time frames and temporary nature of the event infrastructure mean that the comparatively lengthy contracting process found in other industries cannot be realistically undertaken.

As the event will have unique aspects to it, there will be unique goods and/or services. There may be a unique combination of suppliers. Some of the suppliers would not be familiar with events. All of this leads to uncertainty. A small change in one of the suppliers, the goods or services can influence all other areas of the event. This problem can flow into other areas such as costing the event. Contact variations are often the normal part of the working environment. Penalties for variation of contract do not work very well in events. It is far more productive to have a good understanding with the suppliers so they can accommodate changes.

According to an informal survey of event managers the characteristics of a good supplier are as follows:

- Organised
- Proactive
- Reliable
- Understand the brief
- What you see is what you get
- Flexible payment
- Understand local protocol
- Absorbs clients anger
- Able to deal at short notice

10.5 HUMAN RESOURCES (HR) PROCESS

HR process is limited in its applicability by the short time frame of most events and the volunteer management including secondment management used in many events. There are two systems of HR running side by side and they need to complement each other. These are the professional staff, part-time or fulltime, and the volunteers or seconded staff. Figure 10.8 shows these two processes in tandem as the event planning and implementation proceeds.

Figure 10.9 shows a simplified standard process for HR management. This process is also recommended by the texts in event management.

This standard process must work under the constraint of the deadline and in a dynamic and complex environment.

In addition, the standard HR process will be moderated by the use of seconded staff and volunteers. The quality of service by the event staff is the part of the event management experienced by the attendees. It is similar to the front of house concept in hotel management. Using seconded staff presents a series of problems. The amount of time and strength of focus they can bring to the event is difficult to control. An internal company event may use staff from marketing and operations. The lines of authority in such a situation are not clear.

Here are a few tips from experienced event managers on keeping the volunteers and seconded staff:

- Use the associations and clubs. Give donations in exchange for work at the event
- 'If the event is fun they will return next year'
- The uniform that they proudly wear to work. It makes them feel smart and special
- By having a fun or themed costume they become part of the event
- For the important government events it is their name in the printed programme
- It is the 'certificate' at the post-event celebration function as well as the tea and biscuits
- It is the seemingly small operational issues that produce return volunteers

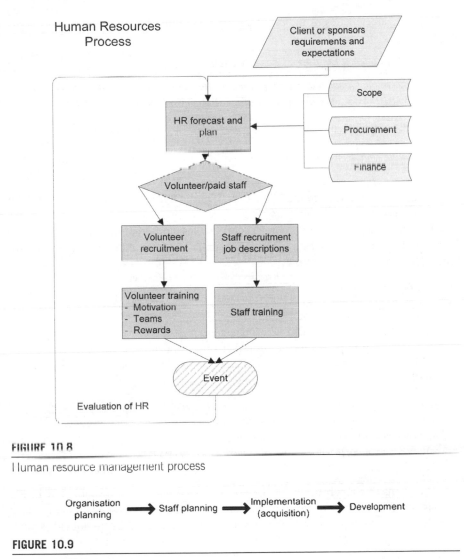

FIGURE 10.8

Human resource management process

Organisation planning ➡ Staff planning ➡ Implementation (acquisition) ➡ Development

FIGURE 10.9

Standard HR process

This is illustrated by Ric Birch when discussing recruitment technique for major ceremonies, such as the opening of the Barcelona Olympics:

> *For Pepo, the selection process started over a meal, because he refused to hire people if he found they were dull over dinner. It's not a bad method either. The creative people best suited to ceremonies have intangible qualities of imagination and ideas that a conversation over dinner will bring out much better that an interview across a desk.*

(Birch, 2004, p. 247)

Other characteristics of the event environment that affect the HR process is the high turnover of paid staff and volunteers.

VANOC Launches Employee Loan Program

Putting on the Games takes a workforce of thousands, and VANOC is looking to fill its 2010 roster with the support of local businesses and organizations.

Jobs are available in 32 of VANOC's 53 departments. Positions will last between eight weeks and six months and the longest terms will begin as early as August. Give your employees the opportunity of a lifetime — join the ultimate Game.

(http://www.vancouver2010.com/)

As can be deduced from the Vancouver Winter Olympics, volunteering can take many forms.

The use of unpaid staff or seconded staff creates a different training environment compared to the methods used to train paid staff. Two characteristics for successful volunteer training are as follows:

1. Leadership
2. Motivation

Leadership can be regarded as a management solution to a changing environment. Leadership implies motivation rather than control. Motivation is suitable to flexibility provided by teams. 'The Cricket World Cup Volunteers 2003 Training Manual' lists as a benefit of volunteering:

Participation has long been seen as an essential element of good governance and development. Volunteering is a key means by which individuals articulate their engagements as citizens, and by building trust and reciprocity among citizens volunteering contributes to a more cohesive, stable society.

(ICC, 2003, p. 1)

There must be a substitute for the normal incentives given to paid staff in the management of volunteers. Promotion, increase in wages, increase in equity or other rewards will not work with a highly temporary position filled by an unpaid person. The disincentives such as demotion, financial penalties or decrease in value of the company have no application to temporary volunteers or temporary staff.

Identification of the motivators for volunteers is essential in volunteer management.

According to a number of experienced event managers the motivations include the following:

- A strong belief and enthusiasm for the event
- A desire to contribute to the life of the community
- Opportunities to learn new skills and gain valued experiences
- Work experience and references, with a view to paid employment
- Commitment to interests of family members and friends

- Access to an event otherwise beyond personal means
- Sense of obligation
- Joint action with a group of friends
- Desire for meaningful activity
- Opportunity to be recognised and appreciated
- Fun

This presents a complex array. Satisfying one motivator may dissatisfy another. None of these are directly measurable. As can be seen in the quote from the Vancouver Olympics

> *Working at the Vancouver Organizing Committee for the 2010 Olympic and Paralympic Winter Games (VANOC) is more than a job. It's an unparalleled opportunity to become a champion of change, and an ambassador of the possible. Job satisfaction at VANOC isn't measured by the size of your workspace or responsibilities, but in the size of the mountain you help move. Staging an Olympic and Paralympic Games is an enormously complicated and rewarding mission. Every member of the Vancouver 2010 Workforce makes that mission possible.*

(http://www.vancouver2010.com/)

Creating teams and team leaders is identified as important to volunteer management. The possible friction between paid staff and volunteer has to be pre-empted. An event team with a large number of volunteers has to be structured with the roles of the volunteers clearly defined. When the team rapidly grows just before the event the organisation must be able to absorb the increasing number of people.

There is a negative side to using volunteers. As they have given their time freely, there may be problems with succession planning. The volunteers, if they have been with a repeat event for many years, take ownership of the knowledge and may be reluctant to teach others. The thought of reducing cost by using free labour can cloud the mind of the event manager when assessing the real cost of the event. The quality of the event may suffer when amateurs are used instead of fully paid professionals.

Other characteristics of the event management environment that influence the HR include the following:

1. Short-term nature of many event projects that does not allow the time to assimilate and train event personnel
2. The event organisation is 'pulsating' in the size of its human resources. This means that the size of the workforce can increase and decrease dramatically over the event project's life. Most of the staff and volunteers are needed during the event itself. The members of the professional staff are often part-time.
3. Some events are completely run by volunteers.
4. The volunteers are often recruited from the key stakeholders such as the sponsors and local community.

Although the texts discuss the risks associated with volunteers, such as they don't turn up and often require extra resources, the work being done in South Africa is instructive in the use of events to raise the skill of the host population. The training of an unemployed workforce as part of the Black Economic Empowerment can solve many of these problems. Such training is being absorbed into the national education framework. In this way, volunteering for work on an event is part of the national education system.

10.5.1 **HR and delegation**

A core skill for an event team that will suddenly increase in size is the ability to delegate work to their members. Understanding what can be delegated to teams and allowing them to 'get on with it' is vital in event management. The delegation process is fundamental to team and volunteer meetings. The characteristics of good and successful delegation are more than handing the tasks to the available people. The team must be competent. They must have knowledge and experience in the area of work they have been delegated. Also they should have a right attitude — a combination of enthusiasm, determination, understanding, timeliness and the people skills needed to accomplish tasks without causing problems in other areas. To enable delegation to occur the event management should have a transparent and understandable management system. By using a project management approach, for example, the work breakdown structure will identify the areas to be delegated. The system will also identify deliverables, such as the site/venue map, the schedule or the signing of a contract. The deliverables must be clearly defined and have a deadline. A signed contract with the main speaker by the close of business on the first of July is an example of a clearly defined deliverable. There can be nothing ambiguous about the deliverable. A signed contract is an object that can be shown to other people — it is not an opinion. The team must have a system to report on the progress. This system can be 'percentage of task completed'. It is a simple and effective way to find out how the team is progressing. One experienced event manager asks for the percentage of the task that is uncompleted as she feels this will elicit a more accurate answer. If this is combined with a numbered checklist, the team can report what number they are up to. The management system should have a series of checklists developed over the years and continually refined. The checklist can then be given to the team to assist them with the task. For example, the signing of a major event company would include the checklist in Table 10.1.

The delegated team must understand the risk management process and the importance of consultation. It gives them the authority to identify possible problems before they affect other areas of the event management. Risk management skills allow the delegated team to identify, discuss and communicate any concerns to the senior management. Too often problems are hidden by the team particularly if they are volunteers. Appointing a team leader helps with this issue. The team can bring any problems to the attention of the team leader. Their job is to 'upgrade the issue' and bring it to the attention of the management.

> **Table 10.1** Sample of a checklist for engaging an event company
>
> | **Event Company** |
> | --- |
> | 1. Find event companies |
> | 2. Profiles |
> | 3. Proposals |
> | 4. Compare proposals |
> | 5. Meet with them |
> | 6. CV of supervisors |
> | 7. Discuss and negotiation |
> | 8. Draft of contract |
> | 9. Finalise and sign |
> | 10. Send to me Aug 12th |

The delegated teams should be rewarded for excellent work. This should be done as the event is planned and not wait until the event or when it is over. If milestones are set, there can be a small celebration when they are reached.

Finally, the role of informal channels is vital in the delegation process. Not all information can be captured in formal meeting and documentation. Informal get together can uncover all kinds of issues and opportunities as well as enhancing the team spirit.

In summary, the tips on delegation in the event environment are as follows:

- Make sure they are competent
- Identify the deliverable
- Provide them with a numbered checklist
- Ask for a progress report
- Ensure they understand risk management
- Keep the informal channels open
- Reward success before the event

The event management processes charted in this section on management feasibility and development are drawn together by the management of the scope. This is the integration of all the various processes. It has been demonstrated that these processes intertwine and constantly influence each other as well as depend on each others' inputs and outputs. Integration management is the term used to describe this. The event coordinator is often in the position coordinating the efforts of the people in charge of these processes. Marketing and finance are two examples. Risk and time management cross all the other processes and are examples of integrating processes.

The process description may be too technical for the event team which is involved in the day-to-day organisation of an event. It is difficult to take time out to understand the underlying series of tasks and the links when every decision made could lead to a disaster. The event team must be completely focused on the event and will not have time to consider the system. The process model is necessary for the feasibility and development of events. Without a common system for describing competent event management, the industry will never develop. The feasibility of events and an events portfolio ultimately rests on the competence of the team which delivers it. It would be unthinkable for a doctor to be ignorant of the tasks and processes involved in medicine. As has been recently seen in the disasters and deaths at events, the event team is responsible for far more than one person at a time. A result of event management incompetence can lead to multiple deaths, financial disaster and much more. Hence, the last two chapters provide the model and theoretical underpinning of professional event management. It is a collection of interwoven workflows or processes. Some of the processes are involved in all the areas of management. Others appear at certain times over the phases to create the conditions ready for the next process to take over.

DISCUSSION TOPICS

The event management is often compared to film production management with its emphasis on temporary logistics and deadlines. What are the differences in scheduling between shooting a film and managing an event? Can film production software be used for event production?

Discuss the relationship between risk management and insurance. Look at the law of negligence and other torts and discuss how these can apply to different types of events. What is meant by the term 'duty of care' and how far does this apply to events? Does it apply to the attendees as they travel home from an event?

Event companies are well known for being conservative when it comes to subcontracting. Why do they stick to the same suppliers for many years?

Discuss the use of volunteers as opposed to paying staff. Is it better to use the volunteers to raise money and pay for professional staff at the event?

EXERCISE

You have been asked to launch a new ship building yard. You need to come up with an innovative concept that would be acceptable to the client. The budget will depend on your ideas.

1. List the questions you would ask the client at the first meeting (remember that restricting the budget will restrict your profit — be very careful when talking about the finances).
2. The client would like the 300 VIP guests to tour the new shipyard. What are the risks involved in this aspect of the event? Keep in mind the protocol issues and numbers per tour.
3. Where would you place the event and what sort of structures would you use?
4. What would you have as measurable indicators of success?

Queen's Baton Relay 2010, Namibia. Courtesy of Maxxam Events International

Samoan traditional dancers at the Pasifika Festival. Courtesy of Eric Ngan

Dancer. Courtesy of Pan Events

Event metrics and checklists

INTRODUCTION

The mathematics of any business has an allure that is irresistible to many people. Money often provides the numbers necessary for this mathematics. The recent credit crisis and the role of the quants should give all of us a strong warning of relying on figures for certainty. However, metric is an indicator if not the complete measurement of success. In this chapter we look at the various metrics used in events development and feasibility. All events are an investment and the return on investment (ROI) is increasingly used to justify events. An event may satisfy its objectives in which case the return on objectives (ROO) may be a more realistic measure. Finally, the chapter provides examples of the checklist. The simple numbered checklist can give a metric to enable the event team to measure their progress.

11.1 METRICS

Metrics concern identifying characteristics of an event and the event project that can be measured. The measurable elements of events are used to forecast, monitor and assess the event and the event project. These event characteristics are variables. They are aspects of the event such as promotional coverage, replies to invitations or money raised.

The characteristics are often incorrectly called parameters (ancillary measures). Parameters are fixed aspects of the event that constrain the event and its project. The size of a room for a function, once the venue has been booked, is an example of an event parameter. A useful system of event metrics will enable the event team to identify problems and ultimately provide the client with a report on how well the event performed. The event metrics is a system of dependent variables. They are ultimately dependent on management decisions and the event environment. Hence, they are part of the decision support system.

The attraction of event metrics to the client or the host is because they are independent of opinion. They are meant to be objective. However, their appearance of precision can often hide imperfections.

Due to the ease of gathering and collating data that computers have allowed business, metrics now has its own management study called 'business dashboards'. The dashboards are an analogy with the car dashboard. The dials and digital indicators on the dashboard show the driver immediate data on variables of the car such as speed and petrol consumption. The event metrics can work in similar way to give

Events Feasibility and Development. DOI: 10.1016/B978-0-7506-6640-4.10011-1

the management team and the client an idea of the progress of the event project. A combination of milestones, ratios and variables can deliver key information. Event organisation can become very complex. The management team often has to make quick decisions. It is this situation that the metrics can provide support.

The other function of event metrics is report to the client on the success or otherwise of the event. In this case the metrics are related to the objectives. As pointed out in the Strategy section, the event objectives and the event support objectives should have a measurable component. The objectives provide the foundation for the metrics. An example will illustrate their use. For a commercial event, a car rally is a good example. A major objective for the event organisers is to make a profit. As monetary value in an event environment is time-based — a dollar in the hand now is worth more than a dollar in a month — the metric will be time-based as well. The objective may be that the incoming ticket sales will reach the $100,000 by 1 week out from the start of the rally. From this objective, the metrics can be constructed. It is not simple matter of 'counting the cash' as it comes in. There is a lag between management decisions, changes in the plan and their effect on the cash flow. The event company needs metrics to indicate the level of expected cash, long before it actually happens. It is these decisions that the affect of the event deadline is most evident. The metric for anticipating ticket sales has to be set up in the early stage of event development. This could come from the historical data and metrics from marketing.

Historical data are useful if it is a repeat event such as the annual car rally. A graph of ticket sales over time is prepared from the data of the previous events. The graph is compared to the current ticket sales. Extrapolating the time/sales line on the current graph will indicate a profit or loss. The limitation of this type of extrapolation is it assumes similar conditions to the previous events. The event company must be aware of the influence external factors can have on ticket sales.

Marketing metrics can be useful as it exploits the direct link between marketing and ticket sales. The marketing of the event is set to include using techniques that provide a measurable feedback. One way for the annual car rally to anticipate ticket sales figures is to run a web-based competition months before the event. The interest level in the competition may indicate the interest in buying tickets.

The number of presold or reserved tickets is the most common metric to indicate the future level of ticket sales.

11.1.1 Exposure profile

The exposure profile for an event is a map of financial risk over time. It introduces the factor of time into the risk process. Figure 11.1 illustrates and is an example of this. In the car rally as an example, the y-axis is the financial exposure and the x-axis is the time leading up to the event. Although this refers to a specific type of event, a similar graph can be constructed for most events.

The car rally will be showing a new model vehicle to be demonstrated by a famous rally driver. It is the main attraction of the rally. Past data indicate that ticket sales and their timeliness depend on the audience anticipation of a new model

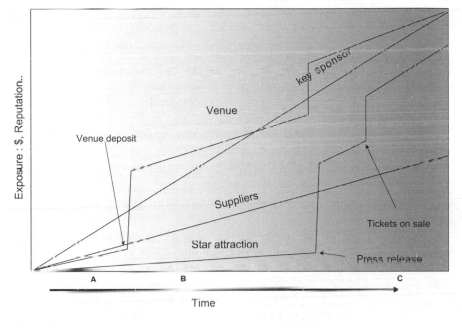

FIGURE 11.1

Risk exposure over time

and the driver. Ticket sales will depend on securing this attraction. The fee paid to the agent of the attraction is part of the negotiation process. This is rarely a simple matter as the event manager wants a product to attract people to the event at minimum cost and the agent wants a maximum fee. It would be simple if the event manager knew how many people the attraction would bring to the event — but this risk is the nature of the entrepreneurial event. As pointed out in the section on operations predicting crowd numbers is difficult. It is in the interest of the event manager to 'lock in' a price for the attraction as early as possible. The agent, on the other hand, may get a better offer. This represents an incentive for the agent to delay the signing of the contract as long as possible. When this is graphed as exposure in Fig. 11.1, the risk to the event team gradually increases as the time progresses. At a certain point the exposure goes markedly vertical. This occurs when the event manager has advertised the attraction at the event. Suddenly, the event is highly exposed to financial loss. If the fee is negotiated after this time, the event manager is at a large disadvantage. The agent knows that the event must hire their vehicle and the star. Therefore, they can ask a much higher figure.

On the surface the solution is simple. Make sure the contract is signed before the attraction is advertised. However, event decisions are often done in a fast-moving environment and it is easy to overlook a day or two or be out of communication. Particularly, when there is an incentive for one side of agreement to delay the negotiations. If this is multiplied over the number of critical decisions that must be made, the complexity of event management becomes apparent.

The complexity of event management can be controlled through employing the exposure profile. The process is to:

1. Graph the timeline or use a tool such as a Gantt chart
2. Decide on the time when critical tasks are completed
3. Place the milestones on the timeline
4. Using the work breakdown structure (WBS) consider the exposure of each category at the time after the critical task

One way to look at the exposure profile is to consider the financial consequence if the aspect of the event is cancelled. If the venue cancels at point A in Fig. 11.1 the consequence is small compared to if it cancels at point B and worse if it cancels at point C.

From the exposure profile, the priority of tasks at specific times becomes obvious. It enables the event team to focus on the important tasks at that time. It introduces 'timeliness' into all decisions.

Returning to the example of the car rally, the estimated exposure for the management areas is shown in the graph. If the venue is cancelled then the financial penalty can be large, depending on the date of cancellation. It affects so many aspects of the event that the relationship between the event company and the venue owners is an important part of stakeholder management. The cost of cancellation is small at the beginning of the event planning and gradually increases as the project progresses. However, there are certain dates when the cancellation can cause enormous problems. Once the event has been announced publicly and when the tickets and promotions is printed is such a date. The signing of the venue contract will be a milestone date as the risk of cancellation will be reduced.

These dates make up the key times for the event team. They create a time-based priority list. In the complicated decisions that are made on a daily basis, the team must keep its collective eye on these dates.

11.2 RETURN ON INVESTMENT

The return on investment (ROI) is the surplus generated by an event divided by the investment. The surplus may come in a variety of forms, be spread over a period of time and depend on who is investing and where the surplus goes. Therefore, the ROI on most events can be difficult to measure. When the initial investment and the surplus are measured in dollar figures, the ROI is a straightforward equation. This section explores the analysis of the ROI for events. The concept of the ROI is used across most parts of the event industry. With the gradual adoption of the corporate model by governments and other organisations, the ROI is one of the major issues facing events at this time. ROI provides a technique from which to compare various events and alternatives to funding events.

To use a straightforward example to illustrate the ROI. A music concert requires an initial investment. The promoter has to have credit or funds to invest. This pays for securing the performers, the venue, the promotion and the audio–visual. These costs are a large part of the investment. The contact negotiation of each of these items will involve reducing the uncertainty for the promoter. There are a number of ways to do this through sharing the financial risk such as profit sharing in exchange for a lower up front cost. Most of the incoming will be a result of ticket sales.

The example has a number of characteristics to enable a simple measurement of the ROI.

Firstly, it is from the promoter's point of view. The promoter is the investor. Next, the measurement is made using money. The investment is the total financial costs, the incoming is money through ticket sales and the profit or surplus is simply taking one away from the other. The equation for the ROI is (income − cost)/cost. Finally, the time period for the measurement is generally before or during the concert.

Compare this to a free outdoor concert paid for by the local authority such as a council. What is the ROI for this? The costs are paid, ultimately, by the taxpayers in the region. There is no income and the surplus becomes a deficit.

Compare this to a software retraining seminar for the staff of a company. The client is the company, the costs are financial but the benefits are very difficult to measure and may not be realised until well after the seminar.

Finally, compare these to an international event such as the Asian Games or the World Cup. The investment is enormous, complex and difficult to measure in financial terms. The benefits, such as tourism spending, may not be realised until many years after the events. The benefits are not all tangible and directly measurable. They may involve numerous organisations and different investors. Even after 10 years there is still disagreement over ROI from the Sydney 2000 Olympics.

The conclusion from these examples is that measuring ROI is not a simple procedure in the event industry. An important feature of the ROI is to compare investments. To allow this to happen there must be a commensurable variable or 'apples with apples'. This is generally achieved by giving every benefit of an event a monetary value. However, as it is noted in the other chapters, the intangible benefits are difficult, and some may argue impossible, to assign a dollar amount. Regardless of the reality, the industry constantly uses the term ROI and it is important that the modern event manager understands it use, benefits and limitations. As mentioned by numerous economic studies of event impacts, a false ROI is too commonly used to promote an event to a client or a city rather than a measure of reality.

11.2.1 Return on objectives (ROO)

As emphasised in most theories of management, the objectives are the foundation of any project. Hence, one way to ascertain the success of the event is if it met the objectives. With some types of events the objectives are all that they supposed to be: clearly stated, measurable and obtainable. The limitation of this theory is that some events are highly complex and involved innumerable stakeholders. The event and its planning is constantly changing and adapting to new conditions. There may be as many objectives as there are stakeholders. New sponsors may be coming online right up to and during the event. This injection of sponsorship can skew the original objectives. Sticking to the original objectives in a dynamic environment can result in failure. One way out of this is to simplify the objectives — but this can defeat the purpose of the objectives which is to give a measure of success. If the objectives are too narrow such as 'have five major speakers' it may miss the more important measures of success. If the objectives are too broad, such as 'keep the sponsor happy', they may be too ill-defined to give direction to the management.

Given these limitations, for certain types of events the ROO can be a highly effective tool in measuring the success.

As exhibitions are commercial events the ultimate return on the investment of the organising company is to make a profit. To do this the company must attract exhibitors as well as buyers. They must promote the event to two very different markets. Part of the promotion of the event is to attract the exhibitors. The exhibitors are interested in their own ROI. This is where it becomes complex as the return on their investment is not only the immediate profit at the exhibition. It is future business. This will be a result of a number of factors that can be easily found at an exhibition. By identifying the factors creating future business, the exhibitor can measure the success of exhibition over time and, to a degree, compare the spend on exhibiting with other ways to expand their business. The generation of leads is perhaps one of the most important. It includes the quality of the leads and how they are turned into future business. Tracing a sale back to a lead at an exhibition is difficult. The use of promotional codes, competitions and surveying the buyers are some of the tools used. There is a system for tracking attendees and the time they spend at each booth. There are other objectives that may have more intangible outcomes. Having a visible presence at important exhibitions and blocking the competition are considerations. The informal networking with other exhibitors can lead to business opportunities.

The modern exhibition company is highly aware of the importance of the ROI decisions for the exhibitors. To attract and retain exhibitors, the company can provide information that would be hard for the individual exhibitor to obtain. This includes attendee surveys to ascertain the awareness of the exhibitor, the brand and its products.

Brand awareness and capturing the human traffic as it passes by the stalls play an important role in exhibitions. The ROI may be significantly increased by having an event within an event. The exhibitors are encouraged to 'engage the visitor'. This can be achieved by everything from a splash event, such as a laser show, robotics and choirs, to the Majlis, the Bedouin hospitality tent set up by the Gulf tourism board at a travel exhibition. In the pursuit of leads, the exhibitor must stand out from the other exhibitors. The event company offers their expertise in event production to develop the event within the exhibition.

The fundraising event seems to be a straightforward application of the ROI. The host charity's aim is to make more money from gifts pledged on the night than is spent in organising the event. There are other objectives for the event such as brand exposure and networking. However, fundraising events have a primary aim of raising funds. Charities have other ways to raise money including bequests, individual gifts, government grants, sale of merchandise and income arising from tax concessions. The ROI is used as a tool to compare these activities. Once again the time horizon is important in establishing the ROI. The charity event may result in an increase in regular annual gifts. Likewise it may take away from the other areas of fundraising. Once a charity has a history of fundraising events they can use the ROI and other measures to establish standards of performance. An ROI of 200%, for example — in other words raising twice the cost of the event — may be the standard. Anything below this would indicate a problem with the efficiency of the events. Anything above this should send out a warning as well.

CASE STUDY 11.1 HIGH-END PRODUCTS

Our product is computer and software for a highly specialist area of the mining industry. The cost to buy is around $200,000 and ongoing cost is around $30,000. In this age of upgrades and redundancy of software, the actual product life is around 2–3 years. So the actual life cycle cost is around $300,000. Due to software and hardware developments, at the end of 3 years, the product is worth very little. We have three international competitors. With the nature of this industry and the amount spent in research and development, the completion is fierce and we 'leap frog' each other with new products and upgrades.

Before we go to the conference we thoroughly research the delegates and their companies. From this a list of key personnel is made and the sales team at the exhibition stand makes sure they meet them. Further, we tailor our extra events such as the hospitably events to these people. Although it is unlikely that we will close a sale at the conference these leads are vital. They are the start of our relationship. Once a customer uses our products and feels they have a good relationship, the 'cost of change' is too high for them. It is a bit like the loyalty programmes of banks and airlines. Once the commitment to a product line is made, it is quite difficult for people to change. They get used to the style and interface of the software. They like our sales, business and maintenance staff. All this is triggered from purchasing an exhibition booth at the conference and thoroughly researching the attendees and delegates. Because we sell a high-end product, we know the value of these events and can trace any sales to a particular conference or exhibition.

Also it is important for the brand to have a presence at these major conferences. Many professional conferences are so established that to *not attend* will start people wondering what has happened to the company.

11.2.1.1 *Seminars and training events*

Seminars and other training events are a large part of the event industry. Almost all major organisations invest money in training their staff. The constant change in business processes such as software upgrades, the change of staff through attrition and promotion and other modern business development demand constant upskilling. Short training, seminar and breakout sessions at a conference are an important investment in the asset of human resources.

The reasons for measuring this return on investment include the need to justify the seminars, gain budget approval and forecast the results. At the same time by providing a measure of the return the training event can be improved. Ideally, the training seminars or conferences will link directly the specific business processes with specific objectives, so that the results can be mapped against the key performance indicators. The benefits must be assessed at the start. They can include:

- Productivity increase
- Increase in sales
- Better compliance
- Personal improvement
- Team improvement
- Reduction of costs
- Networking

The problem is how much of these future benefit can be directly ascribed to the event. The cost of the event must include opportunity cost such as lost productivity during the event. Ultimately, the measure of the benefit and the ROI will depend on an estimation made by the participant staff. In similar way to the measure of consumer surplus, the large part of the value of the benefits will be found through post-event survey of the participants. Fortunately, there is a large body of literature on the ROI for training events. In particular, the J. Phillips and colleagues have written extensively and refined a methodology for assessing the ROI. Unfortunately, setting up a system for ROI for seminars event is time-consuming and can be complex. The main problem is to create a measurement commensurable with other types of investments to allow forecasting and comparisons. A company can set up a draft system and use each event to refine it.

11.2.1.2 *ROI analysis*

The conclusion from the previous discussion of the exhibition, fundraising events and the conference is that the event must have a thorough analysis to establish the objectives, time period and the metrics. The ROI must be broken into its elements that contribute to it. These are revenue raising, costs, timing and efficiencies.

In the fundraising event these include:

- *Revenue raising*: ticket sales, competitions, pledges on the night, merchandise sales
- *Costs*: venue, food and beverage, promotion
- *Timing*: key dates for the planning, contracting and payments
- *Efficiencies*: staff and volunteer work

If the focus of ROI is only on the direct revenue, there can be little improvement over time with repeat events. A charity has a variety of ways to raise revenue —

events are only one type. Hence, the ROI can be used to compare these over the long term. The timing and efficiencies are essential to the long-term success of understanding, measuring and ultimately maximising the ROI.

The general process of ROI analysis is to:

- Establish the client of the ROI
- Establish objective of the client
- Create a system for correctly costing the event
- Analyse the elements of the event that directly contribute to the income
- Analyse the elements that indirectly contribute to the income
- Develop a measure for the intangible aspects
- Establish the time frame of the incoming
- Analyse the efficiency of the elements of the event to deliver the incoming

This can be an involved, time-consuming and complex process. Events have the ability to produce very large ROI in a short period. The music and the sports industry are examples of this. Event investment or underwriting with a fixed return on a certain date is increasing around the world. A government can gain enormous returns as a result of a successful event. Figure 11.12 shows a simple example of the return to a local bank from a car rally in the town. In this country the bank makes most of its money on transaction fees. When the car rally occurs the number of transactions at the bank's electronic teller machines increases suddenly to produce the spike in the graph. After event the bank has more money and therefore increased

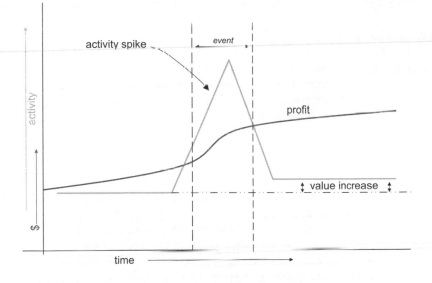

FIGURE 11.2

Spike in economic activity due to an event

in value. The implication of this process is that the event is creating the extra value for the bank. The bank, however, is not investing anything in the event. This presents an excellent opportunity for the event organisation to negotiate with the bank as the preferred bank for the event in exchange for sponsorship. The town has seven banks in competition. Each bank shows an increase in activity during the event. The event company has an opportunity to go into a partnership with a preferred bank. There are a number of strategies. First, the accounts for the event can be moved to the preferred bank. Second the banks automatic teller machines can be allowed onsite as the only cash dispensers. All of this will increase the value of the bank. The event site is unlike many commercial districts that are open to competition. It is exclusive and the trade can be completely controlled. There are many other hospitality opportunities. In summary, the process followed by the event company is:

1. Research the value of the event to all the businesses
2. Identify the businesses that are in competition and offer exclusivity
3. Provide a value-based sponsorship proposal

A risk in the event business is confusing the marketing hype or promotion with the facts. Too many of the assertions of a positive ROI ignore the negative sides of the investments and overlook the long-term effects in the excitement of signing up a new investor. If the aim of the ROI is to compare investments and improve, the figure must be accurate and come from a disinterested party. There are numerous examples of governments being carried away with the forecasted positive economic impact of an event only to find that aspects of the cost have been glossed over. The competitive environment of the tourism industry worldwide combined with an event sellers market does not allow the time necessary for governments to truly assess the claims of many events. The event experts are few and far between to assist with a proper assessment of a proposed event.

A true financial ROI must know the exact investment figure. Fundamental to this is a correct costing of the event and its elements. The figure for the investment occurs twice in the ROI equation. The investment is, in many cases, the cost of the event or part of the event. Hence, correct costing is mandatory for the use of ROI to justify the feasibility of an event. Without the correct costing the ROI is merely a guess.

There are a number of texts on this aspect of events. Event costing is similar to project costing, such as that used in software development and engineering projects. There are major problems with project costing that are not found to the same degree in administration costing. Forecasting the cost of the special or unique aspects of an event is notoriously difficult. For a start the cost of the events needs to be estimated a long before the actual event itself. Even the straightforward elements of the event such as flights, accommodation, venue hire and other supplies will change. This can occur at anytime while the event is being planned. Of course, a signed contract can reduce this uncertainty and this must be weighted against the possibility of prices falling. The sudden and large fall in the price for flights is an example of this. A 30% decrease in the cost of flights will change the ROI for many international events. International changes in the currency rates can affect the cost of an event.

11.3 CASE STUDY FOR INTERNATIONAL ICT (INFORMATION AND COMMUNICATION TECHNOLOGIES) COMPANY

1. **What sort of events do you do for the company?**

I. Organise these events:
- Exhibitions
- Knowledge sharing seminars
- Road shows
- In-house shows

They vary from knowledge sharing events to technical presentations at exhibitions. And these events are regional; Asia except China and Taiwan.

2. **How do they fit into the corporate strategy (or marketing strategy)?**
They fulfil these requirements:
- To brand and position ourselves as technology leaders
- To share knowledge and expertise
- To generate interest in our new products
- To improve relationships with existing customers or prospects

Depending on the requirements of the different regions, we mix the variety of events to achieve our objectives. For instance, if we suffer from low brand awareness in a new country, we would mix the events, from exhibitions and seminars, to generate new leads and also improve relationships with more personal one-to-one contact.

3. **What tests do you have to see if an event will work?**
For every event, we would set certain objectives and targets. Through the responses, which are collected through surveys, we are able to evaluate if we have attracted the right profile of crowd and generated the right impressions through their responses. We analyse the data collected and consolidate insights about the database provided or the selected channel of lead generation.

4. **How does the company go about approving an event? They must have to select the ones — is there a selection criteria? If so what is it?**
Yes, we understand the requirements of the different regions and from that, plan events around it. For instance, if we have decided to generate new leads in India, we would select the most highly recommended exhibition from the sales.
During participation, we would collect data from the leads and analyse if they are the correct profile. If not, we will continue to source for reliable source of recommendations and continue to monitor and track the attendees.

5. **How do you develop the event — by this I mean improve on events each year?**
- We consider all these factors together:
  - i. Target audience
  - ii. Cultural behaviour
  - iii. Region requirements
  - iv. Degree of penetration

v. Competition situation

vi. Political situations

vii. Events occurring at the same time

Through this, the event is conceptualised and reviewed by the product and sales managers. After the event, we evaluate if we have achieved our objectives through interest in topics or ranking of presentation. In addition, we conduct post-event surveys to seek more detailed information about their opinion. Based on the survey results, we tabulate them together which allows us to compare year by year.

As for key performance indicators, we evaluate on these factors:

- Response rate for invites – by number of attendees
- Cost per lead – total amount spent/number of attendees
- Evaluation of topics – from 1 to 5 (1 being the worst)
- Branding metrics

6. How do you know if an event is better?

We use the KPIs (Key Performance Indicators) to compare which events are performing better than others.

11.4 THE EVENT CHECKLIST

The management system outlined in this text demonstrates that the checklist or prompt list is part of best practice in event management. Below are a series of checklists developed by many event managers around the world. A word of warning with regard to these checklists. They are not comprehensive. They are better described as a prompt list as they remind the user of items likely to be overlooked and sometimes do not include the most obvious items. They reflect the work culture and the terminology of the person who created them. As a result these checklists contain the things that have been forgotten or overlooked or have worked very well – the *venue voice over* is an example. In the *Promotion* checklist there could be listed a lot more items. The other lists may seem to miss some of the more obvious items. So the checklists are not exhaustive. These are just a starting point. When setting up the management system during the feasibility phase the checklists can be copied into a spreadsheet. The next step is to check their validity for the specific event and to add, subtract or clarify each of the items. For example, the 'on-the-day' checklist has items on it that will not apply to an exhibition. These items are simply deleted from the list. The exhibitor checklist is elementary for a large and sophisticated exhibition. However, it can easily be amended, added to and subdivided into areas of responsibility. The order of the items in these checklists is random. However, the event manager can order them according to priority or time. If they are then given a number they can become part of the metrics of events. The event manager can keep track of the event team by asking for progress reports describing what number the team is up to on the checklist. Hence, the event manager must be aware that the order may imply that they are a time-based task list or there is a priority of items. As each

Queuing

Set up schedule for queue	Information counters
Public address system	Talk to the people in the queue
Colour-coded tickets for different queues	Registration staff, ticketing staff
Guides and ushers	Enough space for queue and activities
Food and beverage	Sun screen/drinking water
Don't cover the emergency exits	Toilets, water
Barricades	Number of rego desks – pre-registration, VIP, credit card, cash
Children's play area	
Distribute badges	Security checkpoints
Banners for categories – book online, onsite	Emergency exit
	Seats for those who can't stand
Cash machine	Parking
General security	Signage – direction
Big screens – entertain the queue	Shading
Scripts for announcements	Distribute advertising
Trash bins and ash trays	Shelter
Labels and badges	Witches hats (traffic cones)
Entertainment	Special needs queue
Prayer area	Barriers, rope and bollards
Shape and direction of queue	Disable access and areas
Prams	VIP access

VIPs

Database	Hand delivered
Draw up invite list	Send invite with programme and site map
Finalise list of VIPs	Follow up
Prepare info kits for welcome	VIP guest entertainers
Prepare gifts	Brief hosts and hostesses about VIP
Design invitation and print	Seating arrangements
Assign valet	

VIP Transport

Schedule for drivers and map	VIP signs for airport
Brief drivers	VIP sticker
Create a tracking system for vehicles	Plan the route
Vehicle quality	Alternative cars

(Continued)

VIP Transport	
Driver uniforms	Music in cars
Signage for cars	Reception team
Drop off and pick up locations	Contact taxis as a backup
Identification for VIP cars	Police escort service
Quotes for supplier	Place for drivers to meet
Refreshments	VIP expectations
Promotional cars	Mobile numbers of driver to VIP PA

Tickets/Invites	
Locate three design/printing companies	Distribution agency
Receive proposals	Dress code
Sample of print	Font/design/colour
Select company	List of VIPs
Contract signed	Sponsor's logo
Cost of printing	Material – stock quality
Design theme	Name of event
Approval	Names on invitations
Date for proofing artwork	Number on ticket
Estimate quantity	Payments
Final print	Personalised labels
Backup	Programme
"CEO invites you to.."	RSVP date to and by when
Code to identify ticket (barcode)	Status report
Add-ons such as complimentaries	Type of envelope
Dietary requirement	Venue address
Decide distribute methods	Where/how to RSVP
Mail out list	Wording
Info to be sent with ticket, e.g. hotel	

Talent: Artists, Speakers, Stars	
Source talent agent	Send briefing to artists
List of artists	Make sure of site plan, reserved parking
Receive profile/bios	Equipment room
Receive repertoire/tape	Rehearsal/sound check times
Accompanying personnel	Security passes
Transport requirements	Band equipment storage
Any extra equip required	Power lighting facilities needed
Translator	Power rating

Receive their contracts

Sign agreement

Confirm booking

Programme the talent

Name and type of entertainment/date

Information on change room requirements

Special diets

Specs sheet – A/V lighting

Storage requirements

Do they need a seat in VIP area

Send programme and contact details

Any extra requirements

Equipment sound check

Green room

Bump in and bump out times

Security guards

Stage area – needed

Dance floor

Cordoned off areas

Headsets

Run sheet for performers

Water and food

Transport and escorts – bus and police

Media Onsite

Confirm who and contacts

Requirements – room, catering, connections

Brief the media

Give contact details

Give the name of sponsors and VIP

Agenda of day

Media kit

Confirm time on day

Who will they interview

Legal considerations for filming

Exhibitors

Cost

Space needs

Display needs – elect, lighting, tables…

Times – bump in/out

Attendee brief

Other requirements

Agreement

Exhibitor logos

Contact person

Courier times

Courier location

Support staff needed

All staff names

Security requirements

Storage

Parking

Access

After event celebration

Public liability insurance

An invite or event brief sent

Invoicing and other payments

Refreshments

Schedule of main stage activities

Newsletter

Floor plan layout

Promotional material

Collect show bag insert

On the Day	
All signage at decision points	Sound system
Registration desk computers and electricity outlets	Laptop working
	Projector ready
Badges and ribbon	Internet connections working
Branding outside	Smoking area set up
General cleanliness	Bathrooms/toilets clean and available
Lighting	Exits marked and clear
AC working	Access/site/keys
Coffee working	Marquee set up and arrival
Seating and tables set up properly	Paper work sent to suppliers
	A/V arrival
Notepads and pens (working)	Caterers set up
Ash trays	Security brief
Water	Traffic brief
Stage set up	Sponsors signage
Main tables	Communication devices work
Screens are working	Meet with suppliers (status report)
Microphone working	Backstage set up – water, run sheets
Flowers set up	Media door stop set up
Podium/box ready or in position	Check the state of the bins and other rubbish collection
Brochures	
First aid	

Guest Transport	
Method – cars/buses/air	DVD in limos
Transport to airport to hotel and return	Refreshments
Hotel to venue	Tour guide
Venue to gala dinner	Personal escorts
Tour transport	Valet parking
Branding on bus/leaflets	Lighting for all areas
Map to all drivers and hosts	Parking
Emergency contacts	Mark out special parking areas
Beverage	Guides from car park to venue
DVD miniscreen	

Transport	
Car park (disable and VIP)	Limo schedule and drop off
Loading and unloading bays	Towing service
Truck parking	Airline schedules
Emergency bays	Train timetables and info
Drop off zones	Tram timetables and info
Pedestrian access	Bus timetables
Bicycle racks	Shuttle buses
Road closures	Contact taxis
Helipad lighting	Police/traffic control
Bus stops/coach parking	Signage for parking, drop offs

Brochures	
Conceptualisation	Colour separation
Content	Consistency in layout
Spell check especially names and companies	Spec. to printers – paper size, weight, type
Check accuracy on facts and figures	Date brochures
Ensure printers follow colour pantone code	Follow corporate guidelines
Pictures/visuals copyright free	Acknowledge source of information
Disclaimer	

Site Issues	
Road closure permits needed	Information tents/desks
Traffic plan	Lost property
Parking area and access	Facilities
Permits needed	Signage
Site plan	Safety and emergency
Amenities	Incident reporting
Structures/marquees	Cleaning
Safety barriers	Site communications
Office area	VIP area

(Continued)

Venue Issues	
Number of attendees	Position of registration table
Size of rooms	Stage layout
Layout of areas	Lighting
Breakout rooms	Is there a business centre
Size of exhibitors area and layout	Signage
Catering	Security contacts and details
Catering area	Emergency plan
Lecterns	Associated accommodation
Microphones number and type	Deposit date
Projector and screen	Final payment
Whiteboard	Cancellation policy
Technical and computer assistant	Insurance
Lollies, pens, paper and water on desks	Event order – other functions at same time, before and after your event
Bump in and out times	Toilets
Placement of banners	Access to Internet

Promotion	
Agency brief creative	Auction
Creative media	Other events to cross promote
Venue voice overs	Banners
Posters and signage	Cobranding street signs
DL flyer	Celeb training/today show
Media launch	National Calendar
Website development	Approval advert and design
Corporate mail out	Decide on magazines
Supplier mail out	Find sign writer
Media release	Window signage
VIP launch	Cards
Media packs	Post-event flyers
Sourcing designer	Virtual media concepts

event is different, the order of the items should be decided by the event team when adapting these to their specific situation.

Checklists are valuable in all areas of event management. They are easy to use, quick to set up and easy to change. A numbered checklist set out in order of time is essential to the process of delegation.

DISCUSSION TOPICS

A large ROI is often used to justify hosting major sporting events. Compare ROI found in the reports on the South African World Cup and the Commonwealth Games in New Delhi. Compare these to the London Olympic preparations and the claims of a positive legacy.

There are a number of articles and books on the methodology of ROI for training seminars written by J. Phillips. Test if this system can be transferred to other types of events such as sports, exhibitions and public festivals.

There is a theory that objectives are better achieved 'obliquely'. What are the advantages and disadvantages of using measurable objectives in events?

Checklists or prompt list — what are the differences and when should they be used?

Triathlon. Courtesy of IFEA

Operation feasibility and development

3

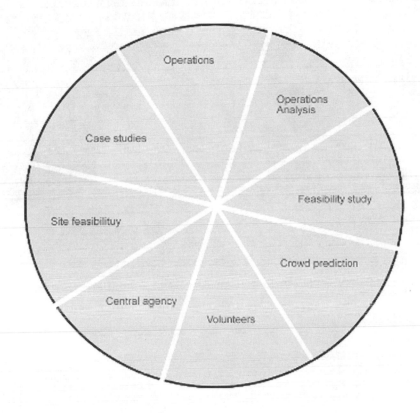

'You can have it faster, you can have it better, you can have it cheaper. Choose two of these. You can't have all three.' A well-known onsite saying regarding any request for changes in the event operations.

The operations of an event are at the heart of any event feasibility and development. Logistics, sites management and staffing take on a large role in the decision to proceed with the events or change the event. The project nature of event management implies that the management is ultimately judged by the success of outcome, the event. The event itself is the visible and most obvious part of the process of the event strategy and event management. In a large part, the operations concerns the attendees at the event and the risks in this area can have consequences that can be far larger than risks in the strategic or management aspect of the event industry. Seemingly small decisions in the operation area can lead to disasters. The

251

event is where all the key stakeholders are focused. The sponsors are concerned the operations run smoothly as their investment and their reputation may depend on it. The media is often present and waiting for a story. One cannot separate the management of an event from the event operations.

Buskers Festival. Courtesy of IFEA

Event operations: upstream design

INTRODUCTION

This chapter concerns the ultimate product of all the strategies and the management — the event itself. The operations of the event are the attendee's main experience. The site, the logistics and the programme are the areas of concern. Any problem in event operations can more often than not be traced back to management decisions made long before the start of the event. By learning from experienced event staff the event team can test the operational feasibility before the day of the event. There are tools that will assist the event team to discuss and test the operational feasibility such as the mud map. There are a number of stories from the frontline of events which, when combined with the case studies of Chapter 13, will give the reader a real world view of event operations. Finally, a method and template to create the event feasibility study are outlined.

12.1 OPERATIONS AS AN OUTCOME

A large part of event development in operations concerns capacity planning. The operational capacity of an event can be defined as its ability to efficiently utilise event resources. Capacity planning enables the event to absorb the changes as the event develops by focusing on the changing requirements for resources. These changes may be a result of the increase in the size of the event. Capacity planning calls on a number of the tools described in the previous chapters. These are as follows:

1. *Operation analysis*: subdividing the event operations into management areas. If a management system is used, such as the event project planning and archive described in Section 2, the analysis is found in the work breakdown structure (WBS).
2. *Sensitivity analysis*: using WBS and analysing the effect of event growth on each aspect of the operations. This can be achieved by computer simulation, using previous experience, asking experts, analysing supporting data and discussion with staff.
3. A thorough understanding of the strategic plans of the major stakeholders. The plans are the framework for the event growth. Stakeholders are committed to their objectives and the event development must assist the stakeholders to meet these objectives.

Events Feasibility and Development. DOI: 10.1016/B978-0-7506-6640-4.10012-3

4. Forecasting the trends in the market, the event environment and assessing their affect on the event and its development.
5. Adjusting the design of the operations so that the major changes can be incorporated, taken advantage of and their risks minimised.

This common process of capacity planning is found in the following chapters. The process is not simple. It involves using all the tools and techniques of event management, as well as employing processes not found in the current event management textbooks. At the same time it must be based on a thorough knowledge and experience of event operations. The complexity of operations is often hidden from view. When an event runs smoothly, the operations are mostly invisible. The operations that are visible at an event are 'above the waterline', hiding the enormous work and expertise that support the event. Figure 12.1 shows the event operations as the core surrounded by the project management working in an event environment.

To enable a complete understanding of event operations, the event team can employ a three-level approach to the analysis of event operations. The aspect of operation that is evident to the attendee is just the first level. For a full understanding, two other levels need to be investigated.

A description of event operations often concerns only the most immediate visceral aspects of it such as the food, waste, toilets and pathways. Because the operations are physically evident at the event, they can easily distract from the cause.

FIGURE 12.1

Level of operations

They are the outcome of the interweaving processes described earlier in this book. In most cases their success or failure will depend on the effectiveness of the processes involved in the planning and ongoing management. In other words, they should be seen as the visible end result of event management. When there is a problem at an event this is most often a symptom or an outcome of a management process. Each aspect of event operation can be traced back to the management system. In risk management terminology this is referred to as upstream design to minimise risk. Understanding the upstream design is essential to event feasibility as it identifies the ultimate results of the decisions made long before the event starts.

For example, long queues at food stations could be a result of not having enough food which can be traced back to a management decision to divert money from the catering to another area of the event. The decision was a result of the management processes including the risk management strategy.

The elements of event operations can be placed into three clusters.

First cluster contains the aspects of operations obvious to the attendee. They are the onsite operations. Their characteristics are that they are used by the attendees or staff at the event and immediate support services for the event.

Second cluster is the aspect of event that may be classified under the term *project operation management*. These are such things as reports and control mechanisms, software systems, work and resource allocation and communication system. They will not be obvious to the attendees and will only be known to some of the staff. They provide the work environment for the on-the-day staff.

Third cluster contains the environment in which the event operations exist. This includes the risk management, corporate culture and organisational structure. These will impact on the whole event operations. It will also include the interface of the operations with the event marketing, overall event organisation and the stakeholders.

To simplify the three clusters one can imagine them as three concentric spheres, as shown in Fig. 12.1. The inner sphere — cluster one — contains the aspects of the events that have an immediate presence to the attendees and staff. They are a consequence of the management system used in the middle sphere and both these spheres operate under the constraints of the outer sphere. In the hotel industry the inner sphere is front-of-house and the middle sphere is back-of-house.

Table 12.1 illustrates this concept with examples of various operational elements.

There are a number of event elements that do not fall clearly into one of the three areas. A thorough analysis of the event operations has to take into account these three levels. A problem that is identified in the first cluster is probably a symptom of the real problem that is found in cluster two or three. This means that any solution to a problem in cluster one will be the same as treating the symptom. For a true solution to be discovered all three clusters must be examined. Any permanent improvements in the onsite event operations will need to take into account and possibly impact on the outer spheres.

Table 12.1 Examples of the Three Levels of Operations

Element of Event Operations	First Cluster	Second Cluster	Third Cluster
Communication system	Public telephones at event Hand helds used by staff Announcements over the PA Information booths, signage, FAQ in event manual	Communication system authority and procedures Communication plot and channel allocation Briefing and reports Signage plan Event manual	Communication during a crisis, linking with stakeholders, communications protocols Sponsors
Power	Cabling, enough outlets, generator, surge protectors and power breakers	Power allocation, backups, integration over the site	OHS and licensing requirements, safety and risk response
Beverage	Drink available on the day Type of service, number of outlets price, type of drinks, glass/plastic	Onsite distribution to maximise profit, integrating with power, refrigeration, lights, training staff, supplier contracts	Regulations – responsible service, stakeholder objections, sponsor's requirements
Transport	Availability of taxis, buses, cost, queues, cleanliness, VIP/audience/logistics separation, blockages	Overall flow through event scheduling and linking with supplies, site plan	Transport Authority timetables and regulations, clearways, risks such as strikes

There are limitations to asking only the event operations staff to assess the capacity planning. As described previously, the onsite staff is responsible for the inner part of the event operations and therefore may miss the actual reasons for any problems or lack of development. However, they provide valuable first-hand experience of these. In particular, understanding the strategic plans of the major stakeholder and forecasting trends in the market are outside the scope of the event operations staff. They will be experts in the onsite effects of any changes.

12.2 THE FEASIBILITY OF THE EVENT SITE

There is much written about the site planning and the constraints and opportunities afforded by a site. They mostly concern the suitability of a site to host the event. For mega events, such as the World Cup with its entertainment and hospitality venues, the site can be the whole city. For the Olympic Torch Relay or a car rally, the site is constantly on the move and can involve a whole country. The mega events often have cities competing to host them. As explained in the section on strategy, complex decision matrices are developed to choose the site/country for the mega events. The large sports events, such as the Olympics, use a combination of weighted decision matrices and fuzzy logic to decide which country will host the event. However, most events do not have venues competing to host them. A large part of finding the right site is matching the event characteristics to those of the venue. Issues such as availability, cost, payment schedule and parking are part of the event manager's checklist. The process for site selection is found in the section on procurement.

Exhibit 12.1 is a sample of part of a site assessment table. The table allows the event manager to use a checklist and demonstrates the professionalism of the event company to the client. In this sample it was an outdoor event. Note how the assessment table relates to the categories in a WBS for the event.

EXHIBIT 12.1 EXAMPLE OF A SITE SELECTION TABLE

Logistics

Element	Ex	Gd	Fr	Bd	Notes
Electricity	A				
Accommodation	A				Caravan park adjacent and many guest houses
Access	A				Easy for audience and suppliers
Communication			A		Mobile coverage limited
Parking	A				Lots of space and access
Seating		A			Tiered fixed and suggest picnic rugs
Attitude of locals		A			Good support from tourism reps and others
Catering		A			Two high-quality caterers
Change rooms (green room)	A				Two large buildings
Security		A			Police station adjacent – but no proper fencing
Drainage	A				
Wet weather				A	Look for alternative in nearby farms
Previous event experience		A			Annual Ag show and NYE event with band on oval
Proximity to town and accommodation	A				Right in town and adjacent to caravan park
Facilities		A			Created for Ag show – 6–8 toilets and shower block
Emergency service		A			Fire brigade nearby
Ticket sales/collection			A		Difficult – need to consult Ag show – perhaps use visible tickets – wrist bands

Ex = excellent, Gd = good, Fr = fair, Bd = bad; A = 100%; B = 80%.

EXHIBIT 12.1 EXAMPLE OF A SITE SELECTION TABLE—*Cont'd*

Broadcast

Element	Ex	Gd	Fr	Bd	Notes
Site suitability		A			Clear site, easy access and power
Programme time availability		B			Need to closely discuss media company
Satellite availability	A				Pencil booked
Audio streaming	A				Engineer contacts but dependent on media company
USA internet		?			Need more communication

Ex = excellent, Gd = good, Fr = fair, Bd = bad; A = 100%; B = 80%; ? = don't know.

EXHIBIT 12.2 EXAMPLE OF VENUE HIRE

When I hired a hall for a function, I went through the usual checklist: parking, time of access, disable access and security. Many of these are a compromise, rather than exactly what you want. The venue checklist is enormous and there are always minor aspects that you do not have the time to cover. The deadline and all the other things are always on your mind. On visiting the site and being taken on a tour of the venue I noticed the lack of ventilation. This of course was not mentioned by the venue manager. I did notice the windows 12 m above the floor near the roof. I insisted that we have access to these so they could be open on the night. This involved an extra ladder. It seemed a minor point at the time and could easily be overlooked, but as it turned out the night of the event was very hot. On the same visit I saw that the venue was used as a theatrical clothing storage and repair centre. A fact I stored away for future use!

An event manager knows that the only way to choose an event site is by seeing it and experiencing it first hand. There are far too many subtle variables that cannot be described in a checklist or a report. Often they only come to mind when actually in the venue. The subtleties can be as small such as staff attitude or cultural issues.

There are situations when the event organiser does not have any choice for the site. The shopping mall promotion must take place in the shopping mall. The launch of the new integrated development must take place at the site. In these cases the feasibility concerns the ability of the site to accommodate the event. If it cannot then aspects of the event must change. Generally, this means a change in the design, quality or time of the programme. The launch of a new product, for example, was to take place on a tennis court. However, the court did not have enough room to hold the guests. The solution was to build a temporary second floor on the tennis court. The extra room was used as a VVIP area. Another event was a film award dinner. The client insisted that it be held in an old cinema. The seating in the cinema was tiered and the tables and chairs would fit into the small area near the screen. The solution was to build a temporary floor over the seats.

EXHIBIT 12.3 SEEMING LACK OF VENUES

In one of the regions I worked, the Tourism Authority said there were no venues to hold events. In their mind a venue for an event was a purpose-built venue. A sports stadium was for sports and a conference venue was for conferences. As a result they did not actively support an events programme. However, a quick look on Google maps of the satellite view of the town showed a large number of areas that could easily be used for events. Once we visited the sites it was obvious that they could be used for other purposes. In particular, the sports oval and stadium had all the facilities needed for a crowd such as parking, security, access, seating, food outlets and fencing. The stadium management could immediately see the advantages of using the grounds during off-season. Their main concern was the state of the oval and the underground sprinkling system. There are an enormous number of events that could benefit from the infrastructure. The real constraint on the development of the events was the thinking of the Tourism Authority. In the past I have seen very successful events that take place in sports arena such as gemology exhibition, circus, mass school examination, product launches, dance performances and concerts.

12.2.1 Success and the event site

In a number of cases, an annual event has outgrown its site. Its success has been sought after for a long time and when it arrives it takes everyone by surprise. Suddenly everyone from suppliers to sponsors to vendors to the attendees wants to be involved. A professional approach to event management must take into account the result of success. The event site will feel these results and new risks will emerge.

In other cases the annual event has slowly diminished in the number of attendees and the amount of general interest and yet hangs on for many years. The event site starts to look tardy and empty. Marketing becomes a chore. The vendors, exhibitors and the attractions are no longer interested in taking part. At the same time there is inertia in the management that keeps it going from year to year, regardless of the changing conditions. The country fair is an example of this in some countries. As a region's economy turns industrial and the farms are amalgamated, mechanised and computerised, the country fair loses its rationale. In many cases the site of the fair, the showground, is owned by the show committee or agricultural association with special status to the local authority. The showground is a purpose-built event site and lies dormant for most of the year. There have been many attempts to brighten up the agricultural fair with themed entertainment and other ways to attract the city people. Unfortunately, the showground management committee are often made up of people with long experience in agricultural shows and not other kinds of events. Often the cheap events selling clothes and other remainders become the replacement for the show. Franchised events that are easy to set up and pay a quick fee become the main events at the showground. This diminishes the reputation of the venue and adds to the long-term losses. In some regions, adding the wine and high-quality food and organic markets and emphasising the freshness of the produce have turned the declining attendee numbers around. Amalgamating the fairs into a regional Ag show with an emphasis on mechanisation and new technology is another development idea for these events.

12.2.2 **The logistics mud map**

The site map can be used to analyse the feasibility of the logistics. One of the major concerns of logistics is the movement of goods and service. In a purpose-built event venue this may be a minor issue as it is part of the way the venue has been constructed. With other sites, good logistics is reflected in the smooth running of the operations and the programme of the event. It is not part of the conscious experience of the attendees, but it makes for a good experience of the event. The logistics mud map is a method to let the event team contribute to the logistics and discuss its feasibility. It is generally made on a large sheet of paper with all the team contributing. A mud map is a conceptual sketch map. It is a way to structure the discussion so there is a visual output. Figure 12.2 shows a simple logistics mud map

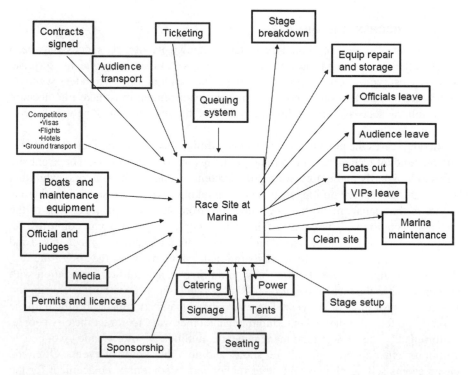

FIGURE 12.2

Logistics mud map

for the feasibility study of a boat race. By employing this technique the organisers were able to identify a number of issues they may have missed.

12.3 THE FEASIBILITY STUDY

The event feasibility study is the document produced as a result of research into the viability of an event. The major purpose of a feasibility study is to provide a choice of various models for the event and to present the cost and benefits of each. The outcome is a decision-making document from which the commensurable pros and cons of the event can be assessed. Even if the event is rejected as unworkable or for any of the other reasons, the research is not wasted. The event may take place somewhere else. The feasibility study may be used as a template for future events. If the event is approved the feasibility study can be used as the starting point for the management system.

There are a number of different feasibility studies that answer specific questions about the event such as should the event grow or be finalised.

There is always a deadline for a feasibility study. For this reason a priority must be drawn up of the important aspects of the event to be researched. It begins with a series of more informal questions to decide on a priority of aspects of the event that will be included in the study.

The questions that frame the study are as follows:

- Is the event concept plausible?
- Is the event practicable?
- Is the event admissible?
- Are the objectives achievable?

At the same time, the opposite perspective must be researched:

- Is it unworkable?
- Are the problems insurmountable?
- Is the concept absurd?

These are some of the many aspects of the term *feasible*. Not all these question can be answered exactly. The event and its management must be within the power of the team and they should be flexible in their management.

The best method to approach a feasibility study is to use a template with headings and a checklist. The study may make use of the headings that come under the five divisions of the Event Management Body of Knowledge (EMBOK); Design, Administration, Risk, Operations and Marketing.

In some cases the two most important headings are the Marketing and the Finance. Marketing, if the event is approved, becomes the basis of the event marketing plan. It would have the headings such as:

- Programme
- Target market

- Competition
- Market trends

The Financial section would form the basis of the financial plan and include:

- Budget
- Sources of income
- Possible sponsors
- Return on investment

In other countries, the competence and experience of the event team are seen as the driving factors for event success. From that point of view the feasibility study would stress the event team's abilities.

The heading of the feasibility study will be determined by the priority of the client as well as the type of event that is proposed.

12.3.1 Research

The feasibility study is not a marketing document. Its aim is not to 'sell' the event to the client or other stakeholders. It is a disinterested and objective assessment of the proposed event or change in the event. Any unpalatable facts that impinge on the event must be included. Exaggeration or omission for the sake of making the project and the event look good is courting disaster. A mistake in the feasibility study can easily be amplified as the event is planned to eventually become a disaster. A knowledgeable client will ask for a risk assessment as part of the feasibility study.

An important part of the feasibility study research is regarding it as a project itself. It has a deadline, milestones, deliverables, stakeholders, resources needed and a budget. All of these should be planned beforehand. Once the research project has been mapped out, the first step is to look for similar events. It is surprising how many times the same event has occurred around the world. It is a matter of looking on the Internet. A standard exhibition, a meeting or a conference has many templates. The marketing and financial feasibilities will take priority. More unusual events such as the case study set out below will have other priorities such as risk.

12.3.2 Feasibility headings

Using the domains of the EMBOK to divide up the study gives the following headings.

12.3.2.1 *Introduction setting out the aims of the study*

The methodology and research should be summarised here so that the reader (client) knows that this has been a thorough project.

12.3.2.2 *Background to event*

For a festival or public event this includes statistics of the region such as income, events history and the similar events.

12.3.2.3 *Administration*

The choice of date and place is highly important to events. It may have to take into account the weather, holidays and other similar events and broadcast opportunities. The location and venue will depend on the type of event could concern anything from nearness to an optical telescope for an astronomy function to distance from an airport, for events using lasers.

The primary stakeholders can be listed at this point. This can form the basis of the stakeholder management. The proposed organisation structure can be illustrated. This could be a committee, a company, a team, seconded staff, volunteers or a combination of these. Contracting suppliers will be the basis of much of the outsourcing done for the event and there should be some research in this area. A draft planning schedule with the major tasks and milestones will give the client an idea of the progress of the event management. It can be used if the event obtains approval.

12.3.2.4 *Risk*

In an era of accountability and compliance, foreseeing possible problems is essential to the feasibility. In a sense the whole document is a risk document. The major legal issues, compliance local laws and insurance can be covered in this heading. The event can be compared to previous similar events and the problems described. The major occupational health and safety (OHS) issues can be covered and the events relationship to the venue and contracts on this issue. Finally any major trends that would affect the event should be covered.

12.3.2.5 *Finance*

Finance is part of the Administration in the EMBOK. However, it takes on a higher priority in a feasibility study. Business events, of course, are primarily concerned with finance. The draft budget is placed in this section. An explanation on the major costs and income sources should be included. If the source of income is ticketed then this should be detailed in terms of ticket scaling and distribution. Expected cash flow with projections will be important to exhibitions and conferences.

12.3.2.6 *Operations*

One of the areas often forgotten in the feasibility is the on-the-ground operations. As mentioned previously, operations are the high-risk areas as the consequences can be disastrous. The sourcing of the major operational elements can be outlined in this section. As well as the general expected logistics with an emphasis on transport. Attendance figure is an important projection. As described in the section estimating numbers, it is part skill and art. It influences almost all other aspects of the event — in particular the risk and finance. A draft staging plan can be included in this section.

12.3.2.7 *Marketing*

The first question to answer is 'Is there a market for this event?' It involves describing the target market and making sure the matches of the region from which the attendees will be drawn. The proposed sponsors or other funding sources are vital to this part of the feasibility. It is here that many feasibility studies make mistakes. It is assumed that sponsors would be interested in the event. A draft promotional schedule can be placed in this section including some promotional ideas and key media.

12.3.2.8 *Design*

The design refers to the programme of the event and the theme. This is the attraction of the event and its creative heart. For the conference it would be a list of proposed important speakers and the topics covered. A festival would include the programme of events. As with the marketing, this section is often exaggerated. It is better to use a percentage of certainty than to say that a performer, for example, will appear.

There may be options for the client to choose in this section. For example, it may be presented as a menu with the cost of each of the items for the programme. It allows the client to have a choice and often engages them in the event.

The feasibility study should conclude with the 'next step'. There should be an action as a result of the study. It should lead to a go or no go decision. If the decision is the 'no go', the information collected and the template of the document are not wasted. It can be used for future events.

CONCLUSION

In the end the event will have to be delivered. At that stage the operations are the priority. Seemingly little problems can be amplified by the number of people at an event to become disasters. Operations are the outcome of management and team expertise and decisions made long before the event occurs. The feasibility of the event site is vital to operations and must have a high priority. This is part of the feasibility study. The study can employ the categories used in the EMBOK to provide its framework. Even if the event is not approved, the feasibility study is a valuable experience and document that can be used for future events.

DISCUSSION TOPICS

There are many disasters at large events. Choose one of these and suggest the upstream design problem that may have caused the disaster.

Create a logistics mud map for one of the major sporting events and compare it to a major music concert. List resources that are required for the operations of each of these events.

Draw a process map of the feasibility study. Show the inputs, tasks necessary, major decisions and the outputs to produce the deliverable − the feasibility report.

Case studies

13

INTRODUCTION

Event operations are an art, science and skill all rolled into one. It requires on the ground experience and the right attitude. Unlike the strategy and the management, it is almost impossible to theorise too broadly. To learn operations the student needs to experience the event first hand and with responsibility for their actions. The case studies presented in this section are written by highly experienced event organisers from real events. They know that the success of their event hinges on the on-the-day decisions backed up by hands-on experience. As has been shown by the disasters at events, the issues raised, such as predicting crowd numbers, are not abstract. The

Rajasthan National Day

Events Feasibility and Development. DOI: 10.1016/B978-0-7506-6640-4.10013-5

case studies are presented as they have been written. Each case study deals with a different operational issue.

CASE STUDY: HERITAGE CONCERT

This was an event proposal put to government environmental authority in response to a request to develop a special event as a promotion. The brief was to come up with an event that reflected the objectives of the authority. It had to be unique and therefore capture the press. The proposal illustrates how an event feasibility document is a method to help the client decide on various options. Also it demonstrates how the operation such as logistics are essential to success.

A celebration of the environment for Earth Day: proposal and feasibility

Special events as focused promotion

It is well recognised in both the corporate world and by governments that a single event can create an awareness of a product, region or service that far outweighs the equivalent resources spent in either long-term marketing or education. The Olympics, Microsoft's 2000 launch and the exponential growth of sponsored public festivals and corporate events attest to this statement.

The country has a juxtaposition of cultures and environment which can provide a fertile ground for unique events. An ancient indigenous culture, a modern multiculture, a frontier culture and an environment that through isolation and separate development has produced a stunning array of flora, fauna and scenery. The world is fascinated with these cultural and environmental resources.

In planning for such an event it is important to keep in mind that it is a promotional event — albeit with a high educational and cultural value. Hence, every aspect of the event needs to be subservient to the promotional aspects. The content, i.e. the programme, the place and the partnership arrangements, all have to have *event as a promotion* as the main aim. Traditionally, the overriding objective of events is to satisfy (and excite) the attendees. With environmental/culture events that are profiling an aspect of the country, the live audience's satisfaction is only one of the objectives — although an important one.

Choice of time and place

The overriding factor in these types of event is the choice of site. This study uses the Bay area as a working example to illustrate the more general considerations. The date suggested, 22nd of April (Earth Day), coincides with the holiday break and a possible world broadcast over the Internet. Both these factors will influence every aspect of the event and its possible success. This feasibility study will give a good grounding in the correct choice of date and venue.

Factors in site choice

The overriding factor in choice of the site is what is the event trying to achieve. If it is to attract a large family style audience (Model 1) of more than 5000 then the following are some of the considerations:

- Transport — public and private
- Facilities — toilets, electricity, food, water…
- Safety issues
- Ticketing and security

If the event is primarily a broadcast with a live audience (Models 2 and 3) in attendance then other factors become important, such as:

- Cable/telecommunication — fibre/wire availability
- An active ISP, radio and possible TV in the region

If the event is to attract a more targeted audience of people who are interested in the Environment and Cultural Heritage then other factors are as follows:

- A culturally interesting area possibly with a surviving indigenous heritage
- An environmentally interesting region

These factors are not necessarily compatible with the each other. To have an event in an interesting and distinct environment which would attract the target audience may mean that the facilities, transport, etc., are not as good — or if at all — as a purpose-built venue. However, using a purpose-built venue — like a local showground or entertainment centre — would not attract the target audience and have less promotional value.

Environmental impact

As the aim of the event is environment heritage, the impact of the event on the event site should be positive. The suppliers and other subcontractors should be evaluated according to their sustainability policies. Organisations such as Wastewise and Leave no Trace can be consulted. The national parks experts can be consulted for an impact statement.

Draft of suggested places

- Bay
- Cape
- Reef
- Mountains
- Desert
- Forests
- Wetland

I have investigated most of these sites for an event. Each has special promotional points. The wetlands, for example, are central to three major cities. As well they have strong link to the present concerns of the environment and would be suitable for the Earth Day aspect of the event.

Factors in the choice of date

This is dependent on the objectives of the event and the choice of site. For Model 1 it should be primarily at a time to maximise attendance at the event. For Models 2 and 3 it should be at a time to maximise broadcast possibilities.

For example, the choice of Bay region on 22nd of April fits into both these categories. Although it clashes with a major holiday festival in terms of popular broadcast, there is no reason that there can't be a radio link to the festivals broadcast. As well, the enormous population increase on the coast during this period brings a ready audience for this type of event. The only other events at this time are nearby at a historical heritage festival. The heritage celebration could be partnered with this event. In preliminary discussions with event organisers, there was obvious enthusiasm for an event that would promote the environmental beauty and cultural heritage of the region.

Logistics

The amount of logistic support for an event in an environmental area is dependent on the choice of site. Obviously, a purpose-built venue will require no extra logistics than the day-to-day operational requirements. However, if we consider a 'remote' area then the logistics can be divided into:

- Sourcing: suitable transportable equipment and artists
- Stage: may or may not be necessary depending on the choice of site
- Sound and lights
- Facilities: toilets, water, food security, etc., will all have to be sourced
- Artist requirements: this will depend on the artists/entertainers involved. Main line acts are expensive in terms of support structure. However, if the promotion is about the region and its history and the event has a world focus there is no need for main acts
- The sourcing of these logistic elements offers no problems as almost every nearby town hosts festivals and event and they are readily available
- Transport: transport of the above logistic elements is fairly straightforward as most suppliers of this equipment are used to supplying to 'remote' areas

Costing

As set out in the draft budget the cost of staging (item 1 — lights, sound, stage and backstage) is a maximum of $50,000. Local council and Parks and Wildlife regulations regarding transport and erection of equipment are a factor to consider. Local council regulations regarding events are found on their website. How these regulations are interpreted depends on the involvement of these organisations in the planning of the event. The draft budget is based on similar events. The site and style of event (model) will affect *every item in this budget*.

Feasibility budget

Heritage Concert: A Celebration of Culture and the Environment

Expenses

Code / Item	Amount	Code / Item	Amount	Code / Item	Amount
1. Staging		4. Site costs		6. Ticketing	
1.1 Lights		4.1 Site hire		6.1 Printing	
1.2 Stage hire		4.2 Cleaning/preparation		6.2 Distribution	
1.3 Sound		4.3 Set up		6.3 Collection	
1.4 Tents		4.4 Security		Subtotal	$8000
Subtotal	$50,000	4.5 Generators, etc.		7. Administration	$50,000
2. Internet		Subtotal	$50,000	8. Permission cost	?
2.1 Equipment		5. On site facilities		9. Contingencies	$10,000
2.2 HR		5.1 Toilets		Subtotal	$25,000
2.3 Communication		5.2 Water		10. Content	
Subtotal	$30,000	5.3 Food		10.1 Artists	
3. Promotion		5.4 Tables/chairs		10.2 MC	
3.1 Artwork		5.5 Hospitality		10.3 Guests	
3.2 Media kit		5.6 Staff/volunteers		10.4 Other	
3.3 Print		Subtotal	$40,000	Subtotal	$35,000
3.4 Radio/TV				11. Recording	$10,000
3.5 Programmes				Subtotal	$15,000
Subtotal	$40,000				
Column totals	$120,000			Column totals	$113,000
Total	$273,000				

Note: *many of these costs can be met by in-kind support from sponsors – in particular the broadcast/recording and Internet costs. Promotion costs can be significantly reduced by publicity if the event has the right ingredients.*

Revenue

Revenue can come from ticket sales. This revenue can be used to pay for the operations of the actual event. A major cost is the *promotion* of the event as it is a first one and the potential audience does not have anything to go by — except the reputations of the stakeholders and event mangers. Hence, it is important to create a high-quality image of the event and target the right media. This can be offset by publicity arising from the unique nature of the event. Models 2 and 3 can create their own publicity and produce a saving in major costs — in particular the Earthday Internet broadcast.

Ticket scaling. Standard prices depending on the event content: $50 per adult and $100 per family of four. If an open air dinner is involved then the ticket prices can be $150 per adult. The ticket prices will also depend on event content.

Ticket distribution. Once again this depends on the model of the event. Tickets can be sold through the local tourism agencies. Prebooked tickets are an important method to judge the size of the event. The best way to do this is by having a limited release of tickets. For tickets at $50 it is not cost-effective to use the professional ticketing agencies.

Funding sources. The national government has a variety of funding. Most cannot fit into the schedule of this event. For example, the Arts Fund's timelines are 1st of November for March. The only fund that fits into this schedule is the Music fund — 15th November for April.

The most suitable programme is the Partnerships programme the purpose of which is 'to encourage new and strategic partnerships with public and private sector organisation…'

Until the date, site and style of event are decided it is difficult to identify funding/sponsorship sources. However, one rule does apply — the larger the media coverage of the event the easier to find sponsors. The suggested partners are shown in Model Matrix.

Event content

If the event is Model 1 then the content should be well-known names that will attract a general family audience. In this case the artists become the attraction. Main artists can cost between $50,000 and $100,000 each for a performance. The risk here is that it deflects attention from the main issue of the Environment and Cultural Heritage. The costs involved with these kinds of artists can far outweigh the expenses in putting the concert on in a special environment.

However, with Model 2 or 3 it is not important to have well-known performers as it is the event and the broadcast that become important. It is the very fact that it is being broadcast from a 'remote' location that attracts the promotion.

In this case the event content does not need a 'star' artist. It can be the winners of the 'Songs of Place' and this could be looked on by the winners as a star event. If the event is decided before the winners are announced then it would be a good publicity pull for the event. It is recommended that the local indigenous people be asked to put together a demonstration or stories from the region and history. This would give a once only opportunity to see and hear such an event. In this case a lot of care and effort is required to gain the correct permission. However, the cultural rewards would be enormous.

It will be important that one music group be used as the core group or backing group such as a symphony orchestra. This group needs experience in outdoor performance and an identification with the issues involved.

Model of the event

Model 1 — Standard family evening concert, primarily aimed at the 'live' audience. The promotion strategy would be to target the region and to a degree the cities. It would then compete with all other family events.

Model 2 — Broadcast from a significant heritage area with a live audience component.

Model 3 — Internet broadcast from a significant heritage area with images and history of the area with a live audience.

Model Matrix			
	Model 1	**Model 2**	**Model 3**
Description	Standard family festival/concert aimed at live audience	Concert and broadcast	Concert and Internet broadcast
Primary costs	Operation Infrastructure and administration	Promotion	Promotion, Internet broadcast and equipment
Primary income	Grant and ticket sales	Sponsors Ticket sales	In-kind support, sponsors, ticket sales
Region of target audience	Regional, holiday makers, families	Country wide with the broadcast	Worldwide
Promotion opportunities	Very little except advertising	Some depends on broadcast partner	Enormous promotion potential which will attract partners and sponsors
Suggested partners	Local council	State funding Public media Parks service State Tourism	Online partner Earth Day council Tourism – regional, state and national, national parks, national media

(Continued)

Significant risks	Model 1	Model 2	Model 3
	Overcoming local suspicion	Broadcast problems – equipment ownership of event	Internet assessment
	No competitive advantage over any other festival in the region		Level of involvement of stakeholders

Administration

The event would need an event manager under the direction of the event committee made up of representatives of the stakeholders. The event needs to be owned by the Heritage Commission. It cannot be seen as a profit-making venture. One must remember that if there were profits to be made in these kinds of events, entrepreneurs would be organising them around the country. It is primarily a promotion or profile event demonstrating the value of the country's heritage. The initial work for the organising committee would be as follows:

1. Work in with local interest groups
2. Gaining permission
3. Working on program and ticket strategy
4. Sourcing extra funding

It is important to have one person who is the event manager who can both see the big picture (i.e. internationally broadcasting culture) and understand the micro-logistics — such as generator hire, ticket collection. The draft schedule of the event planning is attached.

The next step

Based on this study the date, site and model have to be decided. From this all the other decisions follow. In particular what sponsor and funding sources can be approached.

CASE STUDY ONE: DISCUSSION TOPICS

How would the success of this event be measured?
Can a return on investment approach be used to reword this proposal?
If the event went ahead, how could the event team increase the promotion?

CASE STUDY: TUNNEL WALK

Feasibility studies may be undertaken for one aspect of an event. The event may have approval and be well planned only to have a sponsor come up with a new idea.

It is not easy to refuse the main sponsor and an independent feasibility study is often the only way to ensure the new idea will be risk-free. This case study is an example of the situation.

FEASIBILITY OF THE DISTRIBUTION OF PROMOTIONAL COMMEMORATIVE CAPS AT THE OPENING OF NEW CROSS CITY TUNNEL

Background

The opening of new major tunnel for a freeway was to be celebrated by allowing the public to walk on the roadway through the tunnel for the opening day. Cars were not allowed on that day.

The initial parameters:

- Estimates of crowd numbers
- Flow rate
- Period
- Target market
- Site constraints

The crowd numbers were controlled by a registration system. Any person who would like to take part in the walk must register in the weeks prior to the event. Only 200,000 registrations were allowed. The major sponsors assisted with the registration. Two of the sponsors, a utility (gas) company and a media (newspaper) company, were highly suited for this task. The utility company has offices and store fronts in most shopping centres where the public could register. The newspaper used mail-in forms and their website for registration. It added value to the sponsorship. The registration service was a minor cost to the sponsor and added maximum exposure to their brand.

The flow rates, based on previous events and the width of the roadway, was estimated at 20,000 people per hour. Therefore, the event must take place for at least 10 hours if all the registrations were taken up. There was no way of checking the registrations of all the attendees. A simple cost–benefit analysis shows that the cost of checking every person is far outweighed by the benefits of using people's good will. People may show up for this event without registering. So there needs to be a contingency of 10% over the maximum of 200,000. However, not all the people who register will attend, particularly if there are any obstacles such as inclement weather, traffic or competing events.

The target market is found by analysing past similar events and the users of the sponsors' products. There will be some feedforward information gained by the level of interest that the event attracts in the press and the enquiries about the event before hand. This will assist in describing the target market.

The site constraints included the width of the tunnel and the feeding roads to the tunnel entrance and exit. All of this was taken into account when estimating the flow rate of the crowd.

The sponsors would like the caps to be handed out to the public on the day of the event. They have the sponsor's logo on the front.

The problem

The initial computer modelling of a moving crowd queuing for a product in a fixed area demonstrates that there will be bottlenecks rapidly developing into a gridlock. It could lead to crowd control issues and loss of reputation for the sponsor.

Is the above situation feasible?

Analysis

The first questions to ask in operational feasibility is 'What is the ultimate aim of the action?' In the case of the tunnel opening, the key sponsor's requirement is that their logo be visible by all the press covering the event. The sight of a maximum of 200,000 logos on all the TV news and the newspapers is very appealing to the sponsor. Any coverage of the tunnel walk must include the walkers and therefore must include the sponsor's logos. In future any visual reference to the opening of the tunnel will show the walkers and the logos. Operational feasibility always relates to the aims of the event and the stakeholder requirements.

The next step in the feasibility is to analyse the various aspects of the operations to understand what is fixed and what can be altered to allow this aspect of the event to work.

1. Can the caps be sent out in the weeks prior to the event to the registrants?
   This cannot be done as the cost is prohibitive compared to handing out the caps on the day.
2. Can the caps be handed out as the public are coming to the event?
   Most of the public will arrive at the event by public transport. This was closely studied as the numbers of people will put a lot of pressure on the trains and buses on the day of the event. The feeder railway and bus stations were deduced from the address of the registrations received. However, the distribution of the caps to each of the stations and the permissions/permits needed more time than was available. The event had a deadline and the permit process went beyond the deadline.

Recommendation

The complex computer modelling assumed that the walkers formed orderly queues for the caps. However in real life, at most events, people do not all stand in one queue. Looking at similar situations in other events in that country, people will have a number of strategies to obtain a free product. One strategy is to send in one person to obtain a number of products for the group. Therefore, the 1 person in the computer modelling could represent 5 people. Although there are no figures on this, it is safe to assume that most people will come with friends or in groups to this event.

Not everyone wants a free product. If the walkers arrive with their own caps a percentage of them would not be interested in another one. This could be a problem for the sponsors, as their aim is to have everyone wearing their logo. Therefore, the event staff must make sure as many hats are handed out as possible.

This leads to the problem of a crowd crush. There have been events around the world where products are given away or awarded to the first people and the result is a death in the crowd. Crowd crush at this event must be considered a risk and should be part of the risk management strategy. The feasibility part of operations is minimising the possibility of a crowd crush.

An important aspect of crowd behaviour is the type of crowd that is expected. In the case of the tunnel walk, the target market is middle to upper middle class families. At events that attract large numbers of this target market, a product, such as a cap with a logo, does not lead to problems. Most people would judge whether it is worthwhile queuing to get one or moving on.

The analysis shifts the cap distribution strategy to the sponsor. The sponsor would like as many caps to be handed out as possible and at the same time to do this without any crowd problems. Therefore, the feasibility and risk of this aspect of the event must include working with the sponsor.

A large part of the success of this aspect of the event will depend on the staff distributing the caps on the day. They should have the following qualities:

1. Experienced in crowds: it is often a mistake to use volunteers with no experience at events. In this feasibility analysis we have identified a number of risks which implies that the staffing of the distribution points should be taken seriously.
2. Understand the reason for the caps. If the staff know that the caps are there as a logo for the press, they may come up with better ideas for distribution on the day. Otherwise they may feel that a policy of one cap per person is important and hold up the flow of walkers.
3. Be briefed on how to recognise problems quickly and deal with them. In a situation of flow, a small problem can quickly multiply. As the computer modelling illustrated, one obstruction can cause a gridlock. The staff can quickly clear the obstruction and deal with the problem out of the flow channel.

Part of the feasibility of this aspect of the event is to examine what could go wrong and how to minmise its impact and possibly turn it into an advantage. One such problem is that people who want the product will miss out on obtaining one. The solution is to also have distribution points at the end of the tunnel and to have a way of obtaining the commemorative cap after the event. There can be signage telling people this at the beginning of the walk. It can be turned around into a promotion of the utility company as the walkers who missed out can go to their stores to obtain a free hat.

An interesting unintended advantage of the caps was their visibility after the event. The event company could track the crowds after they left the tunnel. This had implication for public transport and gave the event company information about crowd distribution for future events.

DISCUSSION TOPICS

Did the problem of cap distribution warrant a feasibility study?

Would this be a problem with other target markets such as a youth concert day? What are the characteristics of this target market that would create a risk?

It is identified in the feasibility that the volunteers on the day will be important to the success of this venture. What would you say at the volunteer briefing session on the day of the event?

If a crowd crush ensued because of the caps, who would be to blame? List the laws that would be referred to in the court case.

CASE STUDY: PREDICTING CROWD NUMBERS FOR SPECIAL EVENTS

The client is a government agency that would like to hold a very large free festival. It will take place in and around the city. It involves street closures. The feasibility report concerns predicting the crowd numbers that will come to a free event. Many aspects of the event are determined by the size of the crowd and this is a vital part of the planning. In particular the security costs and road closure costs are dependent on numbers of people. A quick estimate showed an inability to predict the crowd size between of around 50% and can double the costs of security and logistic charges.

CROWD NUMBER FORECASTING FOR SPECIAL EVENTS: DISCOVERING THE INDUSTRY STANDARD

Quotes from event professionals:

'There is some 'science': but mostly 'art' to it!'
'It goes without saying that pre-event estimation of crowd capacity is extraordinarily un-predicable'
'My forecasting for the festival involved rain dancing and crossing a lot of fingers'

Crowd number forecasting (CNF) is essential for all events. In a number of replies to the question sent to event professionals, CNF was confused with crowd capacity planning and crowd estimating. CNF occurs over the event planning and implementation phase. To make a generalisation: CNF becomes more accurate the closer to the event but the numbers can spike. Capacity planning will be dependent on CNF.

Many aspects of the proposed event will depend on the expected crown numbers. In particular the risks identified are directly dependent on the ability to forecast the attendance. Numbers of barriers, food and water, logistics, size and direction of pathways, security, parking and almost all operational elements will depend on how many people come to the event. The type of people, i.e. target market, is another factor. However, this report solely concerns predicting, to the standard in the event industry, the number of people who will attend an event.

Methodology

There is little written on the methods to predict crowd numbers for special events. A simple questionnaire was sent to a variety of event and festival professionals and other experts in this area. Event professionals are very busy and the questions needed to be worded so they are answered. The replies are collated in the next section. It is important to realise that the list is compiled from first-hand experience and not detailed research. Currently, there is no disinterested study in this area.

List of factors

This section contains a list of factors the respondents gave as way to predict crowd numbers. As number of the respondents commented, one factor is not enough to use to predict the crowd numbers at a free event and it depends on a combination of factors and research. These are described in the following paragraphs.

Analogy or precedents, i.e. history

CNF for a special event needs to consider events that are similar. The similarity may include:

- Target market
- Geographic area
- Overall size or scope of the event
- Theme
- Events that may be linked to this event but occur before it (this was suggested for sports events where there may be competitions leading up to a final event)

Triggers

There may be actions occurring in the lead up to the event that have a huge influence on the crowd numbers. A news story of a rock star coming to the event is an example. The use of text messaging is another example. Although not the basic communication media of the demographic, the SMS or text communication should be mentioned in crowd forecasting. It has been reported in the press a number of times that SMS messaging can quickly create a crowd. One person is sent to the event to 'check it out' and they relay their opinion to others as a broadcast. They, inturn, rebroadcast and the network becomes exponentially bigger. If the event appealed to this demographic, a free special event is at risk of sudden increases in attendee numbers. The organisers should be aware that their event may attract unwanted satellite events. These are events created by other people and take advantage of the interest in main event.

If any part of the event uses ticket sales or promotional devises, a 'spike' in this may indicate a sudden increase in expected crowd numbers (or the opposite).

Marketing

A primary role of marketing an event is the analysis of the interests of the target market. The crowd numbers can be highly influenced by factors in the marketing of the event.

Response numbers to invitations sent are one way to gauge the interest. RSVP to an invitation will be an indication. But it cannot be assumed that 100% RSVP's will attend.

Other indicators include the following:

- Amount of advertising in comparison to other events
- Website hits – there has to be a reason for the prospective attendee to go to the website
- Pre-purchased vouchers for food or wine
- Bookings of restaurants nearby
- Booking accommodation
- Response to pre-event competitions
- The level of interest at the pre-event press launch

There can be a more formal method of market planning including

- Survey of interest
- Survey of disinterest
- Focus groups

Intangible

It would be incorrect not to include the 'gut feel' of the event team of the level of interest as a measure. This may be a result of the 'vibe' and 'word on the street'. In particular, this works well for the event team if they are in the same demographic as the expected attendees.

External factors

There are a number of external influences on projected audience numbers. The event team must be aware of the flow on influence of an external development. It is easy to overlook factors that are not obviously and directly connected to the event. A rise in the cost of airtickets may create an increase in interest in the event by the surrounding population, for example.

There are variables that the event management can influence and those that are outside the event and part of its 'operating environment'.

In summary, the recommendations are as follows:

1. Research similar events around the world
2. Understand the demographics
3. Work closely with the marketing campaign and being constantly aware of the effect of promotion on crowd numbers.
4. Be aware of triggers that may spike the CNF

Examples of the risk of crowd prediction are as follows:

Love Parade festival in Duisburg, Germany 2010

The expected numbers at the event in Germany were 800,000 and it was estimated that 1.4 million attended. Events for young people have had a long history of mass numbers that arrived unexpectedly. The most publicised have been 1970 Isle of White festival, Woodstock 1969. In their analysis the excellent website crowdsafe. com states

> *Without a reasonably accurate crowd estimate—a key question in a risk assessment plan—neither organizers nor public safety agencies, could properly create a safe site for the event, a safe ingress and egress system (there was only one way in and out!), properly staff the event or develop effective emergency plans*

(http://crowdsafe.com)

Store openings

In two countries, the opening of IKEA stores led to tragedy. In Saudi Arabia three people were killed and in the UK there was crowd crush and a knifing. This is an example where marketing and promotional aims have created a buzz that attracted a large and competitive crowd. The promotional campaign must be aligned with the event planning as simple changes in promotion can lead to disasters at the event.

Olympic Torch Relays

Over the many relays, local authorities are often taken by surprise at the numbers of people who arrive to see the Torch Relay coming through their town or area. It is difficult to predict these numbers and TV coverage of the Torch's progress can create a sudden high level of curiosity in the event.

Below is a list of key factors that influence crowd numbers as compiled and reviewed by event and festival managers. Note that this list is not exhaustive as each event is special and has characteristics unique to the instance.

Promotion

- Quality of publicity
- Targeting promotion correctly
- Quality of PR company
- Timing of press releases

- Existence of other event promotion
- Staff/volunteers talking to the press
- Quality of press contacts

Theme/content
- Quality of suppliers
- Combination of suppliers
- Attractiveness of entrance way
- Attractiveness of site
- Type of entertainment
- Quality of event designer
- Reputation of company for previous events

Operations/staging
- Quality and visibility of parking/transport
- Ability to obtain tickets and other promotional or logistics items
- Managing queues
- Visibility of entrance

Environmental
- Time of year
- Type of weather
- Economic conditions
- Other events at same time for that audience
- Local authorities place last minute restrictions
- Ease of transport conditions and arrival

Capacity

Quite a few respondents replied with statements on crowd capacity planning. The factors concerned with capacity and CNF are linked as capacity will limit the number of people allowed into the event. With a free event such limitations on numbers may be difficult to impose. The perception of the event capacity by the target market will influence the crowd numbers. If the target market knows there are only a limited number of toilets or parking spaces, for example, this may influence their decision to attend. Capacity decision in the planning may directly influence the crowd numbers.

Conclusion

Marketing is the primary tool to reduce the uncertainty in forecasting crowd size. The event team must be highly aware of any developments in marketing of the event. In particular, forecasting should be part of the risk register and continually updated. It can be achieved by scheduling the task of reviewing the CNF over the planning cycle to coincide with the marketing milestones. The event team needs to be aware of the triggers that will produce a spike in crowd numbers. These are difficult to plan for as they are often unexpected. However, the event team needs to be aware of the flow on effect and have a response plan ready. From the CNF will arise the capacity planning. This is a two-way process and is will develop together as the planning progresses.

DISCUSSION TOPICS

The website www.crowdsafe.com has many examples of disasters at events. How many of these were the result of overcrowding or the incorrect prediction of crowd numbers. Compile a list of the reasons given by the website.

There is controversy over the use of terms crowd control and crowd management. What is the difference?

In a climate of budget cutting, the area often targeted for savings is security and crowd management. If the security works then there are no problems and therefore it is difficult to justify the cost. What arguments can be made for keeping security and crowd management as a priority at events?

CASE STUDY: PLANNING A TORCH RELAY AROUND THE WORLD, A DISCUSSION WITH DI HENRY

Managing Director, Maxxam International

Torch Relay Producer, Beijing 2008 Olympic Torch Relay, Beijing Organising Committee

Torch Relay Programme Manager, Doha 2006 Asian Games

Director, The Queen's Jubilee Baton Relay, Manchester 2002 Commonwealth Games

Di Henry has a unique experience in the event industry. Her work crosses the world. Her team has had to create a similar event in countries as diverse as Qatar, UK and China. She has an international perspective on event feasibility and development. Her insights are invaluable as the event industry grows and becomes international. To give an example of the scope of work, the torch around Australia included 27,000 km in Australia, 11,000 torch bearers in Australia, and 2500 escort runners. The Doha Torch Relay of the 15th Asian Games was 55 days on the road, travelling more than 50,000 km in 15 countries and regions. In October 2010, the Commonweath Games baton completed its 85-day tour of 23 Commonwealth countries. Other events include working with the Rugby World Cup and the 2006 Torino Winter Olympics. Each of the relay events took years to organise.

> In lots of ways, it's very life affirming, because a lot of people who are the torch bearers have struggled against great odds and that's what we're seeing, the support there.
>
> People really just cheer on their friend and family who are torch bearers, they're proud of their community, they're showing us what they have on offer in their part of the world.
>
> I think that's all combined to make it a very unifying effect from community to community.

But, you know, there were times when I thought, 'Oh, will it all work, will all the pieces fit together?' But fantastic team, fantastic people helping us, it's a magic sort of system, really.

(ABC Interview 14/9/2000; http://www.abc.net.au/7.30/stories/s176892.htm)

RUNNING AROUND THE WORLD

The first questions I ask when considering the feasibility of my events are 'Does it capture the imagination of the audience? Are you designing something that people want? Or want to go to or want to watch?' You have to have the stakeholders in mind in order to create the event. In the event that I do there are levels of stakeholders. For an Olympic Torch Relay there are levels of government — as you can't run one without government assistance on lots of different levels, policing, community events, as it goes around the countries. Then there is the national Olympic committees, the media, the general public and the torch bearers. If you don't keep them all in mind and consider what they want, the event won't be feasible.

There are internal and external stakeholders. When we are contracted to run a major event we spend a lot of time selling the event back to the client and justifying the work to them. They need at least 50% of our time reporting, justifying and recalculations.

External stakeholders depend on which country you are working in. Generally, it is the body that is putting the most money into the organising committee, such as a government department. Then as you get closer to the day of the event, the media becomes more important.

In the life of a relay there is three distinct worlds:

1. *Front of house*: the event operations
2. *Back of house*: the operations support
3. *Selling the house*: the media and marketing

The front of house or the event operations side is the total focus at the beginning when we are working out the route, negotiating with people about the route and how it will work including all the security and logistics. Operations support comes into its own midway through the planning phase. This is when we are finding and recruiting all the torch bearers, working out the technology, uniforms and, of course, the torches.

Closer to the event it is the media and marketing. Although the marketing has been important earlier in gaining the sponsors, at this stage the sponsors become more involved, advertising has begun and it is when the event must engage the audience. At this stage the event operations staff can feel left out as they were so important at the beginning, but at this part of the life cycle, marketing is getting all the attention.

For a new region or country we have an operational checklist to see if it is feasible. It includes the following:

1. Geography — can we physically get to the area?
2. Do they have enough hotels?
3. Climate — at the time of the event
4. Population — is the size of the population worth it?
5. Are there physical or historical interesting aspect to the area?

First up with feasibility for a relay, you need to come up with a vision of what it is. If it is not well thought out, it can be a pretty ordinary event. But if you discuss what is important to this Olympics in this country's bid, what is their ideal vision in what they are trying to convey. It is about aspiration desire to produce an event that is different and yet fundamentally the same. Pride is important. Then you can come up with a mission, the objective and the theme. At the same time you come up with the information that puts a perimeter around the event.

Australia is a big country and you need a lot of time to travel the country. The Olympic Organising Committee wanted the Torch Relay to communicate to a large percentage of the population with the theme being 'Share the Spirit'. From this theme we decided that the period of the relay would be 100 days around the country. We need to cover 1000 towns. This gives the theme '1000 towns, 100 days and one celebration'. It gives you a 'mould' to develop the event. Next, we need to work out the torch bearers and then the logistical feasibility.

Change is the normal condition of the operations and it can occur on the strategic level as well. An example of strategic development was the change in the relay for the Doha Asian Games. We started with the relay going to 45 countries in 100 days. However, as we progressed with the planning it became obvious to the Doha Asian Organising Committee that it was unfeasible. The work involved in obtaining the visas, other immigration issues and customs would make this untenable. Fear of failure is a powerful agent of change! Unfortunately, this realisation occurred after the announcement of the relay going through 45 countries. It was after our advanced trips, 20 months of work and signed contracts with the countries involved. These difficulties became obvious to the Doha Games Coordination Commission when all the countries came together in Guangzhou, China. There was a possibility of failure, so the Doha Asian Games Organising Committee (DAGOC) scaled the relay back to only include the 15 countries that had previously hosted the Asian Games. Note that the budget was not the issue here.

Goodwill is a way that we often forecast the success of our events in various countries. With the Manchester Baton Relay forecasting was based on goodwill of the various organising committees in each region. In Canada, for example, we depended on the National Olympic Committee. They have been around for a long time and it is staffed with volunteers. They train, kit and send big teams to overseas games every few years. They are highly organised, live for sport and are experts in helping people in this area. So when we contacted these people and suggested they might like to have the baton pass through their region, they readily agreed. We automatically know they will do a good job within their limited resources. In the case of Canada they did not do a relay day, they decided to use the baton relay as a symbol of the games at major promotions and other events. We went to Toronto, Montreal Ottawa and the baton was used to promote the games. It was constant PR launches. They managed it extremely well. The PR for the baton helped them with the positioning of their sports in Canada. In this case, it was a mutually beneficial project.

In fact a large part of our time is spent on communicating goodwill. For the Sydney Olympic Torch Relay we spent a lot of time selling it to the communities, all levels of government and all the media. I would have delivered a presentation about the Olympic Torch Relay at least 20 times a week. This time and effort creates the success. Goodwill must be constantly worked on and never assumed.

The success of such a campaign can produce its own major changes. If the event looks like it is becoming successful, all sorts of people want to be involved. Just a couple of weeks before the Doha Torch Relay we were assigned one of the Qatar royal sons and 20 of his entourage. So suddenly we were running a royal tour and a relay. Two weeks out we needed new logistics and more people and resources. Even for the Sydney Olympics selling the event went so well that an extra 20 media representatives wanted to travel with the torch. This means we needed to service them with extra staff and resources.

Our management system has been developed for the year. I call them the key documents. It is made up of:

1. Executive summary — outlining the structure of the event to the Board
2. Budget for approval
3. Concept of operations or a functional strategy paper that details every programme — in the case of a relay it is 30 programmes. This includes exactly what need to be procured, where its coming from, who will use it and its dependency. What depends on it and what it depends on — such as radios are from technology
4. Master Plan with the timeline including approvals
5. Series of spreadsheets including the following:
    (a) Master Personnel Schedule — details all people, where you are going to hire theme, where they are going to be, what equipment they will have and what uniforms, etc.
    (b) Master Roster — tells the staff what they have to do and where to go
    (c) Master Equipment List
    (d) Master Accommodation Schedule

We use our templates and a database software program that marry the day books with geographic information.
More information:

http://olympic-museum.de/torches/torch2000.htm
http://www.doha-2006.com/gis/menuroot/torchrelay/torchrelay.aspx.html
http://www.bbc.co.uk/manchester/2002/baton/index.shtml

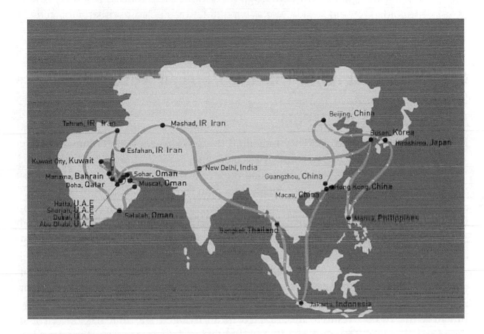

The route of the Doha Torch relay from their website

DISCUSSION TOPICS

List all the changes and their management

List the intangible benefits of these events

Research the history of the torch or baton relay — why is it so effective today?

CASE STUDY: GETTING THE MOST OUT OF VOLUNTEERS

ANZAC DAY AT GALLIPOLI

Following some adverse publicity regarding the 2005 Anzac Day commemorative services at Gallipoli (Turkey), the Australian and New Zealand Departments of Veteran's Affairs, Turkish authorities and the event management company, Definitive Events, formulated a revised management plan for 2006 and beyond. One aspect of that plan was to invite Conservation Volunteers Australia to recruit a team of volunteers to assist with the management of the 10,000 or more visitors who descend on the relatively isolated Anzac Commemorative Site near the south western end of the Gallipoli Peninsula.

The Anzac Day services at Gallipoli present a myriad of event management challenges. Australians and New Zealanders feel such a strong sense of ownership of these events, yet they are on the other side of the world in Turkish sovereign territory. In excess of 10,000 visitors are attracted to an isolated site that has no rail and limited road access. There are no toilets or lighting and there is no shelter or drinking water. Being an unticketed event there is no certainty about the audience size. The site itself is relatively small, being compressed between the Aegean coast and towering ridges that are largely unchanged since the famous landing in 1915. And the event attracts considerable media coverage, with some sections eager to find fault. As leader of the volunteer contingent, I was pleased that overcoming these challenges was the responsibility of the bureaucrats and their contractors.

My challenge was to ensure that the performance of the volunteer team met the expectations of the event organisers, while at the same time meeting the varied expectations of the volunteers themselves. Too often event organisers think only about what volunteers can do for them and then express disappointment that the volunteers are not really committed or are unreliable. If volunteers feel that they have a vested interest in doing an excellent job that is what they will do.

The Gallipoli volunteers paid their own travel and accommodation costs, quite a substantial sum, only to be asked to work a 26-hour straight shift through a freezing cold night with barely time to sit down. How do you make this fun or rewarding? How do you prime people to 'give their all' in a voluntary capacity?

Anzac Cove and the ridges and gullies behind it have a spiritual significance for most Australians, so the challenge was to somehow harness the evocative power of the landscape, and its associated Anzac legend, to motivate the volunteers to feel that the very least they could do to honour the original Anzacs was to 'do their bit' with stamina and good humour. Without exception the volunteers agreed that what they volunteered to do at Gallipoli would be so easy compared with what confronted the volunteers in 1915.

To consolidate the emotional bond with the site, we made sure that there was time to stroll Anzac Cove and Lone Pine, to visit legendary places like Quinn's Post and the Nek and to feel the spirits at Plugge's Plateau and Shrapnel Valley. We laid wreaths at the main Australian, New Zealand and Turkish memorials and made sure that any volunteers wanting to make personal pilgrimages had opportunities to do so.

It is also important that the volunteers know who they are working for, so meetings and social interaction with government and Definitive Events Staff were also arranged. Besides putting faces and personalities to the event organisers, these interactions also put the volunteer tasks in the broader context of the overall plan. By lunchtime on 24th of April, the start of the 'long shift', the volunteers were a close knit team, emotionally, psychologically and intellectually prepared to make sure their contribution was a very positive one. Perhaps, the strongest driver was the personal feeling of needing to do a great job — 'I owe it to the diggers.'

Gallipoli volunteers, at Ari Burnu Cemetery

The volunteers did a sensational job. All through the long, cold night they cheerfully welcomed visitors and encouraged them to respect and care for the site, distributed information packs, helped older visitors to find seats and assisted visitors with general enquiries. When the dawn service was over, some volunteers assisted 'special needs' visitors onto buses for the trip to the Australian service at Lone Pine while other volunteers, 20 hours into their shift, walked with the crowd up Artillery Road to Lone Pine to continue their visitor services roles.

By the time the volunteers joined other event officials at an afternoon barbeque, most of the 10,000 visitors, tired but also uplifted, were making their way back towards Istanbul in a huge fleet of tourist coaches and the commemorative sites were almost litter-free. The Governor General, the Minister for Veterans Affairs and the event manager were generous in their praise of the contribution made by the volunteers. How did the volunteers feel? 'One of the greatest experiences of my life', 'Something I will never forget', 'The most positive aspect for me was being part of a team undertaking such a fabulous life experience' and 'I want to come back next year!' were typical of volunteer responses.

The lesson? Look beyond what volunteers can do for you. Think about what your event or venue has to offer your volunteers. Take the time to think about how to manage and satisfy their expectations and they are likely to reciprocate by giving generously of their time, energy and enthusiasm.

Garry Snowden, Conservation Volunteers Australia, Gallipoli leader

DISCUSSION TOPICS

The case study makes a comment about the media wanting to find fault in the event. Is this the case with many public events? It is a well-known phenomenon for large international sporting events that the media are looking for stories in the lead up. Is this true of the Olympics in Beijing and the World Cup in South Africa? Research the stories in the lead up to these events.

The events commemorating conflicts are common around the world. Compare some of these to this story of Gallipoli.

There is a comment on the volunteers at the event and the volunteers for the actual battle of Gallipoli. Discuss the differences in volunteering for an event and volunteering for war.

CASE STUDY: THE CENTRAL OPERATIONS GROUP

In chapter 1 on Strategy, one of the advanced methods for cities to develop their events is to create an agency to attract events and manage the event portfolio. In this case study the city has gone one step further and gathered all the agencies involved in event operations together. It is a one-stop shop for event operations. Large events require the coordination of numerous agencies some of whom do not normally work together. The events may range from sports events to one-day special events with a million people to political events with major heads of government. The agencies have quite different priorities for each of these types of events.

Background

The Central Sydney Operations Group (CSOG) is an events-based interagency group. It is part of the New South Wales (NSW) Government's strategy to enhance the safety and enjoyment of events for the community and visitors. It was established in 1999 to ensure that Sydney was well prepared for the Millennium fireworks and the Sydney 2000 Olympic Games. The group continues to meet in relation to other events and has been regularly refined.

CSOG is an unusual and creative nexus between government, the community and private industry. The safety of the community and the reputation of the NSW Government face an element of risk every time a major event is held. Major events cannot be conducted without the input of the private sector events industry. Event deadlines cannot be moved so government agencies and event organisers need to resolve planning issues in a timely manner. The CSOG model offers a creative and resource-effective strategy to deliver safe and successful events. By having a central forum where issues are identified with sufficient lead times, planning is effective and resources are saved by not having to do crisis management.

The work of CSOG is governed by the following quality principles:

- Planning is the best prevention
- Decisions should be based on fact
- Progress happens best when there is trust and goodwill
- The best outcomes are achieved when there is shared responsibility in resolving issues and implementing solutions

Description

CSOG is organised and chaired by the NSW Department of Premier and Cabinet. This provides an independent chair and an authoritative, whole-of-government approach. The Department of Premier and Cabinet also oversees government event policies.

CSOG operates through

(i) A monthly forum of senior operational personnel from over 30 NSW Government agencies who share information about upcoming events. Event organisers present their events to the group so issues can be identified. The group also debriefs events from the previous month and identifies areas for improvements in future events. Topics of relevance such as risk management are also presented to the group.

(ii) Event-specific meetings to discuss details such as traffic management plans. These meetings usually involve the event organiser and critical agencies such as the NSW Police Force and the Roads and Traffic Authority.

(iii) A media and communications group. This subgroup looks at how public communications for an event will work, both for those attending an event and, importantly, for the community who are not attending but will be affected by it.

(iv) Desktop exercises to clarify roles, responsibilities and lines of communication. Scenarios are presented to a group that comprises the event organiser and all relevant government agencies, some weeks prior to the staging of the event.

(v) All-agency briefing sessions. These usually occur immediately prior to the staging of an event and involve the event organiser and all relevant government agencies. In some cases, they will be conducted at the site of the event.

(vi) The Government Coordination Centre. During an event, key government agency representatives, as well as the NSW Police Force and a representative of the event organiser, work together in a high technology command centre to monitor the event. This enables a coordinated response to problems arising during an event and is aided by special software developed to track incidents.

Scope

CSOG concentrates on events that have a direct impact on government infrastructure and the operations of agencies, particularly in the Sydney Central Business District and harbour foreshore.

Members

There are five main groups:

1. Landholders: Sydney Opera House, Centennial Parklands, Botanic Gardens Trust, Sydney Harbour Foreshore Authority, Sydney Harbour Federation Trust, Sydney Olympic Park Authority, Sydney Ports, Roads and Traffic Authority, Government House, National Parks and Wildlife and inner metropolitan councils.
2. Emergency services (in the context of events): NSW Police Force, Ambulance Service of NSW, NSW Health, NSW Fire Brigades, District Emergency Management Office, Bureau of Meteorology.
3. Traffic and transport: Ministry of Transport, State Transit Authority, Sydney Ferries, RailCorp, Roads and Traffic Authority, Sydney Ports, NSW Maritime.
4. Volunteer services: St. John Ambulance, Royal Volunteer Coastal Patrol.
5. Other agencies that can advise on events: Department of Local Government, Department of Ageing, Disability and Homecare, Department of State and Regional Development, Tourism NSW, Department of Premier and Cabinet.

Operations

The CSOG group meets on the last Monday of the month for approximately 2 hours. Smaller groups meet on an as-needs basis in the lead up to events.

A reason for the success of the model is the rigour applied to the conduct of the monthly forums. Agenda are consistent, carefully designed and the meetings are chaired in a highly structured manner. Minutes are thorough and distributed quickly. Actions that emerge from the forum are followed through by the staff of Department of Premier and Cabinet.

Event organisers are invited to attend when they are staging an event that will impact on the participating agencies. They are asked to address how their event will impact and what further consultation will take place. The advantage for event organisers is in being able to address a group of government agencies in one session rather than going to each individually. They save time in being introduced to the appropriate personnel for their event.

Examples

An example of CSOG in operation is the annual New Year's Eve event. This is a major event that places Sydney in the spotlight as it receives international press coverage every year. The event organiser is the City of Sydney but the event impacts on the operations of the NSW Police Force, the Roads and Traffic Authority, NSW Maritime, the Sydney Opera House, RailCorp, the Ambulance Service of NSW, the State Transit Authority (buses), Sydney Ferries and all landholders adjacent to the harbour including local councils. Though established for the 1999 Millennium event, CSOG has become the key forum for stakeholder consultation about New Year's Eve. As a result, very successful partnerships have been forged between the government agencies, councils, landholders and event organisers.

The CSOG model has been successfully applied to numerous events including the Sydney 2000 Olympic and Paralympic Games, 2003 Rugby World Cup, 2004 Welcome Home Parades for Athens Olympic and Paralympic Games, the Queen's Baton Relay, Centenary of Federation celebrations, Australia Day events, Sydney Festival, the Mardi Gras Parade, City to Surf, Sydney Marathon, Seniors Week and the 75th Anniversary of the Sydney Harbour Bridge in 2007. These events have been staged without serious incident and have enhanced the national and international reputation of New South Wales and Sydney as a host of successful major events.

The ability to replicate this model was well demonstrated when the project leaders of CSOG were asked to work on issues affecting events in the Moore Park Precinct in Sydney's east. The Moore Park Events Operations Group (MEOG) was established along similar lines to CSOG and after only a few months of operation began delivering benefits to stakeholders. Matters that were intractable matters are now unpacked, reviewed and resolved, and specific operational changes are made.

In 2005, at the invitation of the Singapore Government, 10 of the representatives of CSOG presented a workshop in Singapore to assist in the development of a local version of CSOG.

DISCUSSION TOPICS

There are three core processes involved in this case study; stakeholder management, communication management and risk management. Summarise the case study from these three perspectives.

Create a typology of event or event classification for the events that would be of interest to a central operations group.

Research the latest disasters at events around the world and discuss if these could have been avoided by establishing a central operations group.

CASE STUDY: INTERNATIONAL BUSKERS AND COMEDY FESTIVAL BY THE EVENTS TEAM AT COFFS HARBOUR CITY COUNCIL, AUSTRALIA

The case study illustrates the application of the event management processes to an event. It is not a large event, however, it has the management tools to expand and franchise. It illustrates the way the feasibility and development of the event is highly dependent on a professional system to manage and deliver it.

The Coffs Harbour International Buskers and Comedy Festival will be heading into its eighth year in 2009. Organised by Coffs Harbour City Council, the 2008 festival attracted an estimated 22,000 people throughout the 120 shows that took place over the 8 days. These shows took place in over 15 different venues around Coffs Harbour. Buskers from all over the world attended the festival including acts from the USA, Canada, France, the UK, New Zealand and all corners of Australia. The festival aims to:

- To stimulate greater economic activity throughout the region by encouraging tourists and the community to support local business.
- To create a festival that compliments and builds on the unique natural and built environment of the Coffs Harbour region.
- To create a social outlet that encourages the community to come together in a celebration of culture.
- To create a positive view of Coffs Harbour City Council and the services it provides to the community.

The festival's management team consists of two full-time event coordinators along with a number of part-time roles including operations, marketing, sponsor liaison and performer liaison. The event action plan is the first task for the festival team, with the team meeting as a group to develop the plan. The plan is generally developed from the previous year's plan, with necessary amendments made as a result of the previous year's event evaluation process. On completion of the plan all those with responsibilities assigned to the plan are provided with a copy.

Action plans are designed around the various roles and responsibilities involved in the delivery of an event with sections dedicated to, for example, operations, marketing, sponsor liaison, and performer liaison. This is in line with the festival roles identified above. It is important that the action plan fits with the other project management tools utilised in the project management system including the project budget and project timelines (Gantt chart). As such these tools are generally developed in conjunction with the action plan over a series of meetings, once again following the themes of operations, marketing, sponsors, performers, etc. The action plan generally consists of:

- Festival overview — mission, vision, objectives
- Stakeholders — internal staff, external contractors
- Action sheets — operations, sponsor liaison, performer liaison
- Timeline
- Budget

The roles are broken down into individual steps that need to be completed. It is vital that these steps be accompanied by a timeframe as to when these steps need to be completed by and this ties in with the overall event timeline. Additionally, it is also vital that responsibilities are assigned to the plan to ensure accountability. The steps outlined in the action plan are ideally signed off and completed prior to the implementation of the festival. During the implementation phase of the festival run sheets and contingency plans generally overtake the action plan as being the main working documents during this stage. All of these documents are then compiled at the conclusion of the festival to assist in the evaluation process.

The purpose of the project management plan is twofold. Firstly, the plan aims to ensure that the various individuals involved in the coordination of the event are aware of their roles and responsibilities and the timeframe in which they need to achieve their given tasks, also how these fit with the roles and responsibilities of others in the events team. The second is to ensure that the tasks required to complete the event are well documented for future reference. Past experience has shown that the plan for an event is often stored in the mind of the event coordinator and hence when the coordinators role changes hands, which regularly happens, the incumbent is often left with little or no documentation to guide them through the future development of the festival.

One thing that should be noted is that the action plan is a working document and as such needs to be amended where necessary as issues arise. In most cases the project plan is covered in notes at the conclusion of the event. These notes not only ensure that any additional requirements during the planning process have been recorded, but also that these can be added to the next year's plan. Furthermore as steps are completed these are marked off, or highlighted, to show that they have been completed and the next step moved on to. Meetings are scheduled with their regularity increasing as the festival nears. These meetings are used to check the progress of the overall plan.

At the conclusion of the festival all of the action plans from those involved are collated and any amendments to the original plan noted. These notes and the previous year's plan will then form the basis for the next year's plan. Additionally, these notes can also contribute to the event evaluation process by identifying those actions that were overlooked in the original planning process.

	Action		
	Busker Liaison – To attract suitable Buskers to the festival and to ensure that all the appropriate approvals are in place and that they are well looked after during their stay		
	Steps to completion	**Responsible**	**Completed by**
Step 1	Investigate and shortlist Buskers. Sift through Busker Applications and make a shortlist of those acts considered suitable for the festival	Festival Coordinators, Busker Liaison	*Mid-February*
Step 2	Approach shortlisted acts regarding their availability and interest in attending the festival	Busker Liaison	*Late February*
Step 3	Confirm availability of Buskers and develop a preliminary festival Schedule	Festival Coordinators, Busker Liaison	*Late March*
Step 4	Develop and confirm individual contracts for Buskers	Festival Coordinators, Busker Liaison	*Late April*
Step 5	Confirm Busker's arrangements including airfares, insurances, and travel documentation	Busker Liaison	*Late June*
Step 6	Confirm Busker's festival requirements including accommodation and transport	Busker Liaison	*Late July*
Step 7	Put together information pack for Buskers including tourist information, festival information, run sheets and contact numbers	Busker Liaison	*Late August*
Step 8	Gain access to Busker's Accommodation Facilities to make the necessary arrangements	Busker Liaison	*Festival lead in week*
			Signed off

DISCUSSION TOPICS

The event planing process presented in this case study is an application of some of the processes outlined in Chapters 8 and 9. Which are the processes not used in the festival and why are they not used?

Change this case study into a workflow chart and discuss how it could be employed to franchise the event to other cities.

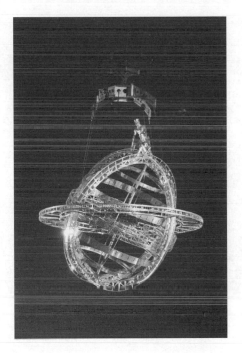

Doha 2006 Asian Games Opening Ceremony: The Astrolabe. Courtesy of David Atkins Enterprises

Doha 2006 Asian Games Opening Ceremony: The Golden Falcon. Courtesy of David Atkins Enterprises

Doha 2006 Asian Games Opening Ceremony: The City of the Future. Courtesy of David Atkins Enterprises

Doha 2006 Asian Games Opening Ceremony: The Wedding Scene. Courtesy of David Atkins Enterprises

A QATARI CEREMONY: OPENING CEREMONY, DOHA 2006 ASIAN GAMES BY MATTHEW LORRIMER 2009

Introduction

The 15th Asian Games was held in Doha, Qatar from 1 to 15 December 2006. It was the largest ever event in the Middle East, attracting approximately 10,500 athletes and team officials from 45 competing nations across 39 sports. Qatar was the first Arab country to host the games and the smallest country in the world in modern history to hold an event of the size, complexity and reputation of the Asian Games.

After its successful bid for the Asian Games, the Qatari Government signed the Host City Contract (HCC) with the Olympic Council of Asia (OCA) the 'owner' of the games. The Asian Games is by far the largest and highest profile event in the OCA calendar. It is the world's second largest multisport event, in terms of athlete and sport competition numbers, after the Summer Olympic Games, in the International Olympic Committee's (IOC) calendar.

The Doha Asian Games Organising Committee (DAGOC), established in 2001 by Emiri decree, was responsible for the planning and execution of the games in accordance with the HCC.

In February 2005, after a lengthy international bidding process, the Sydney, Australia-based major events producer, David Atkins Enterprises (DAE), won the tender to create, produce, construct, stage and dismantle the Opening and Closing Ceremonies for the 15th Asian Games. Led by Producer/Artistic Director, David Atkins, DAE reported to the DAGOC Director of Ceremonies and Cultural Events, the client representative (Client), whose approval was required on all major decisions.

The Opening Ceremony was staged on 1 December 2006 in front of 40,000 spectators and guests at Khalifa Stadium in Doha, with less than 4 days allowed for its 'bump-out'[1] prior to the commencement of the Athletics competition on 7 December.

The television-viewing audience was estimated to be in excess of 3 billion.

DAGOC/DAE CONTRACT

The contract between DAGOC and DAE (Contract) contained an extensive and demanding brief which included the following requirements:

- Enhance and promote the modern image and the 'new era' of Qatar, including its rapid transformation;

---

[1] 'Bump-out' is the term used to refer to the dismantling of staging and equipment and removal from the venue after an event.

- Stage world-class Opening and Closing Ceremonies, exceeding the standards of all previous Asian Games and comparable to, or exceeding, Ceremonies for previous Olympic Games;
- Provide value for money;
- Ensure full integration with DAGOC's planning processes, procedures and operations, both pre and during Games and
- Leave a lasting physical and intellectual legacy for Qatar and its people.

These requirements became seminal to the approach DAE took with the Ceremonies project.

CASE STUDY STRUCTURE

This case study examines how the project and resource management strategies implemented by DAE enabled the Opening Ceremony to meet and exceed the Client's expectations and demanding brief, across three broad perspectives:

- *Creative perspective* – management of the Ceremony's creative content and communicating it to the Client, DAE staff and cast and the performance itself.
- *Logistics perspective* – management of the planning, staffing, contracting, rehearsing and building of the Opening Ceremony.
- *Legacy perspective* – knowledge transfer and skill development imperatives for Qatar's future.

This case study addresses the Opening Ceremony only. It does not address the Closing Ceremony, although most of the management and resourcing issues and solutions discussed in the case study apply equally to it.

PROJECT STRUCTURE AND DOCUMENTATION

In order to focus its event management task, DAE broke down the highly complex project into a Strategic Planning Phase and an Implementation Phase, which was further divided into three stages, each one aligned with the principle documentation requirements and milestones stipulated in the Contract,[2] as follows:

Strategic planning phase

- Strategic stage
  - Focus: ideas generation; *Strategic Plan* implemented (note that the *Strategic Plan* was largely developed for and included in DAE's tender bid documentation)
  - Documentation: *Operational Plan* developed
  - Timing: March–August 2005

---

[2] The Contract required substantial formal documentation. Plans required other than those listed here, included Procurement, IT&T, Quality Assurance Plan and Logistics Plans.

Implementation Phase

- Operational stage
  - Focus: planning; *Operational Plan* implemented
  - Documentation: *Production Plan* developed
  - Timing: September 2005–May 2006
- Production stage
  - Focus: construction/rehearsal; *Production Plan* implemented
  - Documentation: *Event Plan* developed
  - Timing: June–October 2006
- Event stage
  - Focus: delivery/performance: *Event Plan* implemented
  - Documentation
  - Timing: November 2006–January 2007

DAE ORGANISATIONAL STRUCTURE

Drawing on its past experience from other successful mega events, including the Opening and Closing Ceremonies at the Sydney 2000 Olympic Games, DAE structured its organisation into divisions. The head of each division reported either to David Atkins, Producer/Artistic Director, or to the Executive Producer.

Creative Division

Responsible for: artistic direction, creative design, music, choreography, principal performers, livestock, protocol, screen imagery, stage management and three-dimensional animation.

Technical Division

Responsible for: venue and production infrastructure, technical design, lighting, sound, communications, projection, pyrotechnics, staging, construction (scenery, props and costumes) and freight.

Operations Division

Responsible for: venue and site acquisition and management, overlay and temporary facilities, security, accreditation, medical and fire and safety.

Production Services Division

Responsible for: mass casts, volunteers, ground transport, accommodation, information management, flights and catering.

Finance and Administration Division

Responsible for: finance, human resources, information technology, telecommunications, project management, office management, contracts, legal, insurances and administration.

Media Division

Responsible for: publications, programmes and media liaison.

OPERATING ENVIRONMENT

On setting up in Doha, DAE's approach was to first identify the perceived issues arising from the Qatari operating environment.

The following schedule of issues were initially identified and were continually updated, thus providing a useful guide to the way management and resourcing processes needed to be designed and implemented.

Environment	Issues
Climate	The extreme desert climate, including sand storms would: • Reduce working hours for outdoor installations and rehearsals from June to September • Require increased research and development for technical equipment to maintain their performance • Require strict attention to crew health issues • Limit the number of technical personnel available for recruitment • Adversely effect livestock performance
Cultural	Cultural factors would need to be taken into account, including the effect of: • Slower pace of business and government processes and communications (and adherence to other priorities) • Fasting during Ramadan on processes such as customs clearance, as well as procurement, rehearsal schedules and equipment maintenance • Accidental misinterpretation of Qatari cultural taboos and traditions
DAGOC departments	Relationships and interfaces with DAGOC managers would need to be close to: • Facilitate services required by DAE such as IT, telecommunications and accreditation • Ensure facilities were provided, as agreed, to enable DAE to meet its contractual obligations
DAGOC approvals processes	DAGOC approvals would need to be effectively sought and provided within strict time constraints to: • Enable DAE to meet obligations regarding the production budget, expenditure and operational planning • Ensure that the technical schedule was achievable, including time for any required amendments or alterations
Local business	DAE would need to pay particular attention to factors likely to attract complications and delays, including the: • Limited and inflationary accommodation market • Required approvals and licensing for logistical operations, warehousing, customs and freight movements • Immigration and visa processes • Tendering and procurement • Supply limitations for major components

Stadium constraints and opportunities	Khalifa Stadium presented a number of issues for resolution including • Limited functionality and structural limitations in some areas • Requirement for significant infrastructural alterations • Lack of information available regarding the activity in the stadium in 2006 making it difficult to schedule work in the stadium • Adequate space allocation for Ceremonies in the stadium
Khalifa Stadium Precinct	Khalifa Precinct presented challenges including • Coordination of major construction activity prior to the games • Management of logistics, security, transport, spectator services, non-ticketed spectators at games time

OPERATIONAL INTERFACES

Soon after establishing its Doha operations, DAE identified the authorities with which important operational interfaces would need to be established and effectively managed (over and above those with DAGOC and its numerous departments).

The following authorities and interface issues were initially identified. This, along with subsequent revisions, helped DAE shape its approach to communication, reporting and approvals management (e.g. codes and compliance).

Authority/Interface	Issues
Ambulance service	Access to stadium, first aid, hospitalisation, C3[3]
Customs and Ports General Authority	• Importation of all production elements including prohibited goods such as fireworks • Importation Tax Policy • Timeframes during Ramadan
Fire brigade	Access to stadium, C3
Hamad General Hospital	• Emergency Medical requirements • Ambulance access in emergency
Ministry of Education and Culture	Volunteer Student Performer Programme
Ministry of Interior	Visas and residency for: • Performers • Production Personnel • Contractors • Crew
Ministry of Municipal Affairs and Agriculture	Planning and building approvals

(Continued)

---

[3] C3 refers to communications, command and control.

Authority/Interface	Issues
Ministry of Public Health	• Approvals for food service and fit out • Hospitalisation
Labour Department	• Qatari Labour Law • Occupational Health and Safety (OHS) • Weather monitoring advice in the months from June to September
National Council for Culture, Arts and Heritage	• Feedback on creative concept • Qatari cultural input
Police and Security Services	C3
Qatar Telecom	Communications issues include • Bandwidths • Permits for communication licences
Qatar General Electricity and Water Corporation	Interruptions to: • Power supply • Water supply
Khalifa Sports City	Building approvals including for Ceremonies Capital Works Programme

DAGOC MILESTONES

Soon after appointment DAE undertook an analysis of the Contract, and together with subsequent Client instructions, the major milestones were identified and agreed with the Client as follows:

Milestone	Date
Approve draft creative concept	September 2005
Approve implementation milestones	September 2005
Approve Capital Works Programme Concept Design and early engineering design	September 2005
Approve Capital Works Programme budget	October 2005
Approve operational plan	September 2005
Approve first draft production budget	September 2005
Approve 3D animation	November 2005
Confirm protocol requirements	December 2005
Approve final creative concept	December 2005
Approve final production budget	December 2005
Stadium venue team onsite and operational	January 2006
Deliver all Ceremonies site/venue requirements (Doha-wide), fit-for-purpose and ready for occupation	February 2006
Approve production plan	May 2006
Approve event plan	October 2006

CREATIVE PERSPECTIVE

The DAGOC Contract required the Ceremonies to be 'comparable to or exceeding Ceremonies for previous Olympic Games' and stipulated that the they should 'improve on' the previous Olympic Games in Sydney (2000), Salt Lake City (2002), Athens (2004) and Turin 2006, and the Manchester (2002) and Melbourne (2006) Commonwealth Games.

This was a challenging requirement for DAE, especially the creative team, and in order to achieve it, every component of previous major Opening Ceremonies was analysed.[4]

BENCHMARKING AND RESEARCH

DAE determined that the best benchmarks were the Sydney 2000 and Athens 2004 Summer Olympic Games. Athens[5] had taken 'flying'[6] to new levels, so DAE sought to excel in that field, but in almost all other respects, DAE assessed that Sydney 2000 was still far ahead of other Ceremonies, especially in its scenic elements and pure spectacle value, so Doha had to surpass this.

DAE's management approach was to set a number of benchmarks against which to measure the Ceremony's success; the criteria adopted included the following:

- Level of engagement
- Entertainment value
- Innovation

DAE carried out extensive broad-based research,[7] commencing with a series of Cultural Symposia in Doha. The principal aims of the symposia were to ensure that the original DAE creative concept was culturally sensitive and relevant by engaging with the local artistic community; to procure creative Qatari talent and to gain insight into technical resource capabilities available in Qatar.

---

[4] Generally, a ceremony comprises Welcome, Cultural Display and Cauldron Lighting as well as a number of components mandated by the OCA — Pre-Show (warm-up), Welcome and Arrival of Head of State and Dignitaries (when the national flag is raised and national anthem sung), Athletes Parade and Protocol elements (including the OCA hymn and flag, athletes oath, various speeches and the arrival of the Torch Relay).

[5] Athens was thought to be a little esoteric, short on entertainment value and not worth the reported cost of three or four times that of Sydney.

[6] 'Flying' is the term used to refer to the suspension of parts of the Ceremony at heights above the Stadium floor on cables.

[7] The DAE bid had contained detail as to how this would be achieved, but the on-the-ground reality required this to undergo considerable amendment.

SCRIPT AND ANIMATION

The script is the datum from which all other creative development work progresses — design, animation, choreography, music, lighting and sound. DAE's Stage Management Department managed the Opening Ceremony script which was subject to a strict version-control regime. They also managed its distribution and confidentiality, in tandem with the Administration Division, which was responsible for intellectual property protection and legal.

To ensure that the Client, DAE staff and performers well understood all proposed creative content for the Ceremony, DAE made extensive use of CAD data, especially relating to the stadium, and computer-animated the complete Ceremony. This also aided the technical design process.

This was a world-first, as typically a ceremony producer would only provide artists' impressions for their client. But DAE animated all segments of the creative concept, both cultural and protocol — approximately 95% of the concept — and animated the lighting of the cauldron in real time. Even the pyrotechnic sequences were animated to demonstrate their appearance, timing and trajectory.

These measures gave the Client (and DAE) confidence that the creative concept would be delivered 'on the night' and enabled the Client to communicate important sequences and politically sensitive concepts to the Emir of Qatar, HH Sheikh Hamad Bin Khalifa Al-Thani, DAE's ultimate client.

TESTING 'THE CREATIVE'

To ensure ideas and concepts, 'The Creative', were practical and achievable, DAE continually tested them in Khalifa Stadium, at its purpose-built production and rehearsal facilities adjacent to the stadium and at the various contractors' factories in Greece, Macedonia, Australia (Sydney, Adelaide and Brisbane), Switzerland, USA, China, Canada, Germany and UK.

STAGE MANAGEMENT

DAE's Stage Management Department was responsible for show planning and management, including coordinating its resource requirements, as well as 'stage management'.[8] In doing so, Stage Management developed:

- Master Rehearsal Schedule for the Ceremonies in tandem with the creative team, incorporating the integrated movement plans for performers, scenery and props throughout rehearsals and performance and bump out

---

[8] 'Stage management' refers to the management of the Ceremonies performance.

- Requirements and planning for audition and casting, Athletes Parade and protocol in consultation with the Production Services Division
- Rehearsal and performance technical requirements in consultation with the Technical Division
- Operational requirements in consultation with the Operations Division, e.g. transport, site facilities and security.

Stage Management also liaised with the host broadcaster to develop the Ceremony's Television Scripts and Timings.

PERFORMERS

The Opening Ceremony was brought to life by about 5000 performers; inevitably, casting was a mammoth worldwide task. In order to procure an adequate cross-section of performers from the Middle East and Asia, DAE sent its team of choreographers to Egypt, Syria, Lebanon, Phillipines, Kazakhstan, India and Japan to audition performers.

In the final line-up the Ceremony deployed about 500 paid performers from Qatar, Egypt, China, HK, Indonesia, Japan, Thailand, India, Kazakhstan, Phillipines, Australia, UK, Syria and Lebanon, providing dancers, acrobats, aerialists and character performers.

In addition, paid 'headline talent' included: international orchestra of 70 players, Arabic orchestra of 12 players, lead children and adults, Qatari singers, rock/pop stars, opera singers and a famous classical Arabic singer.

This in addition to the volunteer performers, comprising 2000 children from 47 schools (including a 200-voice children's choir) and 2500 adults. Attracting such large numbers of performers from a society not attuned to public performance (especially among girls and women) was achieved by a national outreach programme to educate people about 'Olympic'-style Ceremonies, which preceded the DAE recruitment and audition effort.

One hundred and fifty buses were required to transport all volunteers and performers to and from the Ceremony.

'CHARTING' THE MOVEMENTS

Accurately predicting when thousands of performers need to enter onto a large stadium in order to end up in the desired formation and then dissolve into a series of patterns requires precise planning and a deep understanding of human movement.

DAE achieved this unfolding of the desired image by 'charting' all movements on computer, and these were communicated to all parties on charts, thus mapping the movement of performers and scenic elements. In this way, any given scene or sequence could be rehearsed, at speed, and accurately married with the specially commissioned and recorded music.

MUSIC

The Opening Ceremony contained three and a half hours of music. The challenge was to present Qatar to the world through music that felt 'Arabic' yet worked on a large scale and made sense to the huge worldwide television audience. This was achieved by the Musical Director's lengthy research process, beginning in Sydney with invaluable help from the Sydney's Arabic radio station and then progressing to Doha, where he immersed himself in Qatari culture and met with local composers and performance groups. The Cultural Symposia in Doha were an important part of this research process.

DAE realised that there is no symphonic orchestral tradition in Qatar, but use of the orchestra is essential as it matches the epic scale of such an event. The solution chosen was to use an Asian orchestra — the Guangzhou Symphony Orchestra — and feature Qatari musicians.

Neither is there a tradition of harmony in Arabic music, something that the Musical Director needed, to give a sense of scale to the performance. The solution determined was to introduce the concept of a 150-voice children's choir, and commencing with simple rounds such as Freres Jacques teach the children the basics of harmony. This allowed the Choir to be used during the Ceremony to the desired effect.

For the major set pieces, composers were brought together from Australia, Qatar, Germany, Singapore, Malaysia, Egypt and USA. The orchestral pieces were recorded in Prague with the Slovak National Symphony Orchestra.

LOGISTICS PERSPECTIVE

The Contract stipulated that DAE should achieve 'full integration with DAGOC's planning processes, procedures and operations, both pre and during Games'.

In essence, DAGOC required DAE to become a department of DAGOC, conforming to DAGOC corporate norms. This necessitated effective horizontal liaison between the DAE Heads of Divisions and their equivalent managers inside DAGOC. Functional areas of particular importance and where such collaboration was essential to the success of the Ceremony included finance, HR policy, accreditation, information technology, telecommunications, site management and security, facilities and overlay, supplier selection, tender assessment and award, volunteer recruitment and management, immigration, customs clearance and freight.

DAE's process management task was simplified to some extent as it had already developed number of procedures which, although they needed to be tailored for the Qatari cultural, climatic and legal environments, were nevertheless sound. For example, staff contracts had to align with Qatari Labour Law. However, from a resourcing standpoint, DAE had to start from scratch as there were very limited technical event professionals and resources in Doha at that time.[9]

Staff and Recruitment

The core project team — Executive Producer, Artistic Director, Producer, Stage Manager and the Heads of Design, Music and Administration — was assembled in Sydney in early in 2005. A dozen or so DAE personnel took up residence in Doha in April 2005.

At full strength DAE had over 500 staff and consultants in Doha and 150 in Sydney. Artists, special talent, headline talent (including their entourages) and unpaid performers — students, choirs and clubs (including their teachers and minders) — numbered approximately 9000. In addition, a crew of 800 was required to operate the Ceremony. By any measure this was a very large undertaking.

The exponential growth of the Ceremonies organisation — in this case from a dozen or so to over 10,000 in a 22-month period — is typical of the dynamics of major events. The growth at DAE mirrored that of DAGOC and such growth, and swift dispersal after the Closing Ceremony, required sound management from all DAE Divisions, particularly DAE's HR Department with responsibility for recruitment, relocation and mobilisation procedures.

To achieve this, DAE designed and implemented a sophisticated system comprising modules for:

- Forecasting the staff numbers required
- Identifying required staff and potential candidates by HODs
- Formal requests for staff to the Executive Office
- Approval of such requests
- Engaging, mobilising and contracting staff
- Demobilisation

CAST MANAGEMENT

The assembling, scheduling, management and control of the enormous cast required for the Ceremonies and the services to facilitate their rehearsal and movement necessitated close teamwork between DAE's Divisions which provided services and equipment as detailed:

- *Creative Division*: artistic direction (vision), choreography (spatial sense), stage management (rehearsal and cast management)
- *Technical Services Division*: rehearsal props, staging, flying and technical equipment
- *Operations Division*: site management (facilities) and security

---

[9] However, the Doha Ceremonies production effort did leave a lasting legacy of this expertise (see later commentary under Legacy).

- *Production Services Division*: cast management, accommodation and transport
- *Administration Division*: technology development (databases, animation and charting), legal/contracting, immigration and HR

The biggest single cast group was the 3000 + school students. In order to recruit the numbers required for the Ceremonies, 47 schools were visited in DAE's Schools Programme over 9 months prior to the Ceremonies. All schools participated.

Turning these school children into performers was undertaken by the choreographic team, operating in DAE's column-free rehearsal halls half the size of the stadium arena. DAE provided a bus transport system, complete with a dedicated terminal, to get the children to rehearsals and home again at the right times. Food and standby medical supervision was also provided.

A large team of stage managers was deployed to schedule and control the huge-scale rehearsals. School children were divided into groups and identified with large variously coloured bibs with numbers on them. The charts mapped them all, so the choreographers were able to place each performer at the right coordinates on the arena at the right time.

VOLUNTEERS

No large Ceremony can be staged without volunteers, both children and adults. The adult volunteer performers went through a public audition process and in order to ensure its smooth implementation the DAE staff tested the system first, through the various stages:

- Registration
- Measurement
- Audition
- Final assessment

The main groups of volunteer performers, in order of size, were from: Egypt, Qatar, Yemen, Phillipines, India and Oman. There were also significant numbers of volunteers from Pakistan, Sri Lanka, Sudan, Syria and Nepal in support roles and as performers.

In order to ensure that volunteers were continually motivated and did not drop out half way through rehearsals, DAE developed an Incentive Programme, aligned to DAGOC's Incentive Programme, which included gifts and attendance at dress rehearsals.

HUMAN RESOURCES AND STAFF FACILITIES

A significant task for the HR Department was the smooth mobilisation of staff and performers from the 35 source countries. This required the development of a sophisticated management system to ensure that all personnel quickly adapted to their new environment in Doha without lengthy acclimatisation periods.

The system included the following:

- Streamlined visa, health check, fingerprinting and residency processing (this included advanced applications for visas in 'bulk' — defined by nationality and gender only — before staff were recruited
- Comprehensive 'Welcome Manual', complete with sections on Qatari culture (including expectations during the Holy Month of Ramadan), the Asian Games, the DAE Ceremonies creative concept, finance and banking, work guidelines and codes of conduct, health, insurance, immigration, communications, entertainment, shopping and useful Arabic phrases
- Regular Orientation Programmes for new staff included screenings of the animated creative concept

DAE paid particular attention to securing quality accommodation for its huge staff numbers. At peak DAE occupied 11 separate facilities and these were serviced by DAE's dedicated bus network operating 18 hours a day.

A subsidised staff canteen was constructed at the Ceremonies Compound, which served into the evening. It ensured that valuable time was not lost during rehearsals which generally took place in the evenings and weekends.

Bank accounts were opened for all staff to enable their salaries to be directly deposited and the bank was required to visit the Ceremonies Compound to service all staff requirements.

Special arrangements were made with the local health authorities to ensure adequate health services were available; these in tandem with DAE's onsite nursing staff.

CULTURAL LIAISON

A key challenge faced by DAE was operating in a cultural environment largely foreign to many staff and contractors. DAE's Liaison Department implemented processes to allow staff to function in a culturally acceptable way. Liaison also assisted DAE to efficiently and effectively deliver the Ceremonies in accordance with a number of stringent provisions in the contract; their services and processes included the following:

- Cultural advice to all DAE staff and Divisions in areas such as artistic, procurement/tendering, legal, contractual, human resources, political, insurance, OHS and industrial relations
- Interpretation and translation of documents, including contracts
- Cultural interface where DAE needed to 'get beneath the surface' of challenging relationships, difficult issues and communication problems
- Research and/or analysis when required, in fields such as Qatari culture, local/regional customs and issues, local politics and legal issues
- Guidance through bureaucratic situations and processes, including with government departments, agencies, authorities, utilities, institutions and instrumentalities

FACILITIES AND SITE MANAGEMENT

In January 2006, DAGOC established a 125,000 m^2 construction workshop in Sydney for the early commencement of major scenic elements and stage props[10] there, and contractors were progressively appointed for all the other elements: stages, central chamber and lift, flying system, cauldron, cyclorama, and giant LED screen.

Construction of the Doha facilities required for the Ceremonies commenced in early 2006 and the facilities were completed in April 2006. In doing so, DAGOC provided a world-first, with all required facilities in a single 80,000 m^2, compound adjacent to Khalifa Stadium. Of this, 26,000 m^2 of space was airconditioned, comprising costume workshops, four 10-m high construction workshops, rehearsal spaces, canteen and office space for over 300 DAE operations, creative, administrative and management staff.

A full-size outdoor rehearsal space of 1900 m^2, mirroring the dimensions of the stadium, was constructed in tarmac with viewing platforms around it, as well as two half-size indoor rehearsal halls. A bus terminal (for mass cast rehearsals) was also constructed.

In September 2006, DAGOC added a 30,000 m^2 livestock compound for the 64 horses in the Opening Ceremony, complete with living quarters for their grooms.

TECHNOLOGY

Technology played a significant role in the preparation and implementation of the Ceremonies. To document its requirements, DAE drafted an IT&T Plan in June 2005, which was updated as requirements were better defined. The Plan outlined:

- Capacity planning, e.g. bandwidth and storage
- Network design, e.g. LAN configurations
- DAGOC–DAE interaction, e.g. confidentiality
- Telephony
- Technical specifications, e.g. servers, storage and backup, network appliances, structured wiring, wireless networking, printing/scanning/fax/copying, server room and fire protection
- Administration, e.g. responsibility for access, device management, UPS and fire and safety.

Innovation was a mandatory part of the brief and therefore new technologies were high on the agenda. All such innovations required strict confidentiality at all times and staff, consultants, performers and contractors were required to sign Confidentiality Agreements prior to viewing any confidential information or technological developments associated with the Ceremonies.

---

[10] 'Props' are the hand-held or portable elements used to support the performers.

The huge light-emitting diode (LED) cyclorama was the largest ever built at 4500 m^2 and providing an adequate signal to all parts of the screen required developing a purpose-built system to 'drive' it from a farm of computers. DAE conducted extensive field testing to select the most reliable system with the required definition.

The structure to support the cyclorama comprised 2500 tonnes of steel manufactured in Macedonia. As with everything created for the Ceremonies, the LED cyclorama was designed to cope with the desert climate; each of its ribs was engineered to expand 7 mm between the cool of the night and the heat of the day.

In order to surpass Athens 2004, the DAE Ceremonies pushed aerial 'flying' performance, rigging techniques and the use of the vertical dimension to its limit, and thus required the introduction of technical and performance innovations.

The Cauldron was the most complicated element. Enormously heavy, the hydraulics had to lift 150 tonnes into the air. Pumping gas through the moving rings required innovative engineering solutions. To cool the insides of the three revolving concentric steel rings and stop them distorting with the extreme heat of the flame and the desert climate, airconditioning was installed to pump cold air around inside them.

DAE's IT Department was required to develop computerised and web-based solutions to assist the effort in areas such as: information management; staff forecasting, recruitment and management; mass cast recruitment and management; animation; communications; scheduling; contract management and data storage.

CEREMONIES CAPITAL WORKS PROGRAMME

A regime of Project Control Group meetings was initiated by DAE for the Ceremonies Capital Works Programme (CCWP).

The CCWP was essential because the Ceremonies required significant alterations to Khalifa Stadium, principally a hydraulic stage lift in the centre of the arena with a tunnel connecting it to back-of-house[11] areas; enlargement of performer/athlete entrances; foundations for the LED cyclorama and foundations and gas supply lines for the cauldron.

These alterations required DAE to detail its requirements early on, so that the stadium authorities, who were managing the CCWP, could engineer their design to suit the Ceremonies and the stadium's existing structural limitations.

CONTRACTING AND LEGAL

DAE's subcontracting regime had to satisfy the DAGOC imposed codes of practice, but at the same time attract interest from the international event market. This was

---

[11] The term 'back-of-house' (BOH) refers to the areas isolated from spectator areas required to manage a stadium and its events.

particularly difficult where a limited number of qualified contractors (or in some cases a single contractor) were available to bid.

DAE achieved this by drafting a Procurement Plan, which, after negotiation with the Client, was accepted. Central to the Plan was DAE's approach to fair and open tendering procedures (including expressions of interest, pre-qualification, tender submission requirements, pricing, tenderer selection, award and contracting). The process was supervised by the Ceremonies Tender Review Committee and DAE had a representative on the Committee.

A suite of contracts was devised and approved by DAGOC, with legal advice from local lawyers to ensure all aspects of Qatari law were taken into account and the risks to the Client (and DAE) were minimised. These contracts covered staff, contractors, suppliers, consultants, composers and arrangers and performers. The provisions concerning protection of intellectual property, both for DAE and its creative consultants and partners and the payment of royalties, were drafted by a specialist in the contracting of recorded and live performance.

By the time that the Ceremonies went into production over 1200 entities had been contracted, including 170 major suppliers and consultants from 15 countries, 420 performers and composers from the Middle East, Asia, Europe and Australasia and 660 DAE staff

Insurance

Insurance provisions were thoroughly researched, especially with respect to local Qatari conditions, where insurance is a developing, immature market. Insurance cover effected for: public liability; professional indemnity; contract risk; data loss; group health and loss of income; workers compensation; theft (including cash-in-transit); livestock; vehicles and travel.

FREIGHT AND CUSTOMS

The Ceremonies alone required the importation of over 500 containers through Qatari customs. Each forecast Ceremony shipment was entered onto DAGOC's freight schedule to minimise the risk of delays in the customs clearance procedures. The re-export of goods and equipment used for the Ceremonies after the event was also coordinated in this way, to ensure that DAE and contractors were not burdened with unnecessary import/export duties and taxes.

LEGACY PERSPECTIVE

The Contract stipulated that the Ceremonies should 'leave a lasting physical and intellectual legacy for Qatar and its people'.

DAE gave considerable attention to this important element in the DAGOC Ceremony brief in the tender, planning and implementation stages.

School Children

DAE discovered that there were few organised movement programmes in Qatari schools and none of the dance schools that proliferate in the West. In order to involve school children in the Opening Ceremony, DAE undertook a training programme in schools with the support of Qatar's Ministry of Education and Supreme Education Council.

In June 2005, members of the DAE casting and choreographic departments visited 47 Doha schools to introduce the concept of the Ceremonies to teachers, pupils and their parents and explain the exciting opportunity for the students to represent their country and culture by participating.

The choreography team returned to conduct simple movement classes and returned again a few weeks later to see how the teachers and their students were progressing.

After consulting their parents, about 2000 students were selected from the preliminary classes to participate in the Ceremonies. During a 5-week training workshop, the children were introduced to the rehearsal process and they started to familiarise themselves with the required props and dance routines. Initially, boys and girls were required to rehearse separately, but then the Qatari Government gave DAE special permission for the conduct of co ed rehearsals.

A simpler process, relying solely on those wanting to attend open auditions, would not have achieved the school-wide attitudinal change that DAE initiated. Additionally, those children choosing not to attend such open auditions, or restricted by their parents from attending, would have felt excluded and gained no new skills.

DAE's process ensured that many more school children are now fitter and better equipped and motivated to combat the effects of a sedentary life-style coupled with having to stay indoors through the hot summer months.

THEATRICAL PRODUCTION SKILLS AND TRAINED STAFF

DAE involved as many local staff and volunteers as possible in the technical, operations, creative and performance areas of the Ceremonies. For example, this included the following:

- Stage management: where local and regional stage managers were engaged to manage cast and scenery movements
- Operations: where staff were involved in areas such as accreditation, data management and costume fitting and making
- Performance itself

In the final analysis, 30% of DAE's staff were either local or regional expatriates.

FACILITIES

The DAGOC-built Ceremonies facilities now exist to be used as production facilities for events, films and media or to be converted for other light industrial purposes. At the close of the project a printing press was being considered as a possible use for parts of the facilities.

DANCERS AND ACROBATS

The Ceremonies provided valuable experience for dance companies and acrobatic troupes from China, India, Japan, Thailand, Egypt, Kazakhstan, Syria, Indonesia and the Phillipines. They learnt new forms of performance and some were exposed for the first time to a highly professional creative management regime. Many dancers had never been exposed to an environment where issues of contracting, IP protection, insurance, working conditions and safe practices were professionally managed and resolved.

SUBCONTRACTORS

The Ceremonies created a new niche market for local Qatari and Gulf companies to expand their market and develop their technical and management skills. Many local companies teamed up with more experienced overseas companies in joint ventures to bid on contracts for the Ceremonies. This exposed them to the rigours of international tendering and opened them out to the broader worldwide market.

CULTURAL EXCHANGE

The Ceremonies brought many 'Western' expats to Qatar for their first time in the Middle East. As a result they were exposed to Qatari and Islamic culture set in the Gulf environment. On return to their home countries these expatriates had a better understanding of the region and were equipped to pass this on to their colleagues, families and friends. This provided a significant contribution to the elimination of stereotyping of the people of the Middle East, benefiting Qatar and the Gulf countries in particular.

MEGA EVENT BIDDING PLATFORM

As a result of producing the two Ceremonies at the 2006 Asian Games, Qatar is now better equipped to bid for mega events in the international market; substantial Ceremonies are now on it's national track record.

SYNOPSIS OF THE OPENING CEREMONY
Pre-show entertainment: Sadu — tribute to children of Qatar

A cast of 1500 Qatari children in traditional costume, from 29 Doha schools, play traditional games from their grandparent's era and using huge pieces of cloth they create a massive Sadu[12] carpet.

Contemporary-clad children create a modern carpet with bicycles, kites, balls and balloons. There are acoustic percussion and dance performances.

Orry[13] the mascot has fun and games with 100 students from the Aspire Academy of Sport.

ARRIVAL OF HH SHEIKH HAMAD BIN KHALIFA AL-THANI, THE EMIR OF THE STATE OF QATAR

The cyclorama shows footage of Doha as the camera sweeps over the city of Doha and the Emir takes his place in the royal box, joining heads of state from Syria, Saudi Arabia, Palestine, UAE, Iran, Oman and Jordan, as well as representatives from the Olympic Council of Asia and the International Olympic Committee.

COUNTDOWN AND WELCOME

The countdown features different numerical systems from Asia projected onto the arena floor and lit up by the LED cyclorama. The massed Welcome cast of 2400 adult volunteers ignite hand-held fireworks to form the Qatari flag and the Arabic greeting 'Al-salam alaikom' ('Peace be upon you').

RAISING THE FLAG AND THE QATARI NATIONAL ANTHEM

Seventy fanfare trumpeters accompany the raising of the Qatari flag. A single Qatari boy commences the National Anthem and is joined by the 150-voice Children's Choir. The Guangzhou Symphony Orchestra swells the sound and the many faces of Qatari are projected onto the stadium floor.

THE JOURNEY BEGINS

A pulsating atom streaks across the massive LED cyclorama. A ray of light is followed through the universe, past galaxies, into our solar system, flying past

---

[12] Al-Sadu is the traditional Bedouin craft of hand weaving.
[13] Orry, the official mascot of the Doha 2006 Asian Games, is an oryx, the national animal of Qatar.

asteroids, hurtling towards earth. Panning around the globe we settle on the Arabian peninsular, then Qatar, then Doha.

A boy (The Seeker) appears on the Pillar of Aspiration, a hydraulic lift, projecting 15 m above the stadium floor. He will lead us through the journey of the Opening Ceremony. He holds a magical astrolabe,[14] laser beams exploding from it.

The floor is transformed into the lapping waters of the Gulf.

SEA OF LIFE: PEARL DIVERS

Now a grown man, the Seeker prepares to set sail with the pearl divers to hunt for pearls. His family bids him a tearful farewell. The Seeker's boat, constructed in fibreglass to resemble luminous glowing 'crystal', circles the stadium and comes to rest. Above him appear 11 pearling boats 'flying' at 40 m above the floor. In an underwater ballet 18 pearl divers 'swim' down from their boats to retrieve pearls and return.

SEA OF LIFE: THE STORM

A storm gathers and the boats are rocked back and forth. Huge menacing sea creatures appear on the projection screens lowered from the pearling boats. Abu Darya the Old Man of the Sea appears on the cyclorama, but he is furious with these mortals who have dared to plunder the sea and he hurls his trident at them. The Seeker falls from his boat but is rescued by a golden falcon which swoops down and takes him to a rock outcrop in a faraway new land.

The flying falcon, complete with flapping wings of 15 m, is constructed from kevlar carbon fibre and controlled by a computerised three-dimensional flying system operated from a technician hidden in its stomach.

WONDERS OF ASIA: THE PANORAMA OF ASIAN HISTORY

The Seeker is introduced to Asia as six large bamboo and rice paper screens rise, each shaped into an iconic building from Asia, representing its many cultures and civilisations. Shadow dancers appear on the screens from Thailand, India, Kazakhstan, Bali, China and Japan, taking us through Asia's 5000 years of history.

WONDERS OF ASIA: THE SILK ROAD

The Silk Road, in the form of a giant gold and red fabric banner held aloft by 75 dancers, is carried across the Asia projected on the floor. The famous trade route

---

[14] An astrolabe or 'star grasper' was an ancient astronomical instrument consisting of a series of discs marked with the orbits of the planets, used for navigation.

reveals six caravans entering the stadium (towed by hidden Pajeros). Each caravan is 22 m long and represents a region of Asia. They are accompanied by elaborately costumed performers. The caravans' doors open and totems rise from within revealing the wonders of Asia. More than 800 headdresses and wigs were used in this sequence alone.

TOB TOB YA BAHAR: ATONE, ATONE O SEA!

Back in his homeland the Seeker is deeply missed by the women who await him including Nura, his betrothed. Faraway in Asia the Seeker feels a great sadness. Nura appears at the top of the eastern stand and descends on a trolley structure, her black abaya[15] flowing out behind her and covering the entire stand. She is joined by a chorus of 130 volunteer singer/dancers who beat the sea with palm fronds and sing Tob Tob Ya Bahar.

UM AL-HANAYA: THE GREAT TRADING SHIP

The Seeker yearns for his homeland. His new friends build him a great trading ship to return to his home. He uses his precious astrolabe to guide him and arriving in Doha is given a hero's welcome. Wedding preparations are made.

HOMECOMING: THE SEEKER RETURNS

The Seeker invites his Asian friends as guests at his marriage to Nura. The eastern stage is transformed into a wedding majlis or reception area. An enormous wedding crown flies across the stadium to hang above the stage and the Seeker and Nura are married. The crown is 12 m in diameter, made of woven aluminium pipes and mesh and its 212 m^2 surface area is clad in ornate jewellery panels, modelled on a traditional Qatari wedding crown.

TRIBUTE TO THE DESERT HORSEMAN

To honour his guests the Seeker presents the unique skills of the desert horseman and the nobility of the Arabian horse; 64 horses and riders perform a choreographic routine.

FROM FATHER TO SON: THE GOLDEN AGE OF ARAB SCIENCE

Years have past and the Seeker now has a son. The time has come to teach his son about his people's glorious past and pass on the magical astrolabe. Father and son

---

[15] 'Abaya' refers to the over clothing worn by Arab women in the Gulf region.

rise up on the central lift on a giant half-armillary sphere[16] and the Seeker hands the astrolabe to his son.

As the Seeker reads to his son from an illustrated scroll, images appear on the cyclorama telling the story of the Golden Age of Arab Science. Various inventions are shown on the screen and then appear, either flying or on motorised trucks, in the stadium as giant physical manifestations. They are enlivened by 52 acrobats performing in and around them and represent the March of Science.

CITY OF THE FUTURE

Together, the father and son see their heritage and the future of their country before them. As the March of Science continues, renaissance inventions enter the arena, followed by scientific props, telescopes, microscopes, movie cameras, test tubes, moon buggies and satellite dishes. We understand that modern science is built on the foundations laid by great Arab scientists.

The objects swirl around the stadium and assemble into a long line across the stadium floor in the shape of a gas-to-liquid plant. It transforms into the skyline of a futuristic city. Aerial fireworks light up the city and the gas plant comes alive with massive flames leaping skywards.

TOGETHER NOW

We prepare to welcome the athletes to the Games. A lone drummer begins the beat and gradually 40 other percussionist join in, followed by another 1150 percussionists in the audience aisles and then the full orchestra.

The percussion reaches its climax and Jacky Cheung enters to sing 'Together Now'. During the song 88 flag bearers and 928 field marshals create a human fence to guide the athletes into their positions for the formal opening of the Games.

PARADE OF ATHLETES

The athletes march into the arena, 12 abreast, country-by-country, led by Afghanistan. Between groups of countries a series of drum carts enters, 8 in all, representing different Asian regions; each cart has 10 musicians on it. Finally Qatar enters into the stadium and salutes the Emir.

REACH OUT

Indian singer Sunidhi Chauhan takes her place on the eastern stage to sing 'Reach Out', a tribute to Olympic ideals of aspiration and sportsmanship. During the song

---

[16] The armillary sphere, along with the sextant and astrolabe, is a navigational instrument.

1900 Qatari children carrying illuminated peace doves on poles run into the stadium to form the word 'Salaam' ('Peace').

OPENING OF THE 15TH ASIAN GAMES, DOHA 2006

The Chairman of the Doha Asian Games Organising Committee, HH Sheikh Tamim Bin Hamad Al-Thani, and the President of the Olympic Council of Asia, HH Sheikh Ahmad Al-Fahad Al-Sabah, deliver the official speeches of welcome from the eastern stage.

A musical fanfare announces the arrival of HH Sheikh Hamad Bin Khalifa Al-Thani, the Emir, at a special podium on the western stage, where he declares the Games officially open.

OLYMPIC COUNCIL OF ASIA FLAG AND OATHS

The orchestra plays the official hymn of the Olympic Council of Asia and the OCA flag is carried into the stadium, where it is hoisted. The athlete's oath is taken on behalf of all athletes and the judge's oath on behalf of all judges.

LIGHT THE WAY: ARRIVAL OF THE TORCH

After its 55-day journey of over 500,000 km through 15 Asian countries, the Torch Relay approaches the stadium. As we await it, Spanish tenor Jose Carreras and Lebanese vocalist Magida El Roumi perform a specially composed operatic ballad 'Light the Way', from the eastern stage. The final approach of the Torch is seen on the cyclorama and the torchbearer enters the stadium.

LIGHTING THE CAULDRON

Five Qatari athletes carry the torch around the stadium and it finally passes to the last athlete who salutes the Emir. As he turns back towards the centre of the stadium, the central lift ascends bearing a lone horseman, Sheikh Mohammed Bin Hamad Al-Thani; the Emir is unaware that his son is to perform the lighting of the Cauldron.

Sheikh Mohammed ascends from his chrome and bronze stage from which radiate the sun's rays and takes the torch from the final runner. Then begins the most anticipated sequence of the Opening Ceremony as Sheikh Mohammed rides his horse up the stadium on a specially constructed ramp above the eastern stage. Meanwhile the Cauldron has appeared behind the stand set at 50 m above the floor. It takes the form of an antique Arabian sun with three concentric revolving rings of steel echoing the design of the astrolabe. It is the first kinetic Cauldron ever created.

Sheikh Mohammed applies the Torch to its centre and the Cauldron's flame leaps 6 m into the air. It will burn 300 kg of gas per hour for the 14 days of the Games.

FINALE

As the cauldron is lit, thirty 50 kW searchlights sweep the Doha sky. Sports City Tower adjacent to the stadium is encased in a mesh of programmable LEDs and these shoot patterns up to its summit, triggering three firework sequences. As the last sequence fires, the flame atop SCT fires 16 m into the night sky. This is followed by the most complex digitally fired stadium fireworks-and-searchlight show ever attempted.

TECHNICAL STATISTICS

A team of over 1000 technicians and artists constructed the Ceremony
Over 600 staff members were required to produce the event
One hundred and forty support volunteers from 20 countries helped with the show
Thirty firework technicians were required, firing 15 tonnes of fireworks up to 200 m
Ten thousand costumes made in Australia, Qatar, China, Thailand, Egypt, USA, UK, Syria, Saudi Arabia, Vietnam, Japan, Hong Kong, India, Indonesia and Korea
One hundred and fifty containers for costumes, props and scenery
Fifty-eight kilometres of steel rope to support flying elements
Cyclorama was 157 m wide and 64 m high, containing over 600,000 LEDs
One thousand automated lighting fixtures
Five hundred and sixty moving lights
Twenty-eight moving image projectors
Twenty-five containers of lighting equipment
Over 100 lighting crew

ACKNOWLEDGMENTS

The author acknowledges the assistance of David Atkins and use of the following source documents:

1. DAGOC/David Atkins Enterprises: Contract, March 2005
2. David Atkins Enterprises: Ceremonies Operational Plan, August 2005
3. DAGOC: Opening Ceremony Media Guide, December 2006
4. DAGOC: Sports Technical Handbook, November 2006

Dictionary of terms

The diverse nature of the event industry has resulted in a plethora of terminology Much of it is highly defined in its specialist area, such as theatre or logistics, but ill-defined when applied to events. Many of the words are almost synonyms. They may be interchangeable. But the subtle differences can have significant implications when magnified by repeated use. Communication is critical in an event management environment.

The list below is not meant to be the dictionary for events. The purpose is to assist the reader of this book.

Business events: conferences, exhibitions, such as conferences, exhibitions and meetings. Their primary purpose is to do business. These almost always occur in purpose-built venues such as Trade, Conference and Exhibition Centres.

Capacity/Financial ability (C/F) circle: the ability to pay for increasing capacity, such as hotels, transport and infrastructure, is dependent on the perceived demand for these assets. However, the demand for the assets can only be attained by attracting events that will use them. Events will only be attracted if the assets are already built. This is a viscous circle and can lead to a downward spiral in quality of events and the assets.

CFEE Certified Festival & Event Executive

Competitive neutrality: the objectives of competitive neutrality (CN) are:

- that significant Government business activities do not enjoy net competitive advantages over their private sector competitors (or potential competitors) simply by virtue of their public sector ownership;
- to eliminate potential resource allocation distortions arising from the public ownership of significant business activities operating in contestable environments and
- to encourage fair and effective competition in the supply of goods and services.

Complexity: a comparatively high number of linked tasks

Corporate event: a celebration event that is used by private companies to further their objectives. Dinners, awards nights, end of year parties and incentives are examples.

CSEP (Certified Special Events Professional): awarded by the International Special Events Society.

Deliverable: the physical (or digital) result or output of a number of tasks in the form of a file or document that is passed on to other people (delivered). The identification of deliverables is useful in the event management as it gives the team a specific outcome of their work. Once it is delivered it is proof that the work has been completed.

EMBOK (Event Management Body on Knowledge): an attempt by event experts to map the knowledge needed for event management. www.embok.org

Event applicant: an event organisation, such as a sports club, exhibition seller, PCO, sponsor, major company, or event company, that is applying to a sponsor or government grant body to obtain support for their event.

Event capability maturity model: a measure of the event development of a region compared to other regions around the world. Events programmes follow similar paths in different countries. At the same time as the events programme is developing the capability of the region to host events develops.

Event leverage: using an existing event to increase the return on investment by expanding aspects of the events. This may include the number of days of the event, the size of the area or widening the programme.

Events plan: a separate report compiled by the consultant outlining the events programme for 3 years.

Event project: the management of the event in terms of the planning and implementation of the plans. It is to distinguish this from the event itself.

Event project life cycle: the phases of a specific event from initiation until shutdown and post-evaluation.

Event programme or programme of events: these terms can easily be confused. The event programme is the schedule of activities during single event such as at the 'what's on' a festival. The programme of events, also called the 'events programme' – is the list of separate events over a period of time. A company's programme of events may include a conference, sponsoring a festival, a number of seminars spread over a year and an incentive event for the staff and suppliers.

Events portfolio: a group of events generally spread over a year. For a corporation this may include conferences, seminars, product launches, incentives and sponsored public events. It is also called the Events Programme.

Event team/event company: these terms are used interchangeably in the text to emphasise that the feasibility and development may take place in the private enterprise world by an event company or within a large organisation such as a government authority of a corporation by the in-house event team.

Event variable: an aspect of the event that is expected to change and influence other aspects in a measurable way. The attendee numbers are an example of a variable that will affect other elements of the event.

Flagship event: an event that is used by the city or town as its main public event. Generally, it is a festival branded with the name of the town, e.g. Glastonbury Festival, Deniliquin Ute Muster and Dubai Shopping Festival.

Host, client or sponsor: the key stakeholder who is responsible for the event and its results. Generally, they are the company, department or government organisation financing the event.

IEMS International Event Management Standard: this was the working title of the project. In 2010 the results were released as Event Management: International Competency Standard.

Event or Events: in this book the term 'event' is used for a single event. Hence event management refers to the management of a single event. In the plural form it is taken to mean a group or portfolio of events. This may also be called a 'programme of events'. Hence the term 'events management' is the management of a portfolio. It does not imply the internal management of each event, such as the project management or the operations management. The Events Unit, therefore, has the responsibility of a number of events.

IFEA Internationals Festival & Events Association

MC Master of Ceremonies

MPI Meeting Professionals International

PCO (Professional Conference Organiser): a term commonly used around the world for the people who organise conference and meetings.

Phase: the project of creating and managing an event will pass through quite different sequential periods. They are characterised by different types of management. These are similar to the phases on any project which are initiation, planning, implementation/delivery and closure. According to the EMBOK, the phases of an event are initiation, planning, implementation, the event and closure.

PR: Public Relations

Purpose-built venue: a venue that has been designed for events such as a theatre, sports centre, conference or exhibition centre. Most festivals and many other events occur in civic spaces rather than purpose-built venues.

RFT (Request for Tender): a request for event companies to submit a proposal to manage an event. It may also be called a Request for Proposal (RFP) or Request for Bid (RFB). These terms are used interchangeably in the text. In some countries, the RFP is a more informal method and implies that the event company assists the event design.

Strategy: a long-term high-level plan for an organisation. Generally, covering 3, 5 or 10 years and involving all the units of the organisation.

Tenderer: a person or company submitting a tender or proposal is response to a Request for Tender (RFT).

Units, departments, divisions: management units within an organisation. Events, such as conferences, seminar, sponsored events and product launches, generally cross all the management divisions.

References, sources and further reading

Published books and academic journal articles:

Arcodia, C., & Reid, S. (2003). Goals and objectives of event management associations. *Journal of Convention and Exhibition Management, 5*(1), 57–75, doi: 10.1300/J143v05n01_05.

Birch, R. (2004). *Master of Ceremonies: Crows Nest*. Allen & Unwin.

Checkland, P., & Scholes, J. (1999). *Soft Systems Methodology in Action*. Chichester, England: John Wiley & Sons.

Gawande, A. (2010). *The Checklist Manifesto: How to Get Things Right*. London: Profile.

Getz, D. (2007). *Event Studies: Theory, Research and Policy for Planned Events*. UK: Elsevier.

Mintzberg, H. (1994). *The Rise and Fall of Strategic Planning*. New York: Prentice Hall.

O'Toole, W. (2010). *EPMS*, CDROM. www.epms.net.

O'Toole, W., & Mikolaitis, P. (2002). *Corporate Event Project Management*. New York: Wiley.

Poundstone, W. (2010). *Priceless*. Carlton, Victoria: Scribe.

Project Management Institute. (2008). *Guide to the Project Management Body of Knowledge: PMBOK Guide* (4th ed.). Newtown Square, PA: Project Management Institute, Inc.

Shone, A., & Parry, B. (2004). *Successful Event Management* (2nd ed.). London: Continuum.

Silvers, J. R. (2004). *Professional Event Coordination*. New York: John Wiley & Sons.

Silvers, J. R. (2008). *Risk Management for Meetings and Events*. London: Elsevier. Butterworth–Heinemann.

Sonder, M. (2004). *Event Entertainment and Production*. New York. John Wiley & Sons.

Sterman, J. (2000). *Business Dynamics: Systems Thinking and Modeling for Complex World* Boston: McGraw-Hill/Irwin.

Tassiopoulos, D. (Ed.). (2009). *Events Management: A Developmental and Managerial Approach* (3rd ed.). South Africa: Juta Claremont.

Tuchman, B. (1970). *Sand Against the Wind: Stilwell and the American Experience in China, 1911–45*. London: Macmillan.

Tum, J., Norton, P., & Wright, J. N. (2006). *Management of Event Operations*. London: Elsevier Event Management Series.

Williams, T. (2002). *Modelling Complex Projects*. West Sussex, UK: John Wiley.

Wunsch, U. (Ed.). (2008). *Facets of contemporary event management*. Bonn: Germany. Bad. Honnef Series on Services Management.

Primary source documents including website publications, white papers and reports:

ACT Auditor General. (July 2002). *V8 Car Races in Canberra — Costs and Benefits Performance Audit Report*. ACT, Auditor-General's Office.

ADTA. (2007). *Abu Dhabi Tourism Authority Entity Plan* 2008–2009. UAE: Abu Dhabi to Abu Dhabi Tourism Authority.

Auckland City Council. (2005). *Auckland City Events Strategy*. NZ: www.aucklandcity.govt.nz/council/documents/events/docs/strategy.pdf.

Banks, G. (2002). *Inter-State Bidding Wars: Calling a Truce*. Australia: Productivity Commission.

BEISG. (2008). The Business Events Industry Strategy Group 2008. *A National Business Events Strategy for Australia 2020*. Australia: BEISG.

CCT. (2008). *City of Cape Town Events Policy (April 2008)*. The City of Cape Town, South Africa.

Christchurch City Council. (2007). *Christchurch Event and Festival Funding Framework*. NZ: Christchurch City Council.

City of Melbourne. (2008). *Strategic Directions for Events 2008–2012 City of Melbourne*. Australia.

Clarence Valley Council. (2006). *Events Management Kit: A Guide to Planning Community Events*. NSW: Clarence Valley Council.

Coffs Coast Tourism. (2007a). *Coffs Coast Tourism Strategy, Final Report, March 2007*. NSW.

Coffs Harbour Council. (2007b). *Coffs Harbour City Council Management Plan 2007–2010*. NSW

Colac Otway Council. (2007). *Colac Otway Festival and Events Strategic Plan 2007–2011*. Victoria: Colac Otway Council.

Confex. (2010). *Addressing the skills and labour needs of the events industry: A position paper for discussion at the Events Skills Seminar*, Confex, 22 February 2010.

Culture 10. (2006). *Evaluation Final Report, August 2006*. UK.

Department of Local Government. (1997). *Pricing and Costing for Council Businesses: A Guide for Competitive Neutrality*. Australia: Department of Local Government.

Devonport City Council. (2007). *Events Strategy 2007–2010*. Tasmania: Devonport City Council.

EKOS Ltd. (2010). *Homecoming Scotland 2009. Economic Impact. Report for Homecoming Scotland*, March 2010. <www.ekosconsultants.co.uk>.

Event Awards. (2009). <http://www.nzaep.co.nz/nzaep_files/File/NZAEP%20Awards%202006.pdf>.

Event Wales. (2010). *Developing a Major Events Strategy for Wales (2010–2020)*. Welsh Assembly Government Consultation Document.

EventScotland. (2008). *Scotland the Perfect Stage, A Strategy for the Events Industry in Scotland 2009–2020*. Scotland: EventScotland.

Gold Coast City Council. (2007). *Gold Coast City Events Strategy 2007–2009*. Australia.

Government of Kenya. (2007). *Kenya Vision 2030: A Globally Competitive and Prosperous Kenya*. Government of Kenya.

GSA. (2007). *Event Tourism Growth Strategy 2007–2010, Draft Document, August 2007*. South Africa Government.

IOC. (2008). *Games of the XXXI Olympiad 2016 (Working Group Report)*. Lausanne: Switzerland.

Johnson, R. (2002). *Event Operations Management, East Timor Independence Day*.

Kaplan, R. (2010). *Conceptual Foundations of the Balanced Scorecard*. HBS, White paper.

KPMG. (2006). *Economic Impact Study of the Melbourne 2006 Commonwealth Games, Post Event Analysis*. KPMG.

Maritz Research Canada. (2008). *The Economic Contribution of Meetings Activity in Canada. Dallas*. Texas, USA: Meeting Professionals International.

Nelson Regional Economic Development Agency. (2005). Events Strategy Summary 2005–2006. *New Zealand*. Nelson.

North East England Tourism Strategy (2005–2010), *Final Report*. UK.

North Shore City. (2008). *Events Strategy North Shore City Draft, June 2008*. New Zealand.

NSW Department of Local Government. (2006). *Asset Management Planning for NSW Local Government 2006*. NSW: Department of Local Government.

NSW Premiers Department. (2005). *Event Starter Guide*. NSW: Government Publication.

NZ Major Events. (2006). *The National Events Strategy: Taking Our Place on the World Stage*. New Zealand.

O'Neill, J. (2007). *Review into a Possible Events Corporation for New South Wales for the Premier of New South Wales. The Hon. Morris Iemma MP*. Australia.

One NorthEast. (2007). *North East England Festival and Events Strategy*. UK. <www.onenortheast.co.uk>.

Port Macquarie/Hastings Council. (2008). *Public Inquiry Report*. NSW: Department of Local Government.

Positioning Auckland as a Major Events Destination (2008). New Zealand.

Remarkable Productions. (2007). *Stoke-on-Trent City Council, Festivals and Events Strategy, Summary Report 2007*. UK.

Rogers, T. (2003). *Business Tourism Briefing: An Overview of the UK's Business Tourism Industry*. UK: Business Tourism Partnership.

Scriven, M. (2007). *The Logic and Methodology of Checklists*. Western Michigan University. <http://www.wmich.edu/evalctr/checklists/papers/logic&methodology_dec07.pdf>.

SOCOG. (2001). *Official Report of the XXVII Olympiad 2001*. Sydney Organizing Committee for the Olympic Games. <http://www.gamesinfo.com.au/postgames>

South Africa Government. (2010). *Safety at Sports and Recreational Events Act*. Government Gazette May 2010, South Africa. <www.info.gov.za>.

South African National Standard. (2009). *Health and Safety at Live Events, National Standard, SANS 10366*. South Africa.

State Investment in Major Events. (2007). Government Report. Australia.

STB. (2009). *Singapore Tourism Board – Tourism 2015*. Available from: <http://app-stg.stb.gov.sg/asp/abo/abo08.asp>.

Stoke on Trent City. (2007). *Council Stoke on Trent 2007 Festival and Events Strategy, Summary Report*. UK.

Strategy for Major Event in England's Northwest March 2004. Report. UK.

Supreme Commission for Tourism. (2002). *National Tourism Development Project in the Kingdom of Saudi Arabia 2002–2020*. Kingdom of Saudi Arabia.

Supreme Commission for Tourism. (2007). *Strategy and Action Plan for the Development of the 'MICE' Market in Saudi Arabia, Final Report*. Kingdom of Saudi Arabia.

Traffic Management for Events Advisory Group. (2008). *Traffic Management for Events: Code of Practice*. WA: Government Publication.

US Department of Transportation. (2003). *Managing Travel for Planned Special Events, Final Report, September 2003*.

Victoria's Tourism and Events Industry. (2007). *Industry Strategic Plan 2007–2016 Discussion paper*. Australia.

WBPDC. (2008). *Western Bay of Plenty District Council Events Strategy 2009–2012*. New Zealand.

Western Bay of Plenty. (2008). *Events Strategy 2008–2014*. New Zealand.

Index